CODEPENDENT NO MORE

ALSO BY MELODY BEATTIE

CODEPENDENT NO MORE

*How to Stop Controlling Others and
Start Caring for Yourself*

Melody Beattie

HAZELDEN®

Hazelden
Center City, Minnesota 55012
hazelden.org

ISBN-13: 978-0-89486-402-5

Library of Congress Card Number: 88-82660

Editor's Note
The Twelve Steps are reprinted with permission of Alcoholics Anonymous World Services, Inc. Permission to reprint the Twelve Steps does not mean that Alcoholics Anonymous has reviewed or approved the contents of this publication, or that AA agrees with the views expressed herein. The views expressed herein are solely those of the author. AA is a program of recovery from alcoholism. Use of the Twelve Steps in connection with the programs and activities that are patterned after AA, but that address other problems, does not imply otherwise.

Cover design by Nick Caruso
Interior design by David Swanson

It is not easy to find happiness in ourselves,
and it is not possible to find it elsewhere.

—AGNES REPPLIER,
The Treasure Chest

For helping make this book possible, I thank:

*God, my mother, David, my children, Scott Egleston,
Sharon George, Joanne Marcuson,
and all the codependent people who have
learned from me and allowed me
to learn from them.*

THIS BOOK IS DEDICATED TO ME.

Contents

A Twenty-fifth Anniversary Message from Melody Beattie

Since I wrote this book, I've been to the top of the mountain, walked through the dark tunnel of my son's death, reached the Light at the end of the tunnel, and given others hope when I got there. I've also put on as many years as this book has. It still carries the same message, one I stand behind and often need to remember myself.

I know when to say no and when to say yes. I take responsibility for my choices. The victim? She went somewhere else. The only one who can truly victimize me is myself, and 99 percent of the time I choose to do that no more. But I need to continue to remember the key principles: boundaries, letting go, forgiveness after feeling my feelings—not before, self-expression, loving others but loving myself, too.

There have been cycles in how this book's messages have been received and applied. For a while, some people grew tired of working on themselves. Medications have helped many people deal with very real symptoms of depression and anxiety—but for others, those same medications can conveniently mask the discomfort that could have pushed them to get help. Even cell phones can mask the pain behind obsessions: people don't have to stay home and become uncomfortable waiting for him or her to call—they can bring their phone and their obsessions with them and act them out anywhere, anytime. We've learned to become therapeutically correct and cover our insecurity with all the right lingo. But many of us have started to see how severe the consequences of these behaviors could be. That cycle is ending.

It's clear now that codependency isn't a fad, as some people once claimed. It's come full circle. As family illnesses, from alcoholism to Alzheimer's disease, continue to become openly discussed by more people, so does the number of people seeking help for codependency increase. This little book still has more work to do.

Don't give up hope. It took many of us twenty years or more to acquire these protective behaviors we umbrella with the word *codependency*. It may take as much time as that to let go of them. I don't know why Life chose me to be the messenger for this, but I'm grateful for the work I've been given to do. Thanks for letting me be of service.

Happy twenty-fifth birthday, *Codependent No More*.

With love and gratitude,
Melody Beattie

Author's Preface to the 2001 Fifteenth Anniversary Edition

Taking care of myself is a big job.
No wonder I avoided it for so long.

—ANONYMOUS

The year was 1986. Pioneers such as Janet Geringer Woititz, Robert Subby, and Earnie Larsen were trying to convince people that the non-drinking person in a relationship with an alcoholic got just as out of control, was in just as much pain, and needed just as much healing as the alcoholic.

Al-Anon groups across the country and the world were quietly trying to bring hope and healing to this same group of people: the codependents.

The message carried by all the pioneers of codependency recovery was the same: Not only can we lovingly detach from other people and take care of ourselves, it is our primary responsibility in life to do that.

To a world that believed in control and victimization, this message was revolutionary. So was the word *codependency.*

My computer refused the recognize *codependency* as a legitimate word as I tapped out the manuscript that was yet to be entitled *Codependent No More.*

Addictions and recovery sections did not yet exist in bookstores.

Codependents were having a difficult time finding the help and healing they needed.

Ground was just being broken.

Now it's 2001.

The World Health Organization reports an increase in illicit drug use. The National Association for Children of Alcoholics reports that about 43 percent of the U.S. population has been exposed to alcoholism in their families. And about one out of every eight American adult drinkers consumes alcohol problematically or alcoholically.

These figures don't include the number of families affected by physical or mental illness, sexual addiction, abuse, neglect, and the myriad of problems that can lead people to cope by behaving codependently, giving themselves and their loved ones less of a chance for living a full life.

My laptop computer now recognizes and offers a suggested spelling for the word *codependency*. The world recognizes it, too. The word, or at least the symptoms and the treatment, appears regularly in novels, television shows, movies, and normal conversations between ordinary people. The addictions and recovery section at the bookstore is overflowing.

The purpose of this preface is simple: I want to say thank you. First, I want to thank the numerous experts and authors who brought groundbreaking information to people who were still suffering. These individuals include Janet Geringer Woititz, Earnie Larsen, Sandra Smalley, Pia Mellody, Robert Subby, Brenda Schaeffer, Gayle Rosellini, Mark Worden, Sharon Wegscheider-Cruse, Terence Gorski, Terry Kellog, Patrick Carnes, John Bradshaw, Rokelle Lerner, Anne Wilson Schaef, Robin Norwood, and Charles Whitfield.

I also want to thank organizations such as Al-Anon and Codependents Anonymous, and publishers such as Hazelden, that bring their healing philosophies and words to millions of people.

I want to thank each person who has the courage to push through and past the set of coping behaviors we've come to label as codependency— who learn what it means to take care of themselves.

"Nobody taught me how to take care of myself," a fifty-year-old woman told me recently. "I didn't have enough money to go to therapy, but I had enough to buy a book."

Codependent No More has had several different jackets since Hazelden originally published it in 1986. But many people, including me, remember with fondness that original book with a bright yellow cover and black lettering.

Happy fifteenth birthday, *Codependent No More*.

And thanks to all of you for naming that pain and making an extraordinary miracle an ordinary one.

AUTHOR'S PREFACE
TO THE 1992 EDITION

Back in the early eighties, when I first envisioned writing a book about codependency—when I was desperately struggling to sort through my own pain—I vowed that if I ever figured out what happened to me and what I needed to do to get better, I'd write a book about it. That book, I decided, would be warm, gentle, nonjudgmental, nontechnical.

It would be kind. Because that's what I needed—information and kindness. I needed help with my healing process from my codependency issues.

About five years later, I sat down to write that book. Just separated from my husband of ten years, I went on welfare for four months, to help me support myself and my two children, Nichole and Shane, while I wrote *Codependent No More*.

When I wondered how I, a nonexpert, could write a book like that, I took comfort by telling myself that it was okay to say what I thought because only a few people would read it anyway. I also spent a great deal of time on the introduction, striving not only to introduce the book, but to introduce the concept of *codependency*—the word—to a world that, for the most part, had not heard about it.

Now, another five years later, I've been asked to write an anniversary preface to a book that has sold over two million copies.

"What do I put in it?" I asked my editor and friend, Rebecca Post, from Hazelden.

"Tell about the changes that have happened—to women, to people in our country, to *you*, since you wrote that book," she suggested.

"Hmmm," I pondered. "What changes have happened besides the Persian Gulf War, the breakdown of communism in the Soviet Union, and the Hill-Thomas hearings?"

I turn on the television. The movie of the week, I can't remember the name, is a story about a teenager struggling to deal with her alcoholism and the impact of being raped. Her mother, a nurse, has worked valiantly to break free from a dysfunctional and abusive relationship with her husband, the girl's father. Throughout the movie, mother and daughter talk directly about not rescuing each other because of the diminishing effects of such behavior. The movie ends with the daughter playing a guitar and singing a song she's written about not being a victim anymore.

I walk into a church, one I haven't attended for a long time. The sermon is somewhat unusual this cold, Sunday winter morning. The minister is speaking from his heart, telling the congregation that he is done leading a church that's based on shame, fear, guilt, and dishonesty. He wants instead, he says, to be part of a church that's based on equality, honesty, intimacy, acceptance, and the healing power of God's love. He wants to be part of a church where he can have his own issues and problems, and where people are functioning in healthy, honest relationships with each other and God.

My daughter comes home from her first week at a new school. "Guess what, Mom?" she says. "We're reading a meditation each day in homeroom class from your book, *The Language of Letting Go.* And at my friend's school, they're talking about codependency issues in health class."

Codependent No More, with a picture of handcuffs broken apart on the front cover, makes the best-seller list in France.

Catdependent No More, parodying the title of my book, makes the 1991 Christmas book list here in Minnesota.

Some things have changed. I've written four more books, traveled the world, divorced (but not remarried), and paid back the welfare department for the financial help they gave me.

I feel more passionately about the importance of healing from our abuse issues. I feel more passionately. I've become more spontaneous, embraced my femininity, and learned new lessons along the way—about boundaries, flexibility, and owning my power. And about love. I'm learning to respect men. My relationships have deepened. Some have changed.

The most significant change in my life has been the loss of my son, Shane. As you may have heard or read, in February of 1991, three days after his twelfth birthday, my beloved Shane—so much a part of my life and work—was killed suddenly in a ski accident on the slopes at Afton Alps.

I'm learning about death and life.

I've grown and changed. I've watched my friends grow and change. Many of you have written to me about your growth and change.

I still struggle with feeling feelings and trusting my process, my path, and my Higher Power. I still feel afraid at times. Sometimes I forget and try to control everything. I may become obsessive, unless I catch myself.

And, despite its years on the best-seller list, the most common question I'm still asked by people and the media is, "Just exactly what is codependency?"

Some things haven't changed, at least not a lot. I still refuse to be an expert and permanently decline the title of "guru." But I'm still willing to tell you what I see, and believe.

Although some things appear not to have changed, things are constantly changing. Our consciousness, as individuals and as a society, has been raised. We've realized that women have souls, and men have feelings.

And I've gone deeper into my healing process than I ever intended.

I don't know how much my writing has contributed to this consciousness-raising, and how much the consciousness-raising has contributed to my writing. But I'm grateful to be part of what's happened.

I'm honored to be part of a movement influenced by people such as Anne Wilson Schaef, John Bradshaw, Patrick Carnes, Earnie Larsen, and led by people such as you, my readers—the real heroes—quietly and profoundly doing your own healing work and carrying the message to others, most significantly by example.

I've met many of you in my travels across the country. Some of you have written to me. Thank you for the love, support, and compassion you've shown me not only over the years, but throughout the rough, raw months of 1991 after Shane's death.

Many of you have written to me, saying how much I've helped you. Well, you've helped and touched me, too.

One woman wrote to me recently, saying she had read all my books and had been recovering from codependency for years. "I want to learn more, though," she wrote. "I want to go deeper into my codependency. Please write more about that."

Maybe we don't need to go deeper into our codependency. We can, instead, march forward into our destinies. We can remember and practice all we've learned about addictions, codependency, and abuse. With compassion and boundaries, we need to commit fully to loving God, ourselves, and others. We need to commit fully to trusting God, ourselves, and or process.

Then we can be open to the next step. We are on time, and we are where we need to be. We can be trusted. So can God. And letting go and gratitude still work. Keep your head up and your heart open. And let's see what's next. Happy five-year anniversary, *Codependent No More*.

CODEPENDENT NO MORE

INTRODUCTION

My first encounter with codependents occurred in the early sixties. This was before people, tormented by other people's behavior, were called *codependents,* and before people addicted to alcohol and other drugs were labeled *chemically dependent.* Although I didn't know *what* codependents were, I usually knew *who* they were. As an alcoholic and addict, I stormed through life, helping create other codependents.

Codependents were a necessary nuisance. They were hostile, controlling, manipulative, indirect, guilt producing, difficult to communicate with, generally disagreeable, sometimes downright hateful, and a hindrance to my compulsion to get high. They hollered at me, hid my pills, made nasty faces at me, poured my alcohol down the sink, tried to keep me from getting more drugs, wanted to know why I was doing this to them, and asked what was wrong with me. But they were always there, ready to rescue me from self-created disasters. The codependents in my life didn't understand me, and the misunderstanding was mutual. I didn't understand me, and I didn't understand them.

My first professional encounter with codependents occurred years later, in 1976. At that time in Minnesota, addicts and alcoholics had become *chemically dependent,* their families and friends had become *significant others,* and I had become a *recovering addict and alcoholic.* By then, I also worked as a counselor in the chemical dependency field, that vast network of institutions, programs, and agencies that helps chemically dependent people get well. Because I'm a woman and most of the significant others at that time were women, and because I had the least seniority and none of my co-workers wanted to do it, my employer at the Minneapolis treatment center told me to organize support groups for wives of addicts in the program.

I wasn't prepared for this task. I still found codependents hostile, controlling, manipulative, indirect, guilt producing, difficult to communicate with, and more.

In my group, I saw people who felt responsible for the entire world, but they refused to take responsibility for leading and living their own lives.

I saw people who constantly gave to others but didn't know how to receive. I saw people give until they were angry, exhausted, and emptied of everything. I saw some give until they gave up. I even saw one woman give and suffer so much that she died of "old age" and natural causes at age thirty-three. She was the mother of five children and the wife of an alcoholic who had been sent to prison for the third time.

I worked with women who were experts at taking care of everyone around them, yet these women doubted their ability to take care of themselves.

I saw mere shells of people, racing mindlessly from one activity to another. I saw people-pleasers, martyrs, stoics, tyrants, withering vines, clinging vines, and, borrowing from H. Sackler's line in his play *The Great White Hope,* "pinched up faces giving off the miseries."

Most codependents were obsessed with other people. With great precision and detail, they could recite long lists of the addict's deeds and misdeeds: what he or she thought, felt, did, and said; and what he or she didn't think, feel, do, and say. The codependents knew what the alcoholic or addict should and shouldn't do. And they wondered extensively why he or she did or didn't do it.

Yet these codependents who had such great insight into others couldn't see themselves. They didn't know what they were feeling. They weren't sure what they thought. And they didn't know what, if anything, they could do to solve their problems—if, indeed, they had any problems other than the alcoholics.

It was a formidable group, these codependents. They were aching, complaining, and trying to control everyone and everything but themselves. And, except for a few quiet pioneers in family therapy, many counselors (including me) didn't know how to help them. The chemical dependency field was flourishing, but help focused on the addict. Literature and training on family therapy were scarce. What did codependents need? What did they want? Weren't they just an extension of the alcoholic, a visitor to the treatment center? Why couldn't they cooperate, instead of always making problems? The alcoholic had an excuse for being so crazy—he was drunk. These significant others had no excuse. They were this way sober.

Soon, I subscribed to two popular beliefs. These crazy codependents (significant others) are sicker than the alcoholics. And, no wonder the alcoholic drinks; who wouldn't with a crazy spouse like that?

By then, I had been sober for a while. I was beginning to understand myself, but I didn't understand codependency. I tried, but couldn't—until years later, when I became so caught up in the chaos of a few alcoholics that I stopped living my own life. I stopped thinking. I stopped feeling positive emotions, and I was left with rage, bitterness, hatred, fear, depression, helplessness, despair, and guilt. At times, I wanted to stop living. I had no energy. I spent most of my time worrying about people and trying to figure out how to control them. I couldn't say no (to anything but fun activities) if my life depended on it, which it did. My relationships with friends and family members were in shambles. I felt terribly victimized. I lost myself and didn't know how it had happened. I didn't know *what* had happened. I thought I was going crazy. And, I thought, shaking a finger at the people around me, it's *their* fault.

Sadly, aside from myself, nobody knew how badly I felt. My problems were my secret. Unlike the alcoholics and other troubled people in my life, I wasn't going around making big messes and expecting someone to clean up after me. In fact, next to the alcoholics, I looked good. I was *so* responsible, *so* dependable. Sometimes *I* wasn't sure I had a problem. I knew I felt miserable, but I didn't understand why my life wasn't working.

After floundering in despair for a while, I began to understand. Like many people who judge others harshly, I realized I had just taken a very long and painful walk in the shoes of those I had judged. I now understood those crazy codependents. I had become one.

Gradually, I began to climb out of my black abyss. Along the way, I developed a passionate interest in the subject of codependency. As a counselor (although I no longer worked full-time in the field, I still considered myself one) and as a writer, my counselor was provoked. As a "flaming, careening codependent" (a phrase borrowed from an Al-Anon member) who needed help, I also had a personal stake in the subject. What happens to people like me? How does it happen? Why? Most important, what do codependents need to do to feel better? And stay that way?

I talked to counselors, therapists, and codependents. I read the few available books on the subject and related topics. I reread the basics— the therapy books that have stood the test of time—looking for ideas that applied. I went to meetings of Al-Anon, a self-help group based on the Twelve Steps of Alcoholics Anonymous but geared toward the person who has been affected by another person's drinking.

Eventually, I found what I was seeking. I began to see, understand, and change. My life started working again. Soon, I was conducting another group for codependents at another Minneapolis treatment center. But this time, I had a vague notion of what I was doing.

I still found codependents hostile, controlling, manipulative, indirect, and all the things I had found them before. I still saw all the peculiar twists of personality I previously saw. But, I saw deeper.

I saw people who were hostile; they had felt so much hurt that hostility was their only defense against being crushed again. They were that angry because anyone who had tolerated what they had would be that angry.

They were controlling because everything around and inside them was out of control. Always, the dam of their lives and the lives of those around them threatened to burst and spew harmful consequences on everyone. And nobody but them seemed to notice or care.

I saw people who manipulated because manipulation appeared to be the only way to get anything done. I worked with people who were indirect because the systems they lived in seemed incapable of tolerating honesty. I worked with people who thought they were going crazy because they had believed so many lies they didn't know what reality was.

I saw people who had gotten so absorbed in other people's problems they didn't have time to identify or solve their own. These were people who had cared so deeply, and often destructively, about other people that they had forgotten how to care about themselves. The codependents felt responsible for so much because the people around them felt responsible for so little; they were just taking up the slack.

I saw hurting, confused people who needed comfort, understanding, and information. I saw victims of alcoholism who didn't drink but were nonetheless victimized by alcohol. I saw victims struggling desperately to gain some kind of power over their perpetrators. They learned from me, and I learned from them.

Soon, I began to subscribe to some new beliefs about codependency. Codependents aren't crazier or sicker than alcoholics. But, they hurt as much or more. They haven't cornered the market on agony, but they have gone through their pain without the anesthetizing effects of alcohol or other drugs, or the other high states achieved by people with compulsive disorders. And the pain that comes from loving someone who's in trouble can be profound.

"The chemically dependent partner numbs the feelings and the non-abuser is doubled over in pain—relieved only by anger and occasional fantasies," wrote Janet Geringer Woititz in an article from the book *Co-Dependency, An Emerging Issue*.[1]

Codependents are that way sober because they went through what they did sober.

No wonder codependents are so crazy. Who wouldn't be, after living with the people they've lived with?

It's been difficult for codependents to get the information and practical help they need and deserve. It's tough enough to convince alcoholics (or other disturbed people) to seek help. It's more difficult to convince codependents—those who by comparison look, but don't feel, normal—that they have problems.

Codependents suffered in the backdrop of the sick person. If they recovered, they did that in the background too. Until recently, many counselors (like me) didn't know what to do to help them. Sometimes codependents were blamed; sometimes they were ignored; sometimes they were expected to magically shape up (an archaic attitude that has not worked with alcoholics and doesn't help codependents either). Rarely were codependents treated as individuals who needed help to get better. Rarely were they given a personalized recovery program for their problems and their pain. Yet, by its nature, alcoholism and other compulsive disorders turn everyone affected by the illness into victims—people who need help even if they are not drinking, using other drugs, gambling, overeating, or overdoing a compulsion.

That's why I wrote this book. It grew out of my research, my personal and professional experiences, and my passion for the subject. It is a personal and, in some paces, prejudiced opinion.

I'm not an expert, and this isn't a technical book for experts. Whether the person you've let yourself be affected by is an alcoholic, gambler, foodaholic, workaholic, sexaholic, criminal, rebellious teenager, neurotic parent, another codependent, or any combination of the above, this book is for you, the codependent.

This book is not about how you can help your alcoholic or troubled person, although if you get better, his or her chance of recovery improves too.[2] There are plenty of good books on how to help the alcoholic. This book is about your most important and probably most neglected responsibility: taking care of yourself. It's about what you can do to start feeling better.

I've tried to round up some of the best, most helpful thoughts on codependency. I've included quotes from people I consider experts, to demonstrate their beliefs. I've also included case histories to show how people dealt with particular problems. Although I've changed names and certain details to protect privacy, all case histories are true and are not composites. I've inserted endnotes to document information, to suggest additional reading, and to attribute material to appropriate sources. But, much of what I've learned has been from many people and their similar thoughts on this subject. Many ideas have been handed down and passed around, and their sources have become indistinguishable. I've tried to attribute accurately, but in this field that is not always possible.

Although this is a self-help, how-to book, please remember it's not a cookbook for mental health. Each person is unique; each situation is unique. Try to tap into your own healing process. That may include seeking professional help, attending self-help groups such as Al-Anon, and calling on the assistance of a Power greater than yourself.

A friend, Scott Egleston, who is a professional in the mental health field, told me a therapy fable. He heard it from someone, who heard it from someone else. It goes:

Once upon a time, a woman moved to a cave in the mountains to study with a guru. She wanted, she said, to learn everything there was to know. The guru supplied her with stacks of books and left her alone so she could study. Every morning, the guru returned to the cave to monitor the woman's progress. In his hand, he carried a heavy wooden cane. Each morning, he asked her the same question: "Have you learned everything there is to know yet?" Each morning, her answer was the same. "No," she said, "I haven't." The guru would then strike her over the head with his cane.

This scenario repeated itself for months. One day the guru entered the cave, asked the same question, heard the same answer, and raised his cane to hit her in the same way, but the woman grabbed the cane from the guru, stopping his assault in midair.

Relieved to end the daily batterings but fearing reprisal, the woman looked up at the guru. To her surprise, the guru smiled. "Congratulations," he said, "you have graduated. You now know everything you *need* to know."

"How's that?" the woman asked.

"You have learned that you will never learn everything there is to know," he replied. "And you have learned how to stop the pain."

That's what this book is about: stopping the pain and gaining control of your life.

Many people have learned to do it. You can, too.

Part I

What's Codependency, and Who's Got It?

1

JESSICA'S STORY

The sun was shining, and it was a beautiful
day when I met him.
Then, everything went crazy.

—GEORGIANNE, MARRIED TO AN ALCOHOLIC

This is Jessica's story. I'll let her tell it.

I sat in the kitchen, drinking coffee, thinking about my unfinished house-work. Dishes. Dusting. Laundry. The list was endless, yet I couldn't get started. It was too much to think about. Doing it seemed impossible. Just like my life, I thought.

Fatigue, a familiar feeling, overtook me. I headed for the bedroom. Once a luxury, naps had become a necessity. Sleeping was about all I could do. Where had my motivation gone? I used to have an excess of energy. Now, it was an effort to comb my hair and apply makeup daily—an effort I frequently didn't put forth.

I lay on my bed and fell into a deep sleep. When I awoke, my first thoughts and feelings were painful. This, also, was not new. I wasn't sure which hurt most: the raw ache I felt because I was certain my marriage was over—the love was gone, extinguished by the lies and the drinking and the disappointments and the financial problems; the bitter rage I felt toward my husband—the man who had caused it all; the despair I felt because God, whom I had trusted, had betrayed me by allowing this to happen; or the mixture of fear, helplessness, and hopelessness that blended into all the other emotions.

Damn him, I thought. Why did he have to drink? Why couldn't he have sobered up earlier? Why did he have to lie? Why couldn't he have loved me as much as I had loved him? Why didn't he stop drinking and lying years ago, when I still cared?

I never intended to marry an alcoholic. My father had been one. I had tried so hard to carefully choose my husband. Great choice. Frank's problem with drinking had become apparent on our honeymoon when he left our hotel suite late one afternoon and didn't return until 6:30 the next morning. Why didn't I see then? Looking back, the signs were clear. What a fool I had been. "Oh, no. He's not an alcoholic. Not him," I had defended, time and again. I had believed his lies. I had believed my lies. Why didn't I just leave him, get a divorce? Guilt, fear, lack of initiative, and indecision. Besides, I had left him before. When we were apart, all I did was feel depressed, think about him, and worry about money. Damn me.

I looked at the clock. Quarter to three. The kids would soon be home from school. Then he would be home, expecting supper. No housework done today. Nothing ever got done. And it's his fault, I thought. HIS FAULT!

Suddenly, I shifted emotional gears. Was my husband really at work? Maybe he had taken another woman to lunch. Maybe he was having an affair. Maybe he had left early to drink. Maybe he was at work, creating problems there. How long would he have this job, anyway? Another week? Another month? Then he'd quit or be fired, as usual.

The phone rang, interrupting my anxiety. It was a neighbor, a friend. We talked, and I told her about my day.

"I'm going to Al-Anon tomorrow," she said. "Want to come along?"

I had heard about Al-Anon. It was a group for people married to drunks. Visions charged into my mind of "the little women" huddled at this meeting, making the most of their husbands' drinking, forgiving them, and thinking of little ways to help them.

"I'll see," I lied. "I've got a lot of work to do," I explained, not lying.

Outrage poured through me, and I barely heard the rest of our conversation. Of course I didn't want to go to Al-Anon. I had helped and helped. Hadn't I already done enough for him? I felt furious at the suggestion that I do more and continue giving to this bottomless pit of unmet needs we called a marriage. I was sick of shouldering the burden and feeling responsible for the success or failure of the relationship. It's his problem, I railed silently. Let him find his solution. Leave me out of this. Don't ask another thing of me. Just make him better, and I'll feel better.

After I hung up the phone, I dragged myself into the kitchen to fix supper. Anyway, I'm not the one that needs help, I thought. I haven't drunk, used drugs, lost jobs, and lied to and deceived those I loved. I've held this family together, sometimes by the skin of my teeth. I've paid the bills, maintained a home on a scant budget, been there for every emergency (and, married to an alcoholic, there had been plenty of emergencies), gone through most bad times alone, and worried to the point of frequent illness. No, I decided, I'm not the irresponsible one. To the contrary, I've been responsible for everything and everyone. There was nothing wrong with me. I just needed to get going, start doing my daily chores. I didn't need meetings to do that. I'd just feel guilty if I went out when I had all this work to do at home. God knows, I didn't need more guilt. Tomorrow, I'd get up and get busy. Things will be better—tomorrow.

When the kids came home, I found myself hollering at them. That didn't surprise them or me. My husband was easygoing, the good guy. I was the bitch. I tried to be pleasant, but it was hard. Anger was always just beneath the surface. For so long, I had tolerated so much. I was no longer willing or able to tolerate anything. I was always on the defensive, and I felt like I was, somehow, fighting for my life. Later, I learned I was.

By the time my husband came home, I had put a disinterested effort into preparing supper. We ate, barely talking.

"I had a good day," Frank said.

What does that mean? I wondered. What did you really do? Were you even at work? Furthermore, who cares?

"That's nice," I said back.

"How was your day?" he asked.

How in the hell do you think it was? I railed silently. After all you've done to me, how do you expect me to have any day? I flashed him daggers, forced a smile, and said, "My day was okay. Thanks for asking."

Frank looked away. He heard what I wasn't saying, more than what I had said. He knew better than to say anything else; I did too. We were usually one step away from a raving argument, a recount of past offenses, and screamed threats of divorce. We used to thrive on arguments, but we grew sick of them. So we did it silently.

The children interrupted our hostile silence. Our son said he wanted to go to a playground several blocks away. I said no, I didn't want him to go without his father or me. He wailed he wanted to go, he would go, and I never let him do anything. I yelled he wasn't going, and that was that. He yelled please, I have to go, all the other kids get to go. As usual, I backed down. Okay, go ahead, but be careful, I warned. I felt like I had lost. I always felt like I lost—with my kids and with my husband. No one ever listened to me; no one took me seriously.

I didn't take me seriously.

After supper, I washed dishes while my husband watched television. As usual, I work, and you play. I worry, and you relax. I care, and you don't. You feel good; I hurt. Damn you. I walked through the living room several times, purposely blocking his view of the television and secretly flashing him hateful looks. He ignored me. After tiring of this, I promenaded into the living room, sighed, and said I was going outside to rake the yard. It's really the man's job, I explained, but I guess I'll have to do it. He said he'd do it later. I said later never came, I couldn't wait, I was embarrassed by the yard, just forget it, I was used to doing everything, and I would do that, too. He said okay, he would forget it. I stormed outside and stomped around the yard.

As tired as I was, bedtime came too early. Sleeping with my husband had become as strained as our waking moments. We would either not speak, each curling up on opposite sides of the bed as far away from each other as possible, or he would make attempts—as though everything were fine—to have sex with me. Either way, it was tense. If we turned our backs to each other, I would lie there with confused, desperate thoughts. If he tried to touch me, I froze. How could he expect me to make love to him? How could he touch me as though nothing had happened? Usually I pushed him away with a sharp, "No, I'm too tired." Sometimes I agreed. Occasionally, I did it because I wanted to. But, usually, if I had sex with him, it was because I felt obligated to take care of his sexual needs and guilty if I didn't. Either way, sex was psychologically and emotionally unsatisfying. But, I told myself I didn't care. It didn't matter. Not really. Long ago, I had shut off my sexual desires. Long ago, I had shut off my need to give and receive love. I had frozen that part of me that felt and cared. I had to, to survive.

I had expected so much of this marriage. I had so many dreams for us. None of them had come true. I had been tricked, betrayed. My home and family—the place and people who should have been warm, nurturing, a comfort, a haven of love—had become a trap. And I couldn't find the way out. Maybe, I kept telling myself, it will get better. After all, the problems are his fault. He's an alcoholic. When he gets better, our marriage will get better.

But, I was beginning to wonder. He had been sober and attending Alcoholics Anonymous for six months. He was getting better. I wasn't. Was his recovery really enough to make me happy? So far, his sobriety didn't appear to be changing the way I felt, which was, at age thirty-two, dried up, used up, and brittle. What had happened to our love? What had happened to me?

One month later, I began to suspect what I would soon learn was the truth. By then, the only thing that had changed was I felt worse. My life had ground to a halt; I wanted it to end. I had no hope that things would get better; I didn't even know what was wrong. I had no purpose, except to care for other people, and I wasn't doing a good job of that. I was stuck in the past and terrified of the future. God seemed to have abandoned me. I felt guilty all the time and wondered if I was going crazy. Something dreadful, something that I couldn't explain, had happened to me. It had snuck up on me and ruined my life. Somehow, I had been affected by his drinking, and the ways I had been affected had become *my* problems. It no longer mattered whose fault it was.

I had lost control.

I met Jessica at this point in her life. She was about to learn three fundamental ideas.

1) She wasn't crazy; she was codependent. Alcoholism and other compulsive disorders are truly family illnesses. The way the illness affects other family members is called codependency.

2) Once they have been affected—once "it" sets in—codependency takes on a life of its own. It is similar to catching pneumonia or picking up a destructive habit. Once you've got it, you've got it.

3) If you want to get rid of it, *you* have to do something to make it go away. It doesn't matter whose fault it is. Your codependency becomes your problem; solving your problems is your responsibility.

If you're codependent, you need to find your own recovery or healing process. To begin that recovery, it helps to understand codependency and certain attitudes, feelings, and behaviors that often accompany it. It is also important to change some of these attitudes and behaviors and understand what to expect as these changes occur.

This book will search for those understandings and encourage those changes. I'm happy to say Jessica's story had a happy ending or a new beginning. She got better. She started living her own life. I hope you do, too.

2

OTHER STORIES

When I say I'm codependent, I don't mean I'm a little bit codependent. I mean I'm really codependent. I don't marry men who stop for a few beers after work. I marry men who won't work.

—ELLEN, AN AL-ANON MEMBER

Maybe you identified with Jessica in the last chapter. Her story is an extreme example of codependency, but it is one I hear frequently. However, Jessica's experience is not the only type of codependency. There are as many variations of that story as there are codependents to tell them.

Here are a few.

Gerald, a handsome and personable man in his early forties, calls himself "a success in business but a failure in relationships with women." During high school and college, Gerald dated many women. He was popular and considered a good catch. However, after graduation, Gerald stunned his family and friends when he married Rita. Rita treated Gerald worse than any other woman he had dated. She acted cool and hostile toward Gerald and his friends, shared few interests with him, and didn't seem to care much for or about Gerald. Thirteen years later, the marriage ended in divorce when Gerald discovered some things he had suspected for years for true: Rita had been dating other men since they were married, and she was (and had been for some time) abusing alcohol and other drugs.

Gerald was devastated. But, after mourning for about two months, he fell wildly in love with another woman, who was a start-in-the-morning-and-drink-'til-she-passes-out alcoholic. After spending several months worrying about her, trying to help her, trying to figure out what he was doing that caused her to drink, trying to control her drinking, and ultimately getting angry with her because she wouldn't stop drinking, Gerald terminated the relationship. Soon he met another woman, fell in love with her, and moved into her apartment. Within months, Gerald suspected she, too, was chemically dependent.

Soon, Gerald began spending much of this time worrying about his girlfriend. He checked up on her, rummaged through her purse looking for pills or other evidence, and questioned her about her activities. Sometimes, he simply denied she had a problem. During those times, he kept busy, tried to enjoy his time with his girlfriend (although he said he felt uneasy), and told himself, "It's just me. Something's wrong with me."

During one of the many crises in his most recent relationship, when Gerald was temporarily jolted out of denial, he went to a chemical dependency counselor for advice.

"I know I should end the relationship," Gerald said, "but I'm just not ready to let it go. We can talk about anything and everything together. We're such good friends. And I love her. Why? Why does this always happen to me?

"Give me a room full of women, and I'll fall in love with the one with the most problems—the one that will treat me the worst. Frankly, they're more of a challenge," Gerald confided. "If a woman treats me too well, it turns me off."

Gerald considered himself a social drinker who had never had problems as a result of his drinking. Gerald told the counselor he had never used drugs. Gerald's brother, now in his late forties, had been an alcoholic since he was a teenager. Gerald denied that either of his deceased parents was an alcoholic, but reluctantly admitted his dad may have "drunk too much."

The counselor suggested the alcoholism and excessive drinking in Gerald's immediate family may still be affecting him and his relationships. "How could their problems be affecting me?" he asked. "Dad has been dead for years, and I rarely see my brother."

After a few counseling sessions, Gerald began to label himself codependent, but he wasn't sure exactly what that meant or what to do about it. When Gerald became less angry about the immediate problem in his relationship, he discontinued counseling. Gerald decided his girlfriend's problems with drugs weren't that bad. He became convinced his problems with women were due to bad luck. He said he hoped his luck would change someday.

Is Gerald's problem bad luck? Or is it codependency?

Patty was in her mid-thirties and had been married for eleven years when she sought help from a private therapist. She had three children, the youngest of whom had cerebral palsy. Patty had devoted her life to being a good wife and mother. She told her therapist she loved her children, didn't regret her decision to stay home and raise them, but hated her daily routine. Before her marriage, she had many friends and hobbies, worked as a nurse, and was interested in the world around her. However, in the years following the birth of her children, particularly her handicapped child, she had lost her enthusiasm for life. She had few friends, had gained over 80 pounds, didn't know what she was feeling, and if she did, felt guilty for feeling that way. She explained she had tried to stay active by helping her friends and doing volunteer work for various organizations, but her efforts usually resulted in feelings of ineffectiveness and resentment. She thought about returning to work, but she didn't because, "All I know is nursing, and I'm sick of taking care of people."

"My family and friends think I'm a tower of strength. Good ol' dependable Patty. Always there. Always in control. Always ready to help them. The truth is," Patty said, "I'm falling apart, very quietly but very certainly. I've been depressed for years. I can't shake it. I cry at the drop of a hat. I don't have any energy. I scream at the kids all the time. I don't have any interest in sex, at least not with my husband. I feel guilty all the time about everything. I even feel guilty about coming to see you," she told the counselor. "I should be able to solve my own problems. I should be able to just snap out of this. It's ridiculous to waste your time and my husband's money for my problems, problems I'm probably imagining and blowing way out of proportion.

"But I had to do something," Patty confessed. "Lately, I've been thinking about suicide. Of course," she added, "I'd never actually kill myself. Too many people need me. Too many people depend on me. I'd be letting them down. But I'm worried. I'm scared."

The counselor learned Patty and her husband had children, the youngest with cerebral palsy. Patty also said before their marriage, her husband had problems with alcohol. During their marriage, he had drunk less, had held the same job, and had been a good provider. But, upon questioning, Patty told the counselor her husband had not attended Alcoholics Anonymous meetings or any other support group. Instead, he went "on the wagon" for months between weekend drinking binges. When he drank, he acted crazy. When he wasn't drinking, he was angry and hostile.

"I don't know what's happened to him. He's not the man I married. What's even more frightening is I don't know what's happening to me or who I am," Patty said. "It's difficult to explain exactly what the problem is. I don't understand it myself. There's no major problem I can point to and say, 'That's what's wrong.' But it feels like I've lost myself. At times, I wonder if I'm going crazy. What's wrong with me?" Patty asked.

"Maybe your husband is an alcoholic, and your problems are caused by the family disease of alcoholism," the counselor suggested.

"How could that be?" Patty asked. "My husband doesn't drink that often."

The counselor dug into Patty's background. Patty talked with fondness about her parents and her two adult brothers. She came from a good family that was close and successful.

The counselor dug deeper. Patty mentioned her father had attended Alcoholics Anonymous since she was a teenager.

"Dad sobered up when I was in high school," she said. "I really love him, and I'm proud of him. But his drinking years were some pretty crazy years for our family."

Not only was Patty married to someone who was probably an alcoholic, she is what is now called an adult child of an alcoholic. The entire family had been affected by the family disease of alcoholism. Her dad stopped drinking; her mother went to Al-Anon; family life improved. But Patty, too, had been affected. Was she expected to magically overcome the ways she had been affected, just because the drinking stopped?

Instead of additional counseling sessions, Patty's counselor referred Patty to a self-esteem course and an assertiveness class. The counselor also recommended Patty attend Al-Anon meetings or Adult Children of Alcoholics meeting, which are self-help groups based on the Twelve Steps of Alcoholics Anonymous.

Patty followed the counselor's advice. She didn't find an overnight cure, but as the months passed she found herself making decisions with greater ease, feeling and expressing her feelings, saying what she thought, paying attention to her needs, and feeling less guilty. She became more tolerant of herself and her daily routine. Gradually, her depression lifted. She cried less and laughed more. Her energy and enthusiasm for life returned. Incidentally, with no prodding from Patty, her husband joined Alcoholics Anonymous. He became less hostile, and their marriage began to improve. The point here is Patty gained control of her life. Her life started working.

Now, if you ask Patty what her problem is or was, she will answer: "I'm codependent."

Clients who seek help from mental health and chemical dependency agencies are not the only people who suffer from codependency. Randell was a chemical dependency counselor and a recovering alcoholic with several years of sobriety when he found himself having troubles. Randell was also an adult child of an alcoholic; his father and three brothers were alcoholics. An intelligent, sensitive man who enjoyed his work, Randell's problem was his leisure time. He spent most of it worrying about— obsessed with—other people and their problems. Sometimes he tried to untangle messes alcoholics created; other times he felt angry with the alcoholics for creating the messes he felt obligated to clean up; sometimes he felt upset because people, not necessarily alcoholics, behaved in particular ways. He ranted, felt guilty, sorry, and used by people. Rarely, however, did he feel close to them. Rarely did he have fun.

For many years, Randell believed his duty was to worry about people and get involved in their problems. He called his behavior kindness, concern, love, and, sometimes, righteous indignation. Now, after getting help for his problem, he calls it codependency.

Sometimes, codependent behavior becomes inextricably entangled with being a good wife, mother, husband, brother, or Christian. Now in her forties, Marlyss is an attractive woman—when she takes care of herself. Most of the time, however, she's busy taking care of her five children and her husband, who is a recovering alcoholic. She devoted her life to making them happy, but she didn't succeed. Usually, she feels angry and unappreciated for her efforts, and her family feels angry at her. She has sex with her husband whenever he wants, regardless of how she feels. She spends too much of the family's budget on toys and clothing for the children—whatever they want. She chauffeurs, reads to, cooks for, cleans for, cuddles, and coddles those around her, but nobody gives to her. Most of the time, they don't even say, "Thank you." Marlyss resents her constant giving to people in her life. She resents how her family and their needs control her life. She chose nursing as her profession, and she often resents that.

"But I feel guilty when I don't do what's asked of me. I feel guilty when I don't live up to my standards for a wife and mother. I feel guilty when I don't live up to other people's standards for me. I just plain feel guilty," she said. "In fact," she added, "I schedule my day, my priorities, according to guilt."

Does endlessly taking care of other people, resenting it, and expecting nothing in return mean Marlyss is a good wife and mother? Or could it mean Marlyss is codependent?

Alcoholism (or chemical dependency) is not the only family problem that can create a codependent person. Alissa, the mother of two teenagers, worked part-time at a mental health organization when she went to a family counselor. (She had previously gone to many family counselors in her search for help.) She went to counseling because her oldest child, a fourteen-year-old boy, was constantly causing problems. He ran away, broke curfew, skipped school, disobeyed other family rules, and generally did whatever he wanted, whenever he wanted.

"This child," Alissa told the counselor, "is driving me crazy."

She meant it. She was worried sick. Some days she was so depressed and troubled she couldn't get out of bed. Alissa had tried everything she could think of to help this child. She'd placed him in treatment three times, put him in two different foster homes, and dragged the whole family from counselor to counselor. Alissa had tried other techniques, too: She had threatened, cried, hollered, and begged. She had gotten tough and called the police on him. She had tried gentleness and forgiveness. She even tried acting like he hadn't done the inappropriate things he had done. She had locked him out. And she had traveled halfway across the state to bring him home after he ran away. Although her efforts hadn't helped her child, Alissa was obsessed with finding and doing the one thing that would "make him see the errors of his ways" and help him change.

"Why," she asked the counselor, "is he doing this to me? He's running and ruining my life!"

The counselor agreed the problem with Alissa's son was painful, upsetting, and required action. But the counselor also said the problem didn't have to run and ruin Alissa's life.

"You haven't been able to control your son, but you can gain control of yourself," he said. "You can deal with your own codependency."

Sheryl also labels herself codependent. Shortly after marrying the man of her dreams, she found herself in a nightmare. Her husband, she learned, was a sex addict. In his case, that meant he couldn't control his urges to indulge in pornography, he was compulsively drawn into affairs with other women and, as Sheryl put it, "God only knows what and who else." She learned her husband was a sex addict one week after their wedding, when she discovered him in bed with another woman.

Sheryl's first response was panic. Then she got angry. Then she felt concern—for her husband and his problem. Her friends advised her to leave him, but she decided to stay in the marriage. He needed help. He needed her. Maybe he would change. Besides, she wasn't ready to lose her dream of that rosy future they would have together.

Her husband joined Sex Addicts Anonymous, a Twelve Step self-help group similar to Alcoholics Anonymous. Sheryl refused to join Co-SA (similar to Al-Anon) for family members of sex addicts. She didn't want to go public with her problem; she didn't even want to discuss it privately.

Over a period of months, Sheryl, a successful fashion model, found herself accepting fewer work assignments, turning down evenings out with friends, and sticking closer to home. She wanted to answer the telephone, in case women called for her husband. She wanted to be home to see her husband when he left the house and returned. She wanted to see what he looked like, how he acted, and how he talked. She wanted to know exactly what he was doing and with whom he was doing it. She often called his S.A. sponsor to complain, to report, and to inquire about her husband's progress. She refused, she said, to be tricked and deceived again.

Gradually, she alienated herself from her friends and activities. She was too worried to work; she was too ashamed to talk to her friends. Her husband had several more affairs; her friends were frustrated with her for staying with him and constantly whining about how terrible it was to be his wife.

"I couldn't stand the sight of my husband. I had nothing but contempt for him. Yet, I couldn't bring myself to leave him," Sheryl reported later. "I couldn't make myself do much of anything except worry and check up on him."

"My turning point was the night I chased him with a butcher knife," Sheryl said. "It was my lowest point. I was running through the house screaming and raving, when I suddenly became aware, for the first time, of *me*. I had gone mad. I was crazy—completely out of control—and he just stood there, calmly looking at me. I knew then I had to do something to get help for me."

Sheryl joined Co-SA shortly after that incident. It was at those meetings that she began to label herself and her loss of control as codependency. Sheryl is now separated from her husband and seeking a divorce. She is also feeling better about herself.

Although the preceding examples have been dramatic, codependency doesn't necessarily have to be so intense. And it doesn't always involve experiences with deeply troubled people. Kristen is married, has two young children, and knows of no alcoholism or compulsive disorders in her immediate or extended family. Yet, she calls herself codependent. Her problem, she says, is that other people's moods control her emotions; she, in turn, tries to control their feelings.

"If my husband is happy, and I feel responsible for that, then I'm happy. If he's upset, I feel responsible for that, too. I'm anxious, uncomfortable, and upset until he feels better. I try to *make* him feel better. I feel guilty if I can't. And he gets angry with me for trying.

"And it's not only with him that I behave codependently," she added. "It's with everyone: my parents, my children, guests in my home. Somehow, I just seem to lose myself in other people. I get enmeshed in them.

"I'd like to do something about it—this thing called codependency— before it gets any worse. I'm not terribly unhappy," she said, "but I'd like to learn how to relax and start enjoying myself and other people."

A minister summarized the condition this way: "Some people are *really* codependent, and some of us are a *little bit* codependent."

I chose the preceding examples because they're interesting and represent a variety of experiences. They also illuminate a point that needs to be made: No single example illustrates the typical codependent or his or her experience. Codependency is complex. People are complex. Each person is unique, and each person's situation is different. Some people have extremely painful and debilitating experiences with codependency. Others don't and may be only mildly affected. Sometimes codependency is a person's response to another person's alcoholism; sometimes it isn't. Each codependent has a unique experience born from his or her circumstances, history, and personality.

Yet, a common thread runs through all stories of codependency. It involves our responses and reactions to people around us. It involves our relationships with other people, whether they are alcoholics, gamblers, sex addicts, overeaters, or normal people. Codependency involves the effects these people have on us and how we, in turn, try to affect them. As Al-Anon members say, "Identify, don't compare."

ACTIVITY

1. Did you identify with any people in this chapter? What helped you think of yourself? Which relationships did it bring to mind? Why?

2. You might find it helpful to buy a large notebook and record your responses to these activities. You can also write down other thoughts and feelings you have as you read this book.

3

CODEPENDENCY

Relationships are like a dance, with visible energy
racing back and forth between the partners.
Some relationships are the slow,
dark dance of death.[1]

—COLETTE DOWLING

Up to this point, I have been using the words *codependent* and *codependency* as lucid terms. However, the definitions of these words remain vague.

The definition of chemical dependency means being dependent (psychologically and/or physically) on alcohol or other drugs. Overeating and gambling are also words that bring specific ideas to mind. But what is codependency?

The obvious definition would be: being a partner in dependency. This definition is close to the truth but still unclear. It brings no specific image to mind. Codependency is part of treatment center jargon, professional slang that's probably unintelligible to people outside that profession and gibberish to some inside the trade.

Jargon may or may not mean anything in particular. Jargon may mean different things to different people. Or, people may sense what a term means but not be able to clearly define it, because it's never been clearly defined.

Those are some of the problems I've encountered with researching and attempting to define codependency and codependent. Many people haven't heard the terms. Others, who are familiar with the words, can't define them. If they can, each definition is different. Or people define the words by using more jargon. To complicate matters, I can't find the words in any dictionaries. My computer keeps tagging the words as misspelled, trying to convince me they're not words.

Yet, codependency does mean something in particular, something particularly important to me and millions of people. Let's get rid of the jargon and look at that meaning.

WHAT'S CODEPENDENCY?

I have heard and read many definitions of codependency.

In an article from the book *Co-Dependency, An Emerging Issue,* Robert Subby wrote codependency is "an emotional, psychological, and behavioral condition that develops as a result of an individual's prolonged exposure to, and practice of, a set of oppressive rules—rules which prevent the open expression of feeling as well as the direct discussion of personal and interpersonal problems."[2]

Earnie Larsen, another codependency specialist and a pioneer in that field, defines codependency as "those self-defeating, learned behaviors or character defects that result in a diminished capacity to initiate or to participate in loving relationships."

Some less professional definitions follow.

"Codependency means," said one woman, "that I'm a caretaker."

"Being codependent means I'm married to an alcoholic," responded one woman. "It also means I need to go to Al-Anon."

"Codependency," replied another, "means I'm up to my elbows in alcoholics."

"It means I'm always looking for someone to glob onto."

"Codependency? It means I know any man I'm attracted to, fall in love with, or marry will be chemically dependent or have some other equally serious problem."

"Codependency," explained one person, "is knowing all your relationships will either go on and on the same way (painfully), or end the same way (disastrously). Or both."

There are almost as many definitions of codependency as there are experiences that represent it. In desperation (or perhaps enlightenment), some therapists have proclaimed: "Codependency is *anything*, and *everyone* is codependent." So who's got the inside story? Which definition is accurate? A brief history of codependency will help answer this question.

A BRIEF HISTORY

The word codependency appeared on the treatment scene in the late seventies. I don't know who discovered it. Although several people may claim to have done so, the word emerged simultaneously in several different treatment centers in Minnesota, according to information from the office of Sondra Smalley, C.C.D.P., a licensed psychologist and a leader in the codependency field. Maybe Minnesota, the heartland of chemical dependency treatment and Twelve Step programs for compulsive disorders, discovered it.

Robert Subby and John Friel, in an article from the book *Co-Dependency, An Emerging Issue*, wrote: "Originally, it was used to describe the person or persons whose lives were affected as a result of their being involved with someone who was chemically dependent. The codependent spouse or child or lover of someone who was chemically dependent was seen as having developed a pattern of coping with life that was not healthy, as a reaction to someone else's drug or alcohol abuse."[3]

It was a new name for an old game. Professionals had long suspected something peculiar happened to people who were closely involved with chemically dependent people. Some research had been done on the subject, indicating a physical, mental, emotional, and spiritual condition similar to alcoholism seemed to appear in many nonalcoholic or non-chemically dependent people who were close to an alcoholic. Words (more jargon which would later become synonymous for codependent) surfaced to describe this phenomenon: co-alcoholic, nonalcoholic, para-alcoholic.

Codependents certainly felt the effects of codependency long before the word was coined. In the 1940s, after the birth of Alcoholics Anonymous, a group of people—primarily wives of alcoholics—formed self-help support groups to deal with the ways their spouses' alcoholism affected them.[4] They didn't know they would later be called codependents. They did know they had been directly affected by their mates' alcoholism. And, they were envious that alcoholics had a Twelve Step program to recover through. The wives also wanted a program. So they used the A.A. Twelve Step program, revised the A.A. Twelve Traditions, changed its name to Al-Anon, and it worked! Millions of people have since benefited from Al-Anon.[5]

The basic thought then, and in 1979 when the word codependency emerged, was codependents (co-alcoholics or para-alcoholics) *were people whose lives had become unmanageable as a result of living in a committed relationship with an alcoholic.*[6]

However, the definition for codependency has expanded since then. Professionals began to better understand the effects of the chemically dependent person on the family, and the effects of the family on the chemically dependent person. Professionals began to identify other problems such as overeating and undereating, gambling, and certain sexual behaviors. These compulsive disorders paralleled the compulsive disorder, or *illness,* of alcoholism. Professionals also began to notice many people in close relationships with these compulsive people developed patterns of reacting and coping that resembled the coping patterns of people in relationships with alcoholics. Something peculiar had happened to these families, too.

As professionals began to understand codependency better, more groups of people appeared to have it: adult children of alcoholics; people in relationships with emotionally or mentally disturbed persons; people in relationships with chronically ill people; parents of children with behavior problems; people in relationships with irresponsible people; professionals—nurses, social workers, and others in "helping" occupations. Even recovering alcoholics and addicts noticed they were codependent and perhaps had been long before becoming chemically dependent.[7] Codependents started cropping up everywhere.

When a codependent discontinued his or her relationship with a troubled person, the codependent frequently sought another troubled person and repeated the codependent behaviors with that new person. These behaviors, or coping mechanisms, seemed to prevail throughout the codependent's life—if that person didn't change these behaviors.

Was it safe to assume codependency was triggered through relationships with people who have serious illnesses, behavior problems, or destructive compulsive disorders? Alcoholism in the family helped create codependency, but many other circumstances seemed to produce it, also.

One fairly common denominator was having a relationship, personally or professionally, with troubled, needy, or dependent people. But a second, more common denominator seemed to be the unwritten, silent rules that usually develop in the immediate family and set the pace for relationships.[8] These rules prohibit discussion about problems; open expression of feelings; direct, honest communication; realistic expectations, such as being human, vulnerable, or imperfect; selfishness; trust in other people and one's self; playing and having fun; and rocking the delicately balanced family canoe through growth or change—however healthy and beneficial that movement might be. These rules are common to alcoholic family systems but can emerge in other families, too.

Now, I return to an earlier question: Which definition of codependency is accurate? They all are. Some describe the cause, some the effects, some the overall condition, some the symptoms, some the patterns, and some the pain. Codependency either meant, or has come to mean, all the definitions listed earlier.

I'm not trying to confuse you. Codependency has a fuzzy definition because it is a gray, fuzzy condition. It is complex, theoretical, and difficult to completely define in one or two sentences.

Why all this fuss about a definition? Because I'm going to attempt the difficult—define codependent in one sentence. And, I want you to see the broader picture before I show you the narrower one. I hope this approach might help you identify codependency in yourself, if that identification is appropriate. Defining the problem is important because it helps determine the solution. Here, the solution is vital. It means feeling better. It means recovery.

So, here is my definition of a codependent:

A codependent person is one who has let another person's behavior affect him or her, and who is obsessed with controlling that person's behavior.

The *other person* might be a child, an adult, a lover, a spouse, a brother, a sister, a grandparent, a parent, a client, or a best friend. He or she could be an alcoholic, a drug addict, a mentally or physically ill person, a normal person who occasionally has sad feelings, or one of the people mentioned earlier.

But, the heart of the definition and recovery lies not in the *other person*—no matter how much we believe it does. It lies in ourselves, in the ways we have let other people's behavior affect us and in the ways we try to affect them: the obsessing, the controlling, the obsessive "helping," caretaking, low self-worth bordering on self-hatred, self-repression, abundance of anger and guilt, peculiar dependency on peculiar people, attraction to and tolerance for the bizarre, other-centeredness that results in abandonment of self, communication problems, intimacy problems, and an ongoing whirlwind trip through the five-stage grief process.

Is codependency an illness? Some professionals say codependency isn't a disease; they say it's a normal reaction to abnormal people.[9]

Other professionals say codependency is a disease; it's a chronic, progressive illness. They suggest codependents want and need sick people around them to be happy in an unhealthy way. They say, for instance, the wife of an alcoholic needed to marry an alcoholic and chose him because she unconsciously thought he was an alcoholic. Furthermore, she needed him drinking and socking it to her to feel fulfilled. This latter judgment may be overly harsh. I'm convinced codependents need less harshness in their lives. Other people have been hard enough on us. We have been hard enough on ourselves. Friends, we have suffered enough. We have been victimized by diseases and people. Each of us must decide what part we played in our victimization.

I don't *know* if codependency is or isn't an illness. I'm not an expert. But, to tell you what I *believe,* let me complete the brief history of codependency which I started earlier in this chapter.

Although the first Al-Anon groups were formed in the 1940s, I am certain we could go back to the beginning of time and human relationships and find glimmers of codependent behavior. People have always had problems, and others have always cared for their troubled friends and relatives. People have likely been caught up with the problems of others since relationships began.

Codependency probably trailed man as he struggled through the remaining B.C. years, right up to "these generally wretched times of the twentieth century," as Morley Safer of *60 Minutes* says. Ever since people first existed, they have been doing all the things we label "codependent." They have worried themselves sick about other people. They have tried to help in ways that didn't help. They have said yes when they meant no. They have tried to make other people see things their way. They have bent over backward to avoid hurting people's feelings and, in so doing, have hurt themselves. They have been afraid to trust their feelings. They have believed lies and then felt betrayed. They have wanted to get even and punish others. They have felt so angry they wanted to kill. They have struggled for their rights while other people said they didn't have any. They have worn sackcloth because they didn't believe they deserved silk.

Codependents have undoubtedly done good deeds too. By their nature, codependents are benevolent—concerned about and responsive to the needs of the world. As Thomas Wright writes in an article from the book

Co-Dependency, An Emerging Issue, "I suspect codependents have histori-
cally attacked social injustice and fought for the rights of the underdog.
Codependents want to help. I suspect they have helped. But they probably died thinking they didn't do enough and were feeling guilty.

"It is natural to want to protect and help the people we care about.
It is also natural to be affected by and react to the problems of people
around us. As a problem becomes more serious and remains unresolved,
we become more affected and react more intensely to it."

The word *react* is important here. However you approach codependency, however you define it, and from whatever fame of reference you
choose to diagnose and treat it, codependency is primarily a reactionary
process. Codependents are reactionaries. They overreact. They under-
react. But rarely do they *act.* They react to the problems, pains, lives, and
behaviors of others. They react to their own problems, pains, and behaviors. Many codependent reactions are reactions to stress and uncertainty
of living or growing up with alcoholism and other problems. It is normal
to react to stress. It is not necessarily abnormal, but it is heroic and life-
saving to learn how to *not* react and to act in more healthy ways. Most of
us, however, need help to learn to do that.

Perhaps one reason some professionals call codependency a disease is because many codependents are reacting to an illness such as
alcoholism.

Another reason codependency is called a disease is because it is
progressive. As the people around us become sicker, we may begin to
react more intensely. What began as a little concern may trigger isolation, depression, emotional or physical illness, or suicidal fantasies. One
thing leads to another, and things get worse. Codependency may not be
an illness, but it can make you sick. And, it can help the people around
you stay sick.

Another reason codependency is called a disease is because codependent behaviors—like many self-destructive behaviors—become habitual.
We repeat habits without thinking. Habits take on a life of their own.[10]

Whatever problem the other person has, codependency involves a habitual system of thinking, feeling, and behaving toward ourselves and others that can cause us pain. Codependent behaviors or habits are self-destructive. We frequently react to people who are destroying themselves; we react by learning to destroy ourselves. These habits can lead us into, or keep us in, destructive relationships, relationships that don't work. These behaviors can sabotage relationships that may otherwise have worked. These behaviors can prevent us from finding peace and happiness with the most important person in our lives—ourselves. These behaviors belong to the only person each of us can control—the only person we can change—ourselves. These are our problems. In the next chapter, we will examine these behaviors.

ACTIVITY

1. How would you define codependency?

2. Do you know anybody who has significantly affected your life, somebody whom you worry about and wish you could change? Who? Write several paragraphs about that person and your relationship. Later, read what you wrote. What are your feelings?

4

Codependent Characteristics

God, grant me the serenity
To accept the things I cannot change,
Courage to change the things I can,
And wisdom to know the difference.

—THE SERENITY PRAYER

Although two codependents might disagree on the definition of codependency, if they discuss the issues with each other, each will probably sense what the other person means. They will share ideas about things they have in common—things they do, think, feel, and say—that are characteristic of codependency. It is on these points—symptoms, problems, coping mechanisms, or reactions—that most definitions and recovery programs overlap and agree. These points dictate recovery. They are the things we need to recognize, accept, live with, deal with, struggle through, and frequently change.

Before I list the things codependents tend to do, however, I will make an important point: Having these problems does not mean we're bad, defective, or inferior. Some of us learned these behaviors as children. Other people learned them later in life. We may have learned some of these things from our interpretation of religion. Some women were taught these behaviors were desirable feminine attributes. Wherever we learned to do these things, most of us learned our lessons well.

Most of us started doing these things out of necessity to protect ourselves and meet our needs. We performed, felt, and thought these things to survive—emotionally, mentally, and sometimes physically. We tried to understand and cope with our complex worlds in the best ways. It is not always easy to live with normal, healthy people. It is particularly difficult to live with sick, disturbed, or troubled people. It is horrible having to live with a raving alcoholic. Many of us have been trying to cope with outrageous circumstances, and these efforts have been both admirable and heroic. We have done the best we could.

However, these self-protective devices may have outgrown their usefulness. Sometimes, the things we do to protect ourselves turn on us and hurt us. They become self-destructive. Many codependents are barely surviving, and most aren't getting their needs met. As counselor Scott Egleston says, codependency is a way of getting needs met that doesn't get needs met. We've been doing the wrong things for the right reasons.

Can we change? Can we learn healthier behaviors? I don't know if mental, spiritual, and emotional health can be taught, but we can be inspired and encouraged. We can learn to do things differently. We can change. I think most people want to be healthy and live the best lives they can. But many of us don't know it's okay to do things differently. Many of us don't even understand what we've been doing that hasn't been working. Most of us have been so busy responding to other people's problems that we haven't had time to identify, much less take care of, our own problems.

Many professionals say the first step toward change is awareness. The second step is acceptance.[1] With that in mind, let's examine the characteristics of codependency. These characteristics have been compiled from my entire bibliography and from my personal and professional experience.

CARETAKING

Codependents may:

- think and feel responsible for other people—for other people's feelings, thoughts, actions, choices, wants, needs, well-being, lack of well-being, and ultimate destiny.
- feel anxiety, pity, and guilt when other people have a problem.
- feel compelled—almost forced—to help that person solve the problem, such as offering unwanted advice, giving a rapid-fire series of suggestions, or fixing feelings.
- feel angry when their help isn't effective.
- anticipate other people's needs.
- wonder why others don't do the same for them.
- find themselves saying yes when they mean no, doing things they don't really want to be doing, doing more than their fair share of the work, and doing things other people are capable of doing for themselves.
- not know what they want and need or, if they do, tell themselves what they want and need is not important.
- try to please others instead of themselves.
- find it easier to feel and express anger about injustices done to others, rather than injustices done to themselves.
- feel safest when giving.
- feel insecure and guilty when somebody gives to them.
- feel sad because they spend their whole lives giving to other people and nobody gives to them.
- find themselves attracted to needy people.
- find needy people attracted to them.
- feel bored, empty, and worthless if they don't have a crisis in their lives, a problem to solve, or someone to help.
- abandon their routine to respond to or do something for somebody else.

- overcommit themselves.
- feel harried and pressured.
- believe deep inside other people are somehow responsible for them.
- blame others for the spot the codependents are in.
- say other people make the codependents feel the way they do.
- believe other people are making them crazy.
- feel angry, victimized, unappreciated, and used.
- find other people become impatient or angry with them for all the preceding characteristics.

LOW SELF-WORTH

Codependents tend to:

- come from troubled, repressed, or dysfunctional families.
- deny their family was trouble, repressed, or dysfunctional.
- blame themselves for everything.
- pick on themselves for everything, including the way they think, feel, look, act, and behave.
- get angry, defensive, self-righteous, and indignant when others blame and criticize the codependents—something codependents regularly do to themselves.
- reject compliments or praise.
- get depressed from a lack of compliments and praise (stroke deprivation).
- feel different from the rest of the world.
- think they're not quite good enough.
- feel guilty about spending money on themselves or doing unnecessary or fun things for themselves.
- fear rejection.
- take things personally.
- have been victims of sexual, physical, or emotional abuse, neglect, abandonment, or alcoholism.

- feel like victims.
- tell themselves they can't do anything right.
- be afraid of making mistakes.
- wonder why they have a tough time making decisions.
- expect themselves to do everything perfectly.
- wonder why they can't get anything done to their satisfaction.
- have a lot of "shoulds."
- feel a lot of guilt.
- feel ashamed of who they are.
- think their lives aren't worth living.
- try to help other people live their lives instead.
- get artificial feelings of self-worth from helping others.
- get strong feelings of low self-worth—embarrassment, failure, etc.—from other people's failures and problems.
- wish good things would happen to them.
- believe good things never will happen.
- believe they don't deserve good things and happiness.
- wish other people would like and love them.
- believe other people couldn't possibly like and love them.
- try to prove they're good enough for other people.
- settle for being needed.

REPRESSION

Many codependents:

- push their thoughts and feelings out of their awareness because of fear and guilt.
- become afraid to let themselves be who they are.
- appear rigid and controlled.

OBSESSION

Codependents tend to:

- feel terribly anxious about problems and people.
- worry about the silliest things.
- think and talk a lot about other people.
- lose sleep over problems or other people's behavior.
- worry.
- never find answers.
- check on people.
- try to catch people in acts of misbehavior.
- feel unable to quit talking, thinking, and worrying about other people or problems.
- abandon their routine because they are so upset about somebody or something.
- focus all their energy on other people and problems.
- wonder why they never have any energy.
- wonder why they can't get things done.

CONTROLLING

Many codependents:

- have lived through events and with people that were out of control, causing the codependents sorrow and disappointment.
- become afraid to let other people be who they are and allow events to happen naturally.
- don't see or deal with their fear of loss of control.
- think they know best how things should turn out and how people should behave.
- try to control events and people through helplessness, guilt, coercion, threats, advice-giving, manipulation, or domination.
- eventually fail in their efforts or provoke people's anger.
- get frustrated and angry.
- feel controlled by events and people.

DENIAL

Codependents tend to:

- ignore problems or pretend they aren't happening.
- pretend circumstances aren't as bad as they are.
- tell themselves things will be better tomorrow.
- stay busy so they don't have to think about things.
- get confused.
- get depressed or sick.
- go to doctors and get tranquilizers.
- become workaholics.
- spend money compulsively.
- overeat.
- pretend those things aren't happening, either.
- watch problems get worse.
- believe lies.
- lie to themselves.
- wonder why they feel like they're going crazy.

DEPENDENCY

Many codependents:

- don't feel happy, content, or peaceful with themselves.
- look for happiness outside themselves.
- latch onto whoever or whatever they think can provide happiness.
- feel terribly threatened by the loss of any thing or person they think provides their happiness.
- didn't feel love and approval from their parents.
- don't love themselves.
- believe other people can't or don't love them.
- desperately seek love and approval.
- often seek love from people incapable of loving.
- believe other people are never there for them.
- equate love with pain.

- feel they need people more than they want them.
- try to prove they're good enough to be loved.
- don't take time to see if other people are good for them.
- worry whether other people love or like them.
- don't take time to figure out if they love or like other people.
- center their lives around other people.
- look to relationships to provide all their good feelings.
- lose interest in their own lives when they love.
- worry other people will leave them.
- don't believe they can take care of themselves.
- stay in relationships that don't work.
- tolerate abuse to keep people loving them.
- feel trapped in relationships.
- leave bad relationships and form new ones that don't work either.
- wonder if they will ever find love.

POOR COMMUNICATION
Codependents frequently:

- blame.
- threaten.
- coerce.
- beg.
- bribe.
- advise.
- don't say what they mean.
- don't mean what they say.
- don't know what they mean.
- don't take themselves seriously.
- think other people don't take the codependents seriously.
- take themselves too seriously.
- ask for what they want and need indirectly—sighing, for example.
- find it difficult to get to the point.
- aren't sure what the point is.

- gauge their words carefully to achieve a desired effect.
- try to say what they think will please people.
- try to say what they think will provoke people.
- try to say what they hope will make people do what they want them to do.
- eliminate the word *no* from their vocabulary.
- talk too much.
- talk about other people.
- avoid talking about themselves, their problems, feelings, and thoughts.
- say everything is their fault.
- say nothing is their fault.
- believe their opinions don't matter.
- wait to express their opinions until they know other people's opinions.
- lie to protect and cover up for people they love.
- lie to protect themselves.
- have a difficult time asserting their rights.
- have a difficult time expressing their emotions honestly, openly, and appropriately.
- think most of what they have to say is unimportant.
- begin to talk in cynical, self-degrading, or hostile ways.
- apologize for bothering people.

Weak Boundaries

Codependents frequently:

- say they won't tolerate certain behaviors from other people.
- gradually increase their tolerance until they can tolerate and do things they said they never would.
- let others hurt them.
- keep letting people hurt them.
- wonder why they hurt so badly.
- complain, blame, and try to control while they continue to stand there.

- finally get angry.
- become totally intolerant.

LACK OF TRUST

Codependents:

- don't trust themselves.
- don't trust their feelings.
- don't trust their decisions.
- don't trust other people.
- try to trust untrustworthy people.
- think God has abandoned them.
- lose faith and trust in God.

ANGER

Many codependents:

- feel very scared, hurt, and angry.
- live with people who are very scared, hurt, and angry.
- are afraid of their own anger.
- are frightened of other people's anger.
- think people will go away if anger enters the picture.
- think other people make them feel angry.
- are afraid to make other people feel anger.
- feel controlled by other people's anger.
- repress their angry feelings.
- cry a lot, get depressed, overeat, get sick, do mean and nasty things to get even, act hostile, or have violent temper outbursts.
- punish other people for making the codependents angry.
- have been ashamed for feeling angry.
- place guilt and shame on themselves for feeling angry.
- feel increasing amounts of anger, resentment, and bitterness.
- feel safer with their anger than with hurt feelings.
- wonder if they'll ever *not* be angry.

SEX PROBLEMS

Some codependents:

- are caretakers in the bedroom.
- have sex when they don't want to.
- have sex when they'd rather be held, nurtured, and loved.
- try to have sex when they're angry or hurt.
- refuse to enjoy sex because they're so angry at their partner.
- are afraid of losing control.
- have a difficult time asking for what they need in bed.
- withdraw emotionally from their partner.
- feel sexual revulsion toward their partner.
- don't talk about it.
- force themselves to have sex, anyway.
- reduce sex to a technical act.
- wonder why they don't enjoy sex.
- lose interest in sex.
- make up reasons to abstain.
- wish their sex partner would die, go away, or sense the codependent's feelings.
- have strong sexual fantasies about other people.
- consider or have an extramarital affair.

MISCELLANEOUS

Codependents tend to:

- be extremely responsible.
- be extremely irresponsible.
- become martyrs, sacrificing their happiness and that of others for causes that don't require sacrifice.
- find it difficult to feel close to people.
- find it difficult to have fun and be spontaneous.
- have an overall passive response to codependency—crying, hurt, helplessness.

- have an overall aggressive response to codependency—violence, anger, dominance.
- combine passive and aggressive responses.
- vacillate in decisions and emotions.
- laugh when they feel like crying.
- stay loyal to their compulsions and people even when it hurts.
- be ashamed about family, personal, or relationship problems.
- be confused about the nature of the problem.
- cover up, lie, and protect the problem.
- not seek help because they tell themselves the problem isn't bad enough, or they aren't important enough.
- wonder why the problem doesn't go away.

PROGRESSIVE

In the later stages of codependency, codependents may:

- feel lethargic.
- feel depressed.
- become withdrawn and isolated.
- experience a complete loss of daily routine and structure.
- abuse or neglect their children and other responsibilities.
- feel hopeless.
- begin to plan their escape from a relationship they feel trapped in.
- think about suicide.
- become violent.
- become seriously emotionally, mentally, or physically ill.
- experience an eating disorder (over- or undereating).
- become addicted to alcohol and other drugs.

The preceding checklist is long but not all-inclusive. Like other people, codependents do, feel, and think many things. There is not a certain number of traits that guarantees whether a person is or isn't codependent. Each person is different; each person has his or her way of doing things. I'm just trying to paint a picture. The interpretation, or decision, is up to you. What's most important is that you first identify behaviors or areas that cause you problems, and then decide what you want to do.

At the end of Chapter Three, I asked you to define codependency. As Earnie Larsen says, if you defined your problem as "living with an alcoholic," you may think *not* living with an alcoholic is the solution to your problem. That may be partially correct. But our real problems as codependents are our own characteristics—our codependent behaviors.

Who's codependent? I am.

An estimated 80 million people are chemically dependent or in a relationship with someone who is.[2] They are probably codependent.

People who love, care about, or work with troubled people may be codependent.

People who care about people with eating disorders are probably codependent. In her book *Fat Is a Family Affair,* Judi Hollis wrote that one eating disorder person can keep fifteen to twenty codependents busy.[3] Many people with eating disorders are codependents, too. "In an informal survey, I discovered at least 40 percent of the wives of alcoholics were obese," Hollis wrote.[4]

You may be reading this book for yourself; you may be codependent. Or, you may be reading this book to help someone else; if so, you probably are codependent. If concern has turned into obsession; if compassion has turned into caretaking; if you are taking care of other people and not taking care of yourself—you may be in trouble with codependency. Each person must decide for him- or herself if codependency is a problem. Each person must decide for him- or herself what needs to be changed and when that should happen.

Codependency is many things. It is a dependency on people—on their moods, behaviors, sickness or well-being, and their love. It is a paradoxical dependency.[5] Codependents appear to be depended upon, but they are dependent. They look strong but feel helpless. They appear controlling but in reality are controlled themselves, sometimes by an illness such as alcoholism.

These are the issues that dictate recovery. It is solving these problems that makes recovery fun. Many recoveries from problems that involve a person's mind, emotions, and spirit are long and grueling. Not so, here. Except for normal human emotions we would be feeling anyway, and twinges of discomfort as we begin to behave differently, recovery from codependency is exciting. It is liberating. It lets us be who we are. It lets other people be who they are. It helps us own our God-given power to think, feel, and act. It feels good. It brings peace. It enables us to love ourselves and others. It allows us to receive love—some of the good stuff we've all been looking for. It provides an optimum environment for the people around us to get and stay healthy. And recovery helps stop the unbearable pain many of us have been living with.

Recovery is not only fun, it is simple. It is not always easy, but it is simple. It is based on a premise many of us have forgotten or never learned: Each person is responsible for him- or herself. It involves learning one new behavior that we will devote ourselves to: taking care of ourselves. In the second part of this book, we'll discuss specific ideas for doing that.

ACTIVITIES

1. Go through the checklist in this chapter. Mark each characteristic with a 0 if it is never a problem for you. Mark the characteristic with a 1 if it is occasionally a problem. And mark it with a 2 if it is frequently a problem. Later, in another chapter, you will use this to establish goals. You may wish to use it now as a guide to the chapters you want to read.

2. How do you feel about changing yourself? What do you think would happen if you began to change? Do you think you can change? Why or why not? Write several paragraphs answering these questions.

PART II

THE BASICS OF SELF-CARE

5

DETACHMENT

*It (detachment) is not detaching
from the person whom we care about,
but from the agony of involvement.*[1]

—AL-ANON MEMBER

When I was trying to choose the topic for the first chapter in this section of the book, many subjects competed for first place. I chose detachment not because it is significantly more important than the other concepts. I selected it because it is an underlying concept. It is something we need to do frequently, as we strive to live happy lives. It is the goal of most recovery programs for codependents. And, it is also something we must do first—before we can do the other things we need to do. We cannot begin to work on ourselves, to live our own lives, feel our own feelings, and solve our own problems until we have detached from the object of our obsession. From my experiences (and those of others), it appears that even our Higher Power can't do much with us until we have detached.

ATTACHMENT
When a codependent says, "I think I'm getting attached to you," look out! He or she probably means it.

Most codependents are attached to the people and problems in their environments. By "attachment," I don't mean normal feelings of liking people, being concerned about problems, or feeling connected to the world. Attachment is becoming overly-involved, sometimes hopelessly entangled.

Attachment can take several forms:

- We may become excessively worried about, and preoccupied with, a problem or person (our mental energy is attached).
- Or, we may graduate to becoming obsessed with and controlling of the people and problems in our environment (our mental, physical, and emotional energy is directed at the object of our obsession).
- We may become reactionaries, instead of acting authentically of our own volition (our mental, emotional, and physical energy is attached).
- We may become emotionally dependent on the people around us (now we're really attached).
- We may become caretakers (rescuers, enablers) to the people around us (firmly attaching ourselves to their need for us).

The problems with attachment are many. (In this chapter I will focus on worry and obsession. In following chapters I will cover the other forms of attachment.) Overinvolvement of any sort can keep us in a state of chaos; it can keep the people around us in a state of chaos. If we're focusing all our energies on people and problems, we have little left for the business of living our own lives. And, there is just so much worry and responsibility in the air. If we take it all on ourselves, there is none left for the people around us. It overworks us and underworks them. Furthermore, worrying about people and problems doesn't help. It doesn't solve problems, it doesn't help other people, and it doesn't help us. It is wasted energy.

"If you believe that feeling bad or worrying long enough will change a fact, then you are residing on another planet with a different reality system," wrote Dr. Wayne W. Dyer in *Your Erroneous Zones*.[2]

Worrying and obsessing keep us so tangled in our heads we can't solve our problems. Whenever we become attached in these ways to someone or something, we become detached from ourselves. We lose touch with ourselves. We forfeit our power and ability to think, feel, act, and take care of ourselves. We lose control.

Obsession with another human being, or a problem, is an awful thing to be caught up in. Have you ever seen someone who is obsessed with someone or something? That person can talk about nothing else, can think of nothing else. Even if he appears to be listening when you talk, you know that person doesn't hear you. His mind is tossing and turning, crashing and banging, around and around on an endless racetrack of compulsive thought. He is preoccupied. He relates whatever you say, no matter how unrelated it actually is, to the object of his obsession. He says the same things, over and over, sometimes changing the wording slightly, sometimes using the same words. Nothing you say makes any difference. Even telling him to stop doesn't help. He probably would if he could. The problem is he can't (at the moment). He is bursting with the jarring energy that obsession is made of. He has a problem or a concern that is not only bothering him—it is controlling him.

Many of the people I've worked with in family groups have been *that* obsessed with people they care about. When I asked them what they were feeling, they told me what the other person was feeling. When I asked what they did, they told me what the other person had done. Their entire focus was on someone or something other than themselves. Some of them had spent years of their lives doing this— worrying about, reacting to, and trying to control other human beings. They were shells, sometimes almost invisible shells, of people. Their energy was depleted—directed at someone else. They couldn't tell me what they were feeling and thinking because they didn't know. Their focus was not on themselves.

Maybe you've been obsessed with someone or something. Someone does or says something. A thought occurs to you. Something reminds you of a past event. A problem enters your awareness. Something happens or doesn't happen. Or you sense something's happening, but you're not sure what. He doesn't call, and he usually calls by now. He doesn't answer the phone, and he should. It's payday. In the past he always got drunk on payday. He's only been sober three months. Will it happen again today? You may not know what, you may not know why, and you're not sure when, but you *know* something bad—something terrible—has happened, is happening, or is about to happen.

It hits you in the stomach. The feeling fills you up—that gut-twisting, handwringing anxiety that is *so* familiar to codependents. It is what causes us to do much of what we do that hurts ourselves; it is the substance worry and obsession feed upon. It is fear at its worst. Fear usually comes and goes, leaving us in flight, ready to fight, or just temporarily frightened. But anxiety hangs in there. It grips the mind, paralyzing it for all but its own purposes—an endless rehashing of the same useless thoughts. It is the fuel that propels us into controlling behaviors of all sorts. We can think of nothing but keeping a lid on things, controlling the problem, and making it go away; it is the stuff codependency is made of.

When you're obsessed, you can't get your mind off that person or that problem. You don't know what you are feeling. You didn't know what you were thinking. You're not even sure what you should do, but by God, you should do something! And fast!

Worrying, obsessing, and controlling are illusions. They are tricks we play on ourselves. We feel like we are doing something to solve our problems, but we're not. Many of us have reacted this way with justifiably good reason. We may have lived with serious, complicated problems that have disrupted our lives, and they would provoke any normal person to become anxious, upset, worried, and obsessed. We may love someone who is in trouble—someone who's out of control. His or her problem may be alcoholism, an eating disorder, gambling, a mental or emotional problem, or any combination of these.

Some of us may be living with less serious problems, but they concern us anyway. People we love or care about may have mood swings. They may do things we wish they wouldn't do. We may think he or she should do things differently, a better way, a way that we believe wouldn't cause so many problems.

Out of habit, some of us may have developed an attitude of attachment—of worrying, reacting, and obsessively trying to control. Maybe we have lived with people and through events that were out of control. Maybe obsessing and controlling is the way we kept things in balance or temporarily kept things from getting worse. And then we just kept on doing it. Maybe we're afraid to let go, because when we let go in the past, terrible, hurtful things happened.

Maybe we've been attached to people—living their lives for and through them—for so long that we don't have any life of our own left to live. It's safer to stay attached. At least we know we're alive if we're reacting. At least we've got something to do if we're obsessing or controlling.

For various reasons codependents tend to attach themselves to problems and people. Never mind that worrying isn't solving anything. Never mind that those problems rarely have solutions. Never mind that they're so obsessed they can't read a book, watch television, or go for a walk. Never mind that their emotions are constantly in turmoil over what she said or didn't say, what she did or didn't do, or what she will do next. Never mind that the things we're doing aren't helping anyone! No matter what the cost, we will hang on. We will grit our teeth, clutch the rope, and grab more tightly than ever.

Some of us may not even be aware we've been holding on so tightly. Some of us may have convinced ourselves we have to hang on this tightly. We believe there is simply no other choice but to react to this particular problem or person in this obsessive manner. Frequently, when I suggest to people that they detach from a person or problem, they recoil in horror. "Oh, no!" they say. "I could never do that. I love him, or her, too much. I care too much to do *that*. This problem or person is too important to me. I *have* to stay attached!"

My answer to that is, "WHO SAYS YOU HAVE TO?"

I've got news—good news. We don't "have to." There's a better way. It's called "detachment."[3] It may be scary at first, but it will ultimately work better for everyone involved.

A Better Way

Exactly what is detachment? What am I asking of you? (The term, as you may have guessed, is more jargon.)

First, let's discuss what detachment isn't. Detachment is not a cold, hostile withdrawal; a resigned, despairing acceptance of anything life and people throw our way; a robotical walk through life oblivious to, and totally unaffected by people and problems; a Pollyanna-like ignorant bliss; a shirking of our *true* responsibilities to ourselves and others; a severing of our relationships. Nor is it a removal of our love and concern, although sometimes these ways of detaching might be the best we can do, for the moment.

Ideally, detachment is releasing, or detaching from, a person or problem *in love*. We mentally, emotionally, and sometimes physically disengage ourselves from unhealthy (and frequently painful) entanglements with another person's life and responsibilities, and from problems we cannot solve, according to a handout, titled "Detachment," that has been passed around Al-Anon groups for years.

Detachment is based on the premises that each person is responsible for himself, that we can't solve problems that aren't ours to solve, and that worrying doesn't help. We adopt a policy of keeping our hands off other people's responsibilities and tend to our own instead. If people have created some disasters for themselves, we allow them to face their own proverbial music. We allow people to be who they are. We give them the freedom to be responsible and to grow. And we give ourselves that same freedom. We live our own lives to the best of our ability. We strive to ascertain what it is we can change and what we cannot change. Then we stop trying to change things we can't. We do what we can to solve a problem, and then we stop fretting and stewing. If we cannot solve a problem and we have done what we could, we learn to live with, or in spite of, that problem. And we try to live happily—focusing heroically on what is good in our lives today, and feeling grateful for that. We learn the magical lesson that making the most of what we have turns it into more.

Detachment involves "present moment living"—living in the here and now. We allow life to happen instead of forcing and trying to control it. We relinquish regrets over the past and fears about the future. We make the most of each day. Detachment also involves accepting reality—the facts. It requires faith—in ourselves, in God, in other people, and in the natural order and destiny of things in this world. We believe in the rightness and appropriateness of each moment. We release our burdens and cares, and give ourselves the freedom to enjoy life in spite of our unsolved problems. We trust that all is well in spite of the conflicts. We trust that Someone greater than ourselves knows, has ordained, and cares about what is happening. We understand that this Someone can do much more to solve the problem than we can. So we try to stay out of His way and let Him do it. In time, we *know* that all is well because we see how the strangest (and sometimes most painful) things work out for the best and for the benefit of everyone.

Judi Hollis wrote of detachment in a section on codependency in her book *Fat Is a Family Affair.* There she described detachment as "a healthy neutrality."[4]

Detaching does not mean we don't care. It means we learn to love, care, and be involved without going crazy. We stop creating all this chaos in our minds and environments. When we are not anxiously and compulsively thrashing about, we become able to make good decisions about how to love people, and how to solve our problems. We become free to care and to love in ways that help others and don't hurt ourselves.[5]

The rewards from detachment are great: serenity; a deep sense of peace; the ability to give and receive love in self-enhancing, energizing ways; and the freedom to find real solutions to our problems. We find the freedom to live our own lives without excessive feelings of guilt about, or responsibility toward others.[6] Sometimes detachment even motivates and frees people around us to begin to solve their problems. We stop worrying about them, and they pick up the slack and finally start worrying about themselves. What a grand plan! We each mind our own business.

Earlier, I described a person caught in the entanglement of obsessions and worry. I have known many people who have had to (or have chosen to) live with serious problems such as an alcoholic spouse who never sobered up, a severely handicapped child, and a teenager hell-bent on destroying himself through drugs and criminal behavior. These people learned to live with, and in spite of, their problems. They grieved for their losses, then found a way to live their lives not in resignation, martyrdom, and despair, but with enthusiasm, peace, and a true sense of gratitude for that which was good. They took care of their actual responsibilities. They gave to people, they helped people, and they loved people. But they also gave to and loved themselves. They held themselves in high esteem. They didn't do these things perfectly, or without effort, or instantly. But they strived to do these things, and they learned to do them well.

I owe a debt of gratitude to these people. They taught me that detachment was possible. They *showed me* it could work. I would like to pass that same hope on to you. It is my wish that you will find other people to pass that hope on to, for detachment is real and thrives with reinforcement and nurturing.

Detachment is both an act and an art. It is a way of life. I believe it is also a gift. And it will be given to those who seek it.

How do we detach? How do we extricate our emotions, mind, body, and spirit from the agony of entanglement? As best we can. And, probably, a bit clumsily at first. An old A.A. and Al-Anon saying suggests a three-part formula called "HOW": Honesty, Openness, and Willingness to try.[7]

In the chapters ahead, I will discuss some specific concepts for detaching from certain forms of attachment. Many of the other concepts I will discuss later will lead to detachment. You will have to decide how these ideas apply to you and your particular situation and then find your own path. With a little humility, surrender, and effort on your part, I believe you can do it. I believe detachment can become a habitual response, in the same manner that obsessing, worrying, and controlling became habitual responses—by practice. You may not do it perfectly, but no one has. However, and at whatever pace, you practice detachment in your life, I believe it will be right for you. I hope you will be able to detach with love for the person or persons you are detaching from. I think it is better to do everything in an attitude of love. However, for a variety of reasons, we can't always do that. If you can't detach in love, it is my opinion that it is better to detach in anger rather than to stay attached. If we are detached, we are in a better position to work on (or through) our resentful emotions. If we're attached, we probably won't do anything other than stay upset.

When should we detach? When we can't stop thinking, talking about, or worrying about someone or something; when our emotions are churning and boiling; when we feel like we *have* to do something about someone because we can't stand it another minute; when we're hanging on by a thread, and it feels like that single thread is frayed; and when we believe we can no longer live with the problem we've been trying to live with. It is time to detach! You will learn to recognize when detachment is advisable. A good rule of thumb is: You need to detach most when it seems the least likely or possible thing to do.

I'll close this chapter with a true story. One night about midnight my telephone rang. I was in bed and wondered, as I picked up the receiver, who was calling me at that hour. I thought it had to be an emergency.

In a way it was an emergency. It was a stranger. She had been calling various friends all evening, trying to find some kind of consolation. Apparently, she hadn't been able to find it. Someone had given her someone else's phone number, that person had given her someone else's phone number, and the last person had suggested she call me.

Immediately upon introducing herself, the woman exploded in a tirade. Her husband used to go to Alcoholics Anonymous. He had separated from her, and now he was seeing another woman because he wanted to "find himself." Furthermore, before he left her, he had been acting really crazy and didn't go to meetings. And she wondered, isn't he acting crazy now by dating a woman who is *that much younger than him?*

I was speechless at first, then found it hard to find a chance to talk. She went on and on. Finally she asked, "Don't you think he's sick? Don't you think he's acting crazy? Don't you think something should be done about him?"

"That could be," I replied. "But obviously I can't do it, and neither can you. I'm more concerned about you. What are *you* feeling? What do *you* think? What do *you* need to take care of *yourself?*"

I shall say the same thing to you, dear reader. I know you have problems. I understand that many of you are deeply grieved over, and concerned about, certain people in your lives. Many of them may be destroying themselves, you, and your family, right before your eyes. But I can't do anything to control those people, and you probably can't either. If you could, you probably would have done it by now.

Detach. Detach in love, or detach in anger, but strive for detachment. I know it's difficult, but it will become easier with practice. If you can't let go completely, try to "hang on loose."[8] Relax. Sit back. Now, take a deep breath. The focus is on you.

ACTIVITIES

1. Is there a problem or person in your life that you are excessively worried about? Write about that person or problem. Write as much as you need to write to get it out of your system. When you have written all you need to write about that person or problem, focus on yourself. What are you thinking? What are you feeling?

2. How do you feel about detaching from that person or problem? What might happen if you detach? Will that probably happen anyway? How has staying "attached"—worrying, obsessing, trying to control—helped so far?

3. If you did not have that person or problem in your life, what would you be doing with your life that is different from what you are doing now? How would you be feeling and behaving? Spend a few minutes visualizing yourself living your life, feeling and behaving that way—in spite of your unsolved problem. Visualize your hands placing in God's hands the person or problem you are concerned about.[9] Visualize His hands gently and lovingly holding that person or willingly accepting that problem. Now, visualize His hands holding you. All is well for the moment. All is as it should be and as it needs to be. All will be well—better than you think.

6

Don't Be Blown About
by Every Wind

Easy Does It.

—TWELVE STEP PROGRAM SLOGAN

I am a reactionary.

That thought burned deeply into my consciousness one day while I was sitting in my office. I had heard people discuss reacting, but until that moment I didn't understand how much I reacted.

I reacted to other people's feelings, behaviors, problems, and thoughts. I reacted to what they *might* by feeling, thinking, or doing. I reacted to my own feelings, my own thoughts, my own problems. My strong point seemed to be reacting to crises—I thought almost everything was a crisis. I overreacted. Hidden panic (which bordered on hysteria) brewed in me much of the time. I sometimes underreacted. If the problem I faced was significant, I often used the tool of denial. I reacted to almost everything that came into my awareness and environment. My entire life had been a reaction to other people's lives, desires, problems, faults, successes, and personalities. Even my low self-worth, which I dragged around like a bag of stinking garbage, had been a reaction. I was like a puppet with strings hanging out, inviting and allowing anyone or anything to yank them.

Most codependents are reactionaries. We react with anger, guilt, shame, self-hate, worry, hurt, controlling gestures, caretaking acts, depression, desperation, and fury. We *react with fear and anxiety*. Some of us react so much it is painful to be around people, and torturous to be in large groups of people. It is normal to react and respond to our environment. Reacting is part of life. It's part of interacting, and it's part of being alive and human. But we allow ourselves to get *so* upset, and *so* distracted. Little things, big things—anything—have the power to throw us off the track. And the way we respond after we react is frequently not in our best interests.

We may have started reacting and responding urgently and compulsively in patterns that hurt us. Just *feeling* urgent and compulsive is enough to hurt us. We keep ourselves in a crisis state—adrenaline flowing and muscles tensed, ready to react to emergencies that usually aren't emergencies. Someone does something, so we must do something back. Someone says something, so we must say something back. Someone feels a certain way, so we must feel a certain way. WE JUMP INTO THE FIRST FEELING THAT COMES OUR WAY AND THEN WALLOW IN IT. We think the first thought that comes into our heads and then elaborate on it. We say the first words on our tongues and sometimes regret them. We do the first thing that comes to mind, usually without thinking about it. That is the problem: we are reacting without thinking—without honest thought about what we need to do, and how we want to handle the situation. Our emotions and behaviors are being controlled—triggered—by everyone and everything in our environment. We are indirectly allowing others to tell us what to do. That means we have lost control. We are being controlled.

When we react we forfeit our personal, God-given power to think, feel, and behave *in our best interests*. We allow others to determine when we will be happy; when we will be peaceful; when we will be upset; and what we will say, do, think, and feel. We forfeit our right to feel peaceful at the whim of our environments. We are like a wisp of paper in a thunderstorm, blown about by every wind.

Here is an example of a way I tend to react (one of many): My office is in my home, and I have two young children. Sometimes when I'm working they start going wild in the other rooms—fighting, running, messing up the house, and eating and drinking everything in the kitchen. My first, instinctive reaction is to screech at them to "Stop that!" My second reaction is to holler some more. It comes naturally. Reacting that way appears to be easier than leaving my office, working my way through the laundry room, and walking upstairs. It also appears easier than taking the time to think about how I want to handle the situation. The problem is: bellowing and screaming do not work. It is not really easier. It makes my throat sore and teaches the children how to make me sit in my office and screech.

Reacting usually does not work. We react too quickly, with too much intensity and urgency. Rarely can we do our best at anything in this state of mind. I believe the irony is that we are not called upon or required to do things in this state of mind. There is little in our lives we need to do that we cannot do better if we are peaceful. Few situations—no matter how greatly they appear to demand it—can be bettered by us going berserk.

Why do we do it, then?

We react because we're anxious and afraid of what has happened, what might happen, and what is happening.

Many of us react as though everything is a crisis because we have lived with so many crises for so long that crisis reaction has become a habit.

We react because we think things *shouldn't* be happening the way they are.

We react because we don't feel good about ourselves.

We react because most people react.

We react because we think we have to react.

We don't have to.

We don't have to be so afraid of people. They are just people like us.

We don't have to forfeit our peace. It doesn't help. We have the same facts and resources available to us when we're peaceful that are available to us when we're frantic and chaotic. Actually we have more resources available because our minds and emotions are free to perform at peak level.

We don't have to forfeit our power to think and feel for anyone or anything. That is also not required of us.

We don't have to take things so seriously (ourselves, events, and other people). We blow things out of proportion—our feelings, thoughts, actions, and mistakes. We do the same thing with other people's feelings, thoughts, and actions. We tell ourselves things are awful, terrible, a tragedy, and the end of the world. Many things might be sad, too bad, and unpleasant—but the only thing that's the end of the world is the end of the world. Feelings are important, but they're only feelings. Thoughts are important, but they're only thoughts—and we all think a lot of different things, and our thoughts are subject to change. What we say and do is important, what others say and do is important, but the world doesn't hinge on any particular speech or action. And if it is particularly important that something gets done or said, don't worry: It'll happen. Lighten up. Give yourself and others room to move, to talk, to be who they are—to be human. Give life a chance to happen. Give yourself an opportunity to enjoy it.

We don't have to take other people's behaviors as reflections of our self-worth. We don't have to be embarrassed if someone we love chooses to behave inappropriately. It's normal to react that way, but we don't have to continue to feel embarrassed and *less than* if someone else continues to behave inappropriately. Each person is responsible for his or her behavior. If another person behaves inappropriately, let him or her feel embarrassed for him- or herself. If you have done nothing to feel embarrassed about, don't feel embarrassed. I know this is a tough concept, but it can be mastered.

We don't have to take rejection as a reflection of our self-worth. If somebody who is important (or even someone unimportant) to you rejects you or your choices, you are still real, and you are still worth every bit as much as you would be if you had not been rejected. Feel any feelings that go with rejection; talk about your thoughts; but don't forfeit your self-esteem to another's disapproval or rejection of who you are or what you have done. Even if the most important person in your world rejects you, you are still real, and you are still okay. If you have done something inappropriate or you need to solve a problem or change a behavior, then take appropriate steps to take care of yourself. But don't reject yourself, and don't give so much power to other people's rejection of you. It isn't necessary.

We don't have to take things so personally. We take things to heart that we have no business taking to heart. For instance, saying "If you loved me you wouldn't drink" to an alcoholic makes as much sense as saying "If you loved me, you wouldn't cough" to someone who has pneumonia. Pneumonia victims will cough until they get appropriate treatment for their illness. Alcoholics will drink until they get the same. When people with a compulsive disorder do whatever it is they are compelled to do, they are not saying they don't love you—they are saying they don't love themselves.

We don't have to take little things personally either. If someone has a bad day or gets angry, don't assume it has something to do with you. It may or may not have something to do with you. If it does you'll find out. Usually things have far less to do with us than we think.

An interruption, someone else's bad mood, sharp tongue, bad day, negative thoughts, problems, or active alcoholism does not have to run or ruin our lives, our day, or even an hour of our day. If people don't want to be with us or act healthy, it is not a reflection on *our* self-worth. It reflects on *their* present circumstances. By practicing detachment we can lessen our destructive reactions to the world around us. Separate yourself from things. Leave things alone, and let people be who they are. Who are you to say that the interruption, mood, word, bad day, thought, or problem is not an important and necessary part of life? Who are you to say that this problem won't ultimately be beneficial to you or someone else?

We don't have to react. We have options. That is the joy of recovery from codependency. And each time we exercise our right to choose how we want to act, think, feel, and behave, we feel better and stronger.

"But," you might protest, "why shouldn't I react? Why shouldn't I say something back? Why shouldn't I be upset? He or she deserves to bear the brunt of my turmoil." That may be, but *you* don't. We're talking here about your lack of peace, your lack of serenity, your wasted moments. As Ralph Edwards used to say, "This is your life." How do you want to spend it? You're not detaching for him or her. You're detaching for you. Chances are everyone will benefit by it.

We are like singers in a large chorus. If the guy next to us gets off key, must we? Wouldn't it help him, and us, more to strive to stay on key? We can learn to hold our part.

We don't need to eliminate all our reactions to people and problems. Reactions can be useful. They help us identify what we like and what feels good. They help us identify problems in and around us. But most of us react too much. And much of what we react to is nonsense. It isn't all that important, and it doesn't merit the time and attention we're giving it. Some of what we react to is other people's reactions to us. (I'm mad because he got mad; he got mad because I was angry; I was angry because I thought he was angry with me; he wasn't angry, he was hurt because . . .)

Our reactions can be such a chain reaction that frequently everyone's upset and nobody knows why. They're just upset. Then, everyone's out of control and being controlled. Sometimes people behave in certain ways to provoke us to react in certain ways. If we stop reacting in these certain ways, we take all the fun out of it for them. We remove ourselves from their control and take away their power over us.

Sometimes our reactions provoke other people to react in certain ways. We help them justify certain behaviors. (We don't need any more of that, do we?) Sometimes reacting narrows our vision so much that we get stuck reacting to symptoms of problems. We may stay so busy reacting we never have the time or energy to identify the real problem, much less figure out how to solve it. We can spend years reacting to each drinking incident and resulting crisis, completely failing to recognize that the true problem is alcoholism! Learn to stop reacting in ways that aren't necessary and don't work. Eliminate the reactions that hurt *you*.

Some suggestions follow to help you detach from people and your destructive reactions to them. These are only suggestions. There is no precise formula for detachment. You need to find your own way, a way that works for you.

1. Learn to recognize when you're reacting, when you are allowing someone or something to yank your strings. Usually when you start to feel anxious, afraid, indignant, outraged, rejected, sorry for yourself, ashamed, worried, or confused, something in your environment has

snagged you. (I'm not saying it's wrong to feel these feelings. Probably anybody would feel that way. The difference is, we're learning to decide how long we want to feel that way, and what we want to do about it.) Using the words "he or it or she *made me feel*" often indicates we are reacting. Losing our sense of peace and serenity is probably the strongest indication that we are caught up in some sort of reaction.

2. Make yourself comfortable. When you recognize that you're in the midst of a chaotic reaction, say or do as little as possible until you can restore your level of serenity and peace. Do whatever you need to do (that is not self- or other-destructive) to help yourself relax. Take a few deep breaths. Go for a walk. Clean the kitchen. Go sit in the bathroom. Go to a friend's house. Go to an Al-Anon meeting. Read a meditation book. Take a trip to Florida. Watch a television program. Find a way to emotionally, mentally, and (if necessary) physically separate yourself from whatever you are reacting to. Find a way to ease your anxiety. Don't take a drink or drive the car down a side street at 85 miles per hour. Do something safe that will help restore your balance.

3. Examine what happened. If it's a minor incident, you may be able to sort through it yourself. If the problem is serious, or is seriously upsetting you, you may want to discuss it with a friend to help clear your thoughts and emotions. Troubles and feelings go wild when we try to keep them caged inside. Talk about your feelings. Take responsibility for them. Feel whatever feeling you have. Nobody made you feel. Someone might have helped you feel a particular way, but you did your feeling all by yourself. Deal with it. Then, tell yourself the truth about what happened.[1] Was someone trying to sock it to you? (If in doubt about whether to interpret something as an insult or rejection, I prefer to believe it had nothing to do with me. It saves my time and helps me feel good about myself.) Were you trying to control someone or some event? How serious is the problem or issue? Are you taking responsibility for someone else? Are you angry because someone didn't guess what you really wanted or what you were really trying to say? Are you taking someone's behavior too personally? Did someone push

your insecurity or guilt buttons? Is it truly the end of the world, or is it merely sad and disappointing?

4. Figure out what you need to do to take care of yourself. Make your decisions based on reality, and make them from a peaceful state. Do you need to apologize? Do you want to let it go? Do you need to have a heart-to-heart talk with someone? Do you need to make some other decision to take care of yourself? When you make your decision keep in mind what your responsibilities are. You are not responsible for making other people "see the light," and you do not need to "set them straight." You are responsible for helping yourself see the light and for setting yourself straight. If you can't get peaceful about a decision, let it go. It's not time to make it yet. Wait until your mind is consistent and your emotions are calm.

Slow down. You don't have to feel so frightened. You don't have to feel so frantic. Keep things in perspective. Make life easier for *you*.

ACTIVITY

1. Are you spending too much time reacting to someone or something in your environment? Who or what? How are you reacting? Is that how you would choose to behave or feel if you had a choice?

2. Go through the previous steps on detachment for whatever or whoever is bothering you the most. If you need to talk to someone select a trusted friend. If necessary seek professional help.

3. What activities help you feel peaceful and comfortable? (A Twelve Step meeting, a steaming hot shower, a good movie, and dancing are my favorite ones.)

7

SET YOURSELF FREE

Let Go and Let God.

—TWELVE STEP PROGRAM SLOGAN

People say codependents are controllers.

We nag; lecture; scream; holler; cry; beg; bribe; coerce; hover over; protect; accuse; chase after; run away from; try to talk into; try to talk out of; attempt to induce guilt in; seduce; entrap; check on; demonstrate how much we've been hurt; hurt people in return so they'll know how it feels; threaten to hurt ourselves; whip power plays on; deliver ultimatums to; do things for; refuse to do things for; stomp out on; get even with; whine; vent fury on; act helpless; suffer in loud silence; try to please; lie; do sneaky little things; do sneaky big things; clutch at our hearts and threaten to die; grab our heads and threaten to go crazy; beat on our chests and threaten to kill; enlist the aid of supporters; gauge our words carefully; sleep with; refuse to sleep with; have children with; bargain with; drag to counseling; drag out of counseling; talk mean about; talk mean to; insult; condemn; pray for miracles; pay for miracles; go to places we don't want to go; stay nearby; supervise; dictate; command; complain; write letters about; write letters to; stay home and wait for; go out and look for; call all over looking for; drive down dark alleys at night hoping to see; chase down dark alleys at night hoping to catch; run down alleys at night to get away from; bring home; keep home; lock out; move away from; move with; scold; impress upon;

advise; teach lessons to; set straight; insist; give in to; placate; provoke; try to make jealous; try to make afraid; remind; inquire; hint; look through pockets; peek in wallets; search dresser drawers; dig through glove boxes; look in the toilet tank; try to look into the future; search through the past; call relatives about; reason with; settle issues once and for all; settle them again; punish; reward; almost give up on; then try even harder; and a list of other handy maneuvers I've either forgotten or haven't tried yet.

We aren't the people who "make things happen." Codependents are the people who consistently, and with a great deal of effort and energy, try to force things to happen.

We control in the name of love.

We do it because we're "only trying to help."

We do it because we know best how things should go and how people should behave.

We do it because we're right and they're wrong.

We control because we're afraid not to do it.

We do it because we don't know what else to do.

We do it to stop the pain.

We control because we think we have to.

We control because we don't think.

We control because controlling is all we can think about.

Ultimately we may control because that's the way we've always done things.

Tyrannical and dominating, some rule with an iron hand from a self-appointed throne. They are powerful. They know best. And by God, it will be done this way. They will see to it.

Others do their dirty work undercover. They hide behind a costume of sweetness and niceties, and secretly go about their business—OTHER PEOPLE'S BUSINESS.

Others, sighing and crying, claim inability, proclaim their dependence, announce their overall victimization, and successfully control through weakness. They are *so* helpless. They need your cooperation so badly. They can't live without it. Sometimes the weak are the most power-ful manipulators and controllers.[1] They have learned to tug at the guilt and pity strings of the world.

Many codependents combine tactics, using a variety of methods. Whatever works! (Or, more accurately, whatever doesn't work although we continue to hope it will.)

Despite tactics, the goals remain the same. Make other people do what you want them to. Make them behave as you think they should. Don't let them behave in ways you think they shouldn't, but probably would, without your "assistance." Force life's events to unravel and unfold in the manner and at such times as you have designated. Do not let what's hap-pening, or what might happen, occur. Hold on tightly and don't let go. We have written the play, and we will see to it that the actors behave and the scenes unfold exactly as we have decided they should. Never mind that we continue to buck reality. If we charge ahead insistently enough, we can (we believe) stop the flow of life, transform people, and change things to our liking.

We are fooling ourselves.

Let me tell you about Maria. She married a man who turned out to be an alcoholic. He was a binge drinker. He didn't drink every day, every weekend, or every month, but when he did—look out. He stayed drunk for days, sometimes weeks. He started drinking at eight in the morning and drank until he passed out. He vomited all over, devastated the family's finances, got fired from jobs, and created unbearable chaos each time he drank. Between binges life was not perfect either. A sense of impending doom and unresolved feelings filled the air. Other unresolved problems, residues from the drinking, cluttered their lives. They could never get ahead of the disasters. They were always starting over with a dirty slate. But, it was better—for Maria and her three children—when her husband wasn't drinking. There was hope, too, that this time it would be different.

It never was different. For years, each time Maria turned around or turned her back, her husband went on a binge. When she went away for a weekend, when she went to the hospital to deliver her babies, when her husband left town on a trip, or when he was out of her sight for any reason—he drank.

Whenever Maria returned or retrieved him from wherever he was drinking, he would abruptly quit drinking. Maria decided that the key to her husband's sobriety was her presence. She could control the drinking (and all the pain it caused) by sticking close to home and standing guard over her husband. Because she learned this method of control, and because of increasing feelings of shame, embarrassment, anxiety, and the overall trauma that accompanies codependency, Maria became a recluse. She turned down opportunities to travel, and she refused to attend church conferences she was interested in. Even leaving the house for more than a trip to the grocery store began to threaten the balance she had created—or thought she had created. In spite of her determined and desperate efforts, her husband still found opportunities to drink. He found ways to drink at home without her knowing about it, and he drank when she had no choice but to spend the night away from home.

After one particularly disruptive drinking bout, Maria's husband informed her that the impossible financial predicament they were in caused him to drink. (He neglected to mention that his drinking had caused the impossible financial predicament.) He said if she would take a job and help out financially, he would not feel like he had to drink any more. The pressure would be off. Maria thought about his request, then reluctantly agreed. She was afraid to leave home and felt concerned about setting up appropriate baby-sitting arrangements for the children. She did not feel emotionally or mentally able to work. She especially resented taking a job to earn extra money when her husband was so irresponsible with money. But it was worth a try. Anything to keep this man sober!

Before long Maria located a job as a legal secretary. She did well—better than she thought she would. Codependents make great employees. They don't complain; they do more than their share; they do whatever is asked of them; they please people; and they try to do their work perfectly—at least for a while, until they become angry and resentful.

Maria started feeling a little better about herself. She enjoyed her contact with people—something that had been missing in her life. She liked the feeling of earning her own money (although she still resented her husband's irresponsibility with it). And her employers appreciated her. They gave her increasing amounts of responsibility and were on the verge of promoting her to a paralegal position. But about that time Maria began to feel that old familiar anxious feeling—her cue that her husband was about to drink again.

The feeling came and went for days. Then one day, it hit hard. That handwringing, gut-twisting anxiety came back in full force. Maria started calling her husband on the phone. He was not at work where he was supposed to be. His employer didn't know where he was. She made more phone calls. Nobody knew where he was. She spent the day biting her nails, making frantic phone calls, and hoping her fellow employees wouldn't see through her "everything's fine—no problem" veneer. When she arrived home that evening she discovered that her husband was not at home and had not picked up the children from day care as he was supposed to. Things were out of control again. He was drinking again. The next morning she quit her job—walked out with no appropriate notice. By 10:00 A.M., she was back in her house— guarding her husband.

Years later she said, "I felt like I had to do this. I had to get things under control—MY CONTROL."

My question is this: Who's controlling whom?

Maria learned she was not controlling her husband or his drinking at all. He and his alcoholism were controlling her.

This point was further clarified for me one evening during a family group facilitation I had at a treatment center. (Many of my clients are wise—wiser than I am. I have learned much by listening to them.) During the group, the wife of an alcoholic talked openly to her husband—a man who had spent many years of their marriage drinking, unemployed, and in prison.

"You accuse me of trying to control you, and I guess I have," she said. "I've gone to bars with you so you wouldn't drink so much. I've let you come home when you were abusive and drunk so you wouldn't drink anymore or hurt yourself. I've measured your drinks, drank with you (and I hate drinking), hid your bottles, and taken you to Alcoholics Anonymous meetings.

"But the truth is," she said, "you've been controlling me. All those letters from prison telling me what I've wanted to hear. All those promises, all those words. And every time I'm ready to leave you—to walk out for good—you do or say just the right thing to keep me from leaving. You know just what I want to hear, and that's what you tell me. But you never change. You've never intended to change. You just want to control me."

He smiled a half-smile and nodded when she said that. "Yes," he said, "I have been trying to control you. And I've been doing a pretty good job of it at that."

When we attempt to control people and things that we have no business controlling, we are controlled. We forfeit our power to think, feel, and act in accordance with our best interests. We frequently lose control or ourselves. Often, we are being controlled not just by people but by diseases such as alcoholism, eating disorders, and compulsive gambling. Alcoholism and other destructive disorders are powerful forces. Never forget that alcoholics and other troubled persons are expert controllers. We have met our match when we attempt to control them or their disease. We lose the battles. We lose the wars. We lose our selves—our lives. Borrowing a tidbit from Al-Anon: You didn't cause it; you can't control it; and you can't cure it.

So stop trying! We become utterly frustrated when we try to do the impossible. And we usually prevent the possible from happening. I believe that clutching tightly to a person or thing, or forcing my will on any given situation eliminates the possibility of my Higher Power doing anything constructive about that situation, the person, or me. My controlling blocks God's power. It blocks other people's ability to grow. It stops events from happening naturally. It prevents me from enjoying people or events.

Control is an illusion. It doesn't work. We cannot control alcoholism. We cannot control anyone's compulsive behaviors—overeating, sexual, gambling—or any of their behaviors. We cannot (and have no business trying to) control anyone's emotions, mind, or choices. We cannot control the outcome of events. We cannot control life. Some of us can barely control ourselves.

People ultimately do what they want to do. They feel how they want to feel (or how they are feeling); they think what they want to think; they do the things they believe they need to do; and they will change only when they are ready to change. It doesn't matter if they're wrong and we're right. It doesn't matter if they're hurting themselves. It doesn't matter that we could help them if they'd only listen to, and cooperate with, us. IT DOESN'T MATTER, DOESN'T MATTER, DOESN'T MATTER, DOESN'T MATTER.

We cannot change people. Any attempts to control them are a delusion as well as an illusion. People will either resist our efforts or redouble their efforts to prove we can't control them. They may temporarily adapt to our demands, but the moment we turn our backs they will return to their natural state. Furthermore, people will punish us for making them do something they don't want to do, or be something they don't want to be. No amount of control will effect a permanent or desirable change in another person. We can sometimes do things that increase the probability that people will want to change, but we can't even guarantee or control that.

And that's the truth. It's too bad. It's sometimes hard to accept, especially if someone you love is hurting him- or herself and you. But that's the way it is. The only person you can now or ever change is yourself. The only person that it is your business to control is yourself.

Detach. Surrender. Sometimes when we do that the result we have been waiting and hoping for happens quickly, almost miraculously.

Sometimes it doesn't. Sometimes it never happens. But you will benefit. You don't have to stop caring or loving. You don't have to tolerate abuse. You don't have to abandon constructive problem-solving methods such as professional intervention. You only need to put your emotional, mental, spiritual, and physical hand back in your own pockets and leave things and people alone. Let them be. Make any decisions you need to make to take care of yourself, but don't make them to control other people. Start taking care of yourself!

"But this is so important to me," many people protest. "I can't detach."

If it's that important to you, I suggest that is all the more reason to detach.

I heard some wisdom on detachment out of the mouths of babes—my babies. Sometimes, my youngest son, Shane, hangs on too tightly and too long after a hug. He starts tipping me over. I lose my balance, and become impatient for him to stop hugging me. I begin to resist him. Perhaps he does it to keep me close to him a little longer. Maybe it's a form of control over me. I don't know. One night when he did this my daughter watched until even she became frustrated and impatient.

"Shane," she said, "there comes a time to let go."

For each of us, there comes a time to let go. You will know when that time has come. When you have done all that you can do, it is time to detach. Deal with your feelings. Face your fears about losing control. Gain control of yourself and your responsibilities. Free others to be who they are. In so doing, you will set yourself free.

ACTIVITY

1. Is there an event or person in your life that you are trying to control? Why? Write a few paragraphs about it.

2. In what ways (mentally, physically, emotionally, etc.) are you being controlled by whatever or whomever you are attempting to control?

3. What would happen (to you and the other person) if you detached from this situation or person? Will that probably happen anyway, in spite of your controlling gestures? How are you benefiting by attempting to control the situation? How is the other person benefiting by your attempts to control? How effective are your attempts at controlling the outcomes of events?

8

REMOVE THE VICTIM

We're so careful to see that no one gets hurt.
No one, that is, but ourselves.

—AL-ANON MEMBER

About a year into my recovery from codependency, I realized I was still doing something over and over that caused me pain. I sensed this pattern had something to do with why many of my relationships went sour. But I didn't know what "it" was that I was doing, so I couldn't stop doing it.

One sunny day, as I was walking down the sidewalk with my friend Scott, I stopped, turned to him, and asked, "What is the one thing codependents do over and over? What is it that keeps us feeling so bad?"

He thought about my question for a moment before answering. "Codependents are caretakers—rescuers. They rescue, then they persecute, then they end up victimized. Study the Karpman Drama Triangle," he said. The Karpman Drama Triangle and the accompanying roles of rescuer, persecutor, and victim, are the work and observation of Stephen B. Karpman.[1]

What he said didn't make sense, but I went home, dragged out some therapy books that were collecting dust on my shelves, and studied.[2] After a while, a light went on inside my head. I saw. I understood. And I felt like I had discovered fire.

This was it. This was my pattern. This is *our* pattern. This is what we repeatedly do with friends, family, acquaintances, clients, or anybody around us. As codependents, we may do many things, but this pattern is what we do best and most often. This is our favorite reaction.

We are the rescuers, the enablers. We are the great godmothers or godfathers to the entire world, as Earnie Larsen says. We not only meet people's needs, we anticipate them. We fix, nurture, and fuss over others. We make better, solve, and attend to. And we do it all so well. "Your wish is my command," is our theme. "Your problem is my problem," is our motto. We are the caretakers.

WHAT'S A RESCUE?

Rescuing and *caretaking* mean almost what they sound like. We rescue people from their responsibilities. We take care of people's responsibilities for them. Later we get mad at *them* for what *we've* done. Then we feel used and sorry for ourselves. That is the pattern, the triangle.

Rescuing and caretaking are synonymous. Their definitions are closely connected to enabling. *Enabling* is therapeutic jargon that means a destructive form of helping. Any acts that help an alcoholic continue drinking, prevent the alcoholic from suffering consequences, or in any way make it easier for an alcoholic to continue drinking are considered enabling behaviors.

As counselor Scott Egleston says, we rescue anytime we take responsibility for another human being—for that person's thoughts, feelings, decisions, behaviors, growth, well-being, problems, or destiny. The following acts constitute a rescuing or caretaking move:

- Doing something we really don't want to do.
- Saying yes when we mean no.
- Doing something for someone although that person is capable of and should be doing it for him- or herself.
- Meeting people's needs without being asked and before we've agreed to do so.
- Doing more than a fair share of work after our help is requested.
- Consistently giving more than we receive in a particular situation.

- Fixing people's feelings.
- Doing people's thinking for them.
- Speaking for another person.
- Suffering people's consequences for them.
- Solving people's problems for them.
- Putting more interest and activity into a joint effort than the other person does.
- Not asking for what we want, need, and desire.

We rescue whenever we take care of other people.

At the time we rescue or caretake we may feel one or more of the following feelings: discomfort and awkwardness about the other person's dilemma; urgency to do something; pity; guilt; saintliness; anxiety; extreme responsibility *for* that person or problem; fear; a sense of being forced or compelled to do something; mild or severe reluctance to do anything; more competency than the person we are "helping"; or occasional resentment at being put in this position. We also think the person we are taking care of is helpless and unable to do what we are doing for him or her. We feel needed temporarily.

I am not referring to acts of love, kindness, compassion, and true helping—situations where our assistance is legitimately wanted and needed and we want to give that assistance. These acts are the good stuff of life. Rescuing and caretaking isn't.

Caretaking looks like a much friendlier act than it is. It requires incompetency on the part of the person being taken care of. We rescue "victims"—people who we believe are not capable of being responsible for themselves. The victims actually are capable of taking care of themselves, even though we and they don't admit it. Usually, our victims are just hanging around that corner of the triangle, waiting for us to make our move and jump on the triangle with them.

After we rescue, we will inevitably move to the next corner of the triangle: persecution. We become resentful and angry at the person we have so generously "helped." We've done something we didn't want to do, we've done something that was not our responsibility to do, we've ignored our own needs and wants, and we get angry about it. To complicate matters, this victim, this poor person we've rescued, is not grateful for our help. He or she is not appreciative enough of the sacrifice we have made. The victim isn't behaving the way he or she should. This person is not even taking our advice, which we offered so readily. This person is not letting us fix that feeling. Something doesn't work right or feel right, so we rip off our halos and pull out our pitchforks.

Sometimes, people don't notice or choose not to notice our peeved mood. Sometimes we do our best to hide it. Sometimes we let loose with the full force of our fury; we particularly do this with family members. Something about family tends to bring out the *real* us. Whether we show, hide, or partially hide our agitation and resentment, WE KNOW what's going on.

Most of the time, the people we rescue immediately sense our shift in mood. They saw it coming. It's just the excuse they needed to turn on us. It's *their* turn in the persecution corner. This may precede, happen at the same time as, or follow our feelings of anger. Sometimes, the victims respond to our anger. Usually it is a response to our taking responsibility for that person, which directly or indirectly tells him or her how incapable we believe he or she is. People resent being told or shown they are incompetent, no matter how loudly they plead incompetency. And they resent us for adding insult to injury by becoming angry with them after we point out their incompetency.

Then it's time for our final move. We head right for our favorite spot: the victim corner on the *bottom*. This is the predictable and unavoidable result of a rescue. Feelings of helplessness, hurt, sorrow, shame, and self-pity abound. We have been used—again. We have gone unappreciated—again. We try so hard to help people, to be good to them. We moan, "Why? Why does this ALWAYS happen to me?" Another person has trampled on us, socked it to us. We wonder, shall we forever be victims? Probably, if we don't stop rescuing and caretaking.

Many codependents, at some time in their lives, *were* true victims—of someone's abuse, neglect, abandonment, alcoholism, or any number of situations that can victimize people. We were, at some time, truly helpless to protect ourselves or solve our problems. Something came our way, something we didn't ask for, and it hurt us terribly. That is sad, truly sad. But an even sadder fact is that many of us codependents began to see ourselves as victims. Our painful history repeats itself. As caretakers, we allow people to victimize us, and we participate in our victimization by perpetually rescuing people. Rescuing or caretaking is not an act of love. The Drama Triangle is a hate triangle. It fosters and maintains self-hate, and it hinders our feelings for other people.

The triangle and the shifting roles of rescuer, persecutor, and victim are a visible process we go through. The role changes and the emotional changes come over us as certainly and as intensely as if we were reading a script. We can complete the process in seconds, experiencing only mild emotions as we shift roles. Or, we can take years to complete the triangle and really work up to a major explosion. We can, and many of us do, rescue twenty times in one day.

Let me illustrate a rescue. A friend of mine was married to an alcoholic. Whenever he got drunk, she would drive all over town, enlist the aid of friends, and relentlessly pursue her husband until she found him. She usually felt benevolent, concerned, and sorry for him—a warning that a rescue was about to take place—until she got him home and tucked into bed—taking responsibility for him and his sobriety. When his head hit the pillow, things changed. She charged into the persecutor position. She didn't want this man in her home. She expected him to whine for days about how sick he was. He was unable to assume his responsibilities in the family, and he generally acted pitiful. He had done this so many times! So, she would start in on him, beginning with little snipes and working up to a full-blown blast. He would briefly tolerate her persecution before switching from a helpless victim to vengeful persecutor. She then took a downward dip into the victim role. Self-pity, feelings of helplessness, shame, and despair set in. This was the story of her life, she would moan. After all she had done for him, how could he treat her this way? Why did this always happen to her? She felt like a victim of circumstance, a victim of her husband's outrageous behavior, a victim of life. It never occurred to her that she was also a victim of herself and her own behavior.

Here's another illustration of a rescue. One summer, a friend wanted me to take her to an apple farm. Originally, I wanted to go, and we set a date. By the time that date came, however, I was extremely busy. I called her, and instead of telling her I didn't want to go, I asked to postpone it. I felt guilty and responsible for her feelings—another rescue on the way. I couldn't disappoint her because I thought she couldn't handle or be responsible for her feelings. I couldn't tell the truth, because I thought she might be angry with me—more emotional responsibility—as if someone else's anger is my business. The next weekend rolled around, and I squeezed the trip into my even busier schedule. I didn't even need any apples; I had two drawers in my refrigerator crammed with apples. Before I stopped my car in front of her house, I had already switched into the persecuting role. I seethed with resentful, tense thoughts as we drove to the apple orchard. When we arrived at the orchard and began tasting and looking at apples, it became apparent neither of us was enjoying herself. After a few minutes, my friend turned to me. "I really don't want any apples," she said. "I bought some last week. I only came because I thought you wanted to, and I didn't want to hurt your feelings."

This example is only one of the thousands of rescues I have devoted my life to performing. When I began to understand this process, I realized that I spent most of my waking moments flipping around the jagged edges of this triangle taking responsibility for anybody and everybody besides myself. Sometimes I managed big rescues; sometimes I managed little rescues. My friendships were initiated, maintained, and ultimately discontinued according to the rescue progression. Rescuing infiltrated my relationships with family members and clients. It kept me in a tizzy most of the time.

Two codependents in a relationship can really play havoc with each other. Consider two people-pleasers in a relationship with each other.

Now consider two people-pleasers in a relationship with each other when they both want out of the relationship. They will, as Earnie Larsen says, do horrible things. They'll nearly destroy each other and themselves before one will stop rescuing and say, "I want out."

As codependents, we spend much of our time rescuing. We try to be living proof that people can outgive God. I can usually spot a codependent within the first five minutes of meeting and talking. He or she will either offer me unrequested help, or the person will keep talking to me although he or she is obviously uncomfortable and wants to discontinue the conversation. The person begins the relationship by taking responsibility for me and not taking responsibility for him- or herself.

Some of us become so tired from the enormous burden—total responsibility for all human beings—that we may skip the feelings of pity and concern that accompany the rescue act and move ahead to anger. We're angry all the time; we feel anger and resentment toward potential victims. A person with a need or problem provokes us to feel we have to do something or feel guilty. After a rescue, we make no bones about our hostility toward this uncomfortable predicament. I have frequently seen this happen to people in helping professions. After so many years of rescuing—giving so much and receiving far less in return—many professional helpers adopt a hostile attitude toward their clients. They may continue to hang in there and keep "helping" them, anyway, but they will usually leave their profession feeling terribly victimized, according to some counselors.

Caretaking doesn't help; it causes problems. When we take care of people and do things we don't want to do, we ignore personal needs, wants, and feelings. We put *ourselves* aside. Sometimes, we get so busy taking care of people that we put our entire lives on hold. Many caretakers are harried and overcommitted; they enjoy none of their activities. Caretakers look so responsible, but we aren't. We don't assume responsibility for our highest responsibility—ourselves.

We consistently give more than we receive, then feel abused and neglected because of it. We wonder why, when we anticipate the needs of others, no one notices *our* needs. We may become seriously depressed as a result of not getting our needs met. Yet, a good caretaker feels safest when giving; we feel guilty and uncomfortable when someone gives to us or when we do something to meet our needs. Sometimes, codependents may become so locked into a caretaker role that we feel dismayed and rejected when we can't caretake or rescue someone—when someone refuses to be "helped."

The worst aspect of caretaking is we become and stay victims. I believe many serious self-destructive behaviors—chemical abuse, eating disorders, sexual disorders—are developed through this victim role. As victims, we attract perpetrators. We believe we need someone to take care of us, because we feel helpless. Some caretakers will ultimately present ourselves to somebody or some institution, needing to be taken care of mentally, physically, financially, or emotionally.

Why, you might ask, would apparently rational people do this rescuing? Many reasons. Most of us aren't even aware of what we're doing. Most of us truly believe we're helping. Some of us believe we *have to* rescue. We have confused ideas about what constitutes help and what doesn't. Many of us are convinced that rescuing is a charitable deed. We may even think it cruel and heartless to do something as cold-blooded as allowing a person to work through or face a legitimate feeling, suffer a consequence, be disappointed by hearing "no," be asked to respond to our needs and wants, and generally be held responsible and accountable for him- or herself in this world. Never mind that they will certainly pay a price for our "helping"—a price that will be as harsh as or more severe than any feeling they may be facing.

Many of us do not understand what we are responsible for and what we are not responsible for. We may believe we have to get into a tizzy when someone has a problem because it is our responsibility to do that. Sometimes, we become sick of feeling responsible for so much that we reject all responsibility and become totally irresponsible.

However, at the heart of most rescues is a demon: low self-worth. We rescue because we don't feel good about ourselves. Although the feelings are transient and artificial, caretaking provides us with a temporary hit of good feelings, self-worth, and power. Just as a drink helps an alcoholic momentarily feel better, a rescue move momentarily distracts us from the pain of being who we are. We don't feel lovable, so we settle for being needed. We don't feel good about ourselves, so we feel compelled to do a particular thing to *prove* how good we are.

We rescue because we don't feel good about other people either. Sometimes with justification, sometimes without, we decide other people simply cannot be held responsible for themselves. Although this may appear to be true, it simply is not a fact. Unless a person has brain damage, a serious physical impairment, or is an infant, that person can be responsible for him- or herself.

Sometimes we rescue because it's easier than dealing with the discomfort and awkwardness of facing other people's unsolved problems. We haven't learned to say, "It's too bad you're having that problem. What do you need from me?" We've learned to say, "Here. Let me do that *for* you."

Some of us learned to be caretakers when we were children. Perhaps we were almost forced to as a result of living with an alcoholic parent or some other family problem. Some of us may have started caretaking later in life, as a result of being in a committed relationship with an alcoholic or other person who refused and appeared unable to take care of him- or herself. We decided to cope—to survive—the best way we could, by picking up the slack and assuming other people's responsibilities.

Many codependents have been taught other ways to be caretakers. Maybe someone taught us these lies, and we believed them: don't be selfish, always be kind and help people, never hurt other people's feelings because we "make them feel," never say no, and don't mention personal wants and needs because it's not polite.

We may have been taught to be responsible for other people but not responsible for ourselves. Some women were taught that good, desirable wives and mothers were caretakers. Caretaking was expected and required of them. It was their duty. Some men believe good husbands and fathers are caretakers—superheroes responsible for meeting every need of each family member.

Sometimes a state resembling codependency sets in when a person is taking care of infants or young children. Taking care of infants requires a person to forfeit his or her needs, to do things he or she doesn't want to do, to squelch his or her feelings and desires (4 A.M. feedings usually only meet the needs of the person being fed), and to assume total responsibility for another human being. Taking care of children is not rescuing. That is an actual responsibility and is not the kind of caretaking I'm talking about. But if that person doesn't take care of him- or herself, he or she may begin to feel the codependent blues.

Others may have interpreted religious beliefs as a mandate to caretake. Be cheerful givers, we are told. Go the extra mile. Love our neighbors, and we try. We try so hard. We try too hard. And then we wonder what's wrong with us because our Christian beliefs aren't working. Our lives aren't working either.

Christian beliefs work just fine. Your life can work just fine. It's rescuing that doesn't work. "It's like trying to catch butterflies with a broomstick," observed a friend. Rescuing leaves us bewildered and befuddled every time. It's a self-destructive reaction, another way codependents attach themselves to people and become detached from themselves. It's another way we attempt to control, but instead become controlled by people. Caretaking is an unhealthy parent-child relationship—sometimes between two consenting adults, sometimes between an adult and a child.

Caretaking breeds anger. Caretakers become angry parents, angry friends, angry lovers. We may become unsatisfied, frustrated, and confused Christians. The people we help either are or they become helpless, angry victims. Caretakers become victims.

Most of us have heard the Biblical parable about Mary and Martha. While Mary sat and talked with Jesus and His friends, Martha cleaned and cooked. Before long, the story goes, Martha started banging pans, accusing Mary of being lazy. Martha complained that she had to do everything while Mary relaxed and enjoyed herself. Does this sound familiar? Jesus didn't let this one go by. He told Martha to hush. Mary knows what's important, He said. Mary made the right decision.

His message might be that Mary made the right choice because it's more important to enjoy people than it is to cook and clean. But I also believe there's a message here about taking responsibility for our choices, doing what we *want* to be doing, and realizing how we become angry when we don't. Maybe Mary's choice was right because she acted as she wanted to. Jesus helped many people, but He was honest and straightforward about it. He didn't persecute people after He helped them. And He *asked* them what they wanted from Him. Sometimes He asked why, too. He held people responsible for their behavior.

I think caretaking perverts Biblical messages about giving, loving, and helping. Nowhere in the Bible are we instructed to do something for someone, then scratch his or her eyes out. Nowhere are we told to walk the extra mile with someone, and then grab the person's cane and beat him or her with it. Caring about people and giving are good, desirable qualities—something we need to do—but many codependents have misinterpreted the suggestions to "give until it hurts." We continue giving long after it hurts, usually until we are doubled over in pain. It's good to give some away, but we don't have to give it all away. It's okay to keep some for ourselves.

I believe God wants us to help people and share our time, talents, and money. But I also believe He wants us to give from a position of high self-esteem. I believe acts of kindness are not kind unless we feel good about ourselves, what we are doing, and the person we are doing it for. I think God is in each of us and speaks to each of us. If we absolutely can't feel good about something we're doing, then we shouldn't do it—no matter how charitable it seems. We also shouldn't do things for others that they ought to and are capable of doing for themselves. Other people aren't helpless. Neither are we.

"God told us to lose our lives. He told us to give to people," says the Reverend Daniel Johns, Senior Pastor at Trinity Lutheran Church in Stillwater, Minnesota. "But I don't think He ever intended people to use the Scriptures to behave in unhealthy ways."

Giving to and doing things for and with people are essential parts of healthy living and healthy relationships. But learning when not to give, when not to give in, and when not to do things for and with people are also essential parts of healthy living and healthy relationships. It is not good to take care of people who take advantage of us to avoid responsibility. It hurts them, and it hurts us. There is a thin line between helping and hurting people, between beneficial giving and destructive giving. We can learn to make that distinction.

Caretaking is an act and an attitude. For some of us, it becomes a role, an approach to our entire lives and to all the people around us. Caretaking is, I believe, closely associated with martyrdom (a state codependents are frequently accused of being in), and people-pleasing (another accusation hurled at us). Martyrs, according to Earnie Larsen, "screw things up." We need to keep sacrificing our happiness as well as others' for the good of some unknown cause that doesn't demand sacrifice. People-pleasers, according to Earnie Larsen, can't be trusted. We lie. And as caretakers, we don't take care of ourselves.

The most exciting thing about caretaking is learning to understand what it is and when we are doing it, so we can stop doing it.

We can learn to recognize a rescue. *Refuse to rescue. Refuse to let people rescue us.* Take responsibility for ourselves, and let others do the same. Whether we change our attitudes, our circumstances, our behavior, or our minds, the kindest thing we can do is remove the victims—ourselves.

ACTIVITIES

1. This assignment may take some time, but if caretaking is causing your problems, it may be a breakthrough experience for you. On a sheet of paper, detail all the things you consider your responsibilities. Do this for your participation at work, with children, with friends, and with our spouse or lover. Now, list detail by detail what responsibilities belong to the other people in your life. If any responsibilities are shared, list what percentage you think is appropriate for each person. For instance, if your spouse is working and you have chosen to be a homemaker and work part-time,

list what percentage of the financial responsibilities you assume, and what percentage of the household chores he or she assumes. You may be surprised at how much inappropriate responsibility you have taken on and how little you have allowed others to assume. You may also find you have been so busy with other people's business that you have been neglecting some of your true responsibilities.

2. Become familiar with the Karpman Drama Triangle and how you go through the process in your life. When you find yourself rescuing, watch for the role and mood shifts. When you catch yourself feeling resentful or used, figure out how you rescued. Practice non-rescuing behaviors: Say no when you want to say no. Do things you want to do. Refuse to guess what people want and need; instead insist that others ask you directly for what they want and need from you. Begin asking directly for what you want and need. Refuse to assume other people's responsibilities. When you initially stop taking care of people who are used to having you take care of them, they may become angry or frustrated. You've changed the system, rocked the boat. It means more work for them, and they can't use you anymore. Explain to them what you are doing, and allow them to be responsible for their feelings. They may thank you for it later. They may even surprise you—sometimes the people we thought least able to take care of themselves can, when we stop taking care of them.

9

UNDEPENDENCE

"What is it about me?" she asked.
"Do I need a dead body lying in my bed
in order to feel good about myself?"

—ALICE B., A CODEPENDENT WHO HAS
BEEN MARRIED TO TWO ALCOHOLICS

"I'm real independent—as long as I'm in a relationship," announced a policewoman who has been involved with several emotionally troubled men.

"My husband has been lying on the couch drunk and hasn't brought home a paycheck in ten years," said another woman, the director of a large human services organization. "Who needs this?" she asked. "I must," she said, answering her own question. "But why? And for what?"

A woman who had recently joined Al-Anon called me one afternoon. This married woman worked part-time as a registered nurse, had assumed all the responsibility for raising her two children, and did all the household chores, including repairs and finances. "I want to separate from my husband," she sobbed. "I can't stand him or his abuse any longer. But tell me, please tell me," she asked, "do you think I can take care of myself?"

The words vary, but the thought is the same. "I'm not happy living with this person, but I don't think I can live *without* him (or her). I cannot, for some reason, find it within myself to face the aloneness that every human being must face or continue to run from: that of being ultimately and solely responsible for taking care of myself. I don't believe I *can* take care of myself. I'm not sure I *want* to. I need a person, any person, to buffer the shock of my solitary condition. No matter what the cost."

Colette Dowling wrote about this thought pattern in *The Cinderella Complex*. Penelope Russianoff discussed it in *Why Do I Think I'm Nothing Without a Man?* I've said it many times.

Whether codependents appear fragile and helpless, or sturdy and powerful, most of us are frightened, needy, vulnerable children who are aching and desperate to be loved and cared for.

This child in us believes we are unlovable and will never find the comfort we are seeking; sometimes this vulnerable child becomes too desperate. People have abandoned us, emotionally and physically. People have rejected us. People have abused us, let us down. People have never been there for us; they have not seen, heard, or responded to our needs. We may come to believe that people will never be there for us. For many of us, even God seems to have gone away.

We have been there for so many people. Most of us desperately want someone to finally be there for us. We need someone, anyone, to rescue us from the stark loneliness, alienation, and pain. We want some of the good stuff, and the good stuff is not in us. Pain is in us. We feel so helpless and uncertain. Others look so powerful and assured. We conclude the magic must be in them.

So we become dependent on them. We can become dependent on lovers, spouses, friends, parents, or our children. We become dependent on their approval. We become dependent on their presence. We become dependent on their need for us. We become dependent on their love, even though we believe we will never receive their love; we believe we are unlovable and nobody has ever loved us in a way that met our needs.

I am not saying codependents are peculiar ducks because they want and need love and approval. Most people want to be in a love relationship. They want a special person in their lives. Most people want and need friends. Most people want the people in their lives to love and approve of them. These are natural, healthy desires. A certain amount of emotional dependency is present in most relationships, including the healthiest ones.[1] But many men and women don't just want and need people—we *need* people. We may become driven, controlled by this need.

Needing people too much can cause problems. Other people become the key to our happiness. I believe much of the other-centeredness, orbiting our lives around other people, goes hand in hand with codependency and springs out of our emotional insecurity. I believe much of this incessant approval seeking we indulge in also comes from insecurity. The magic is in others, not us, we believe. The good feelings are in them, not us. The less good stuff we find in ourselves, the more we seek it in others. *They* have it all; we have nothing. *Our* existence is not important. We have been abandoned and neglected so often that we also abandon ourselves.

Needing people so much, yet believing we are unlovable and people will never be there for us, can become a deeply ingrained belief. Sometimes, we think people aren't there for us when they really are. Our need may block our vision, preventing us from seeing the love that is there for us.

Sometimes, no human being could be there for us the way we need them to be—to absorb us, care for us, and make us feel good, complete, and safe.

Many of us expect and need other people so much that we settle for too little. We may become dependent on troubled people—alcoholics and other people with problems. We can become dependent on people we don't particularly like or love. Sometimes, we need people so badly we settle for nearly anyone. We may need people who don't meet our needs. Again, we may find ourselves in situations where we need someone to be there for us, but the person we have chosen cannot or will not do that.

We may even convince ourselves that we can't live without someone and will wither and die if that person is not in our lives. If that person is an alcoholic or deeply troubled, we may tolerate abuse and insanity to keep him or her in our lives, to protect our source of emotional security. Our need becomes so great that we settle for too little. Our expectations drop below normal, below what we ought to expect from our relationships. Then, we become trapped, stuck.

". . . It is no longer Camelot. It is no longer even person to person," wrote Janet Geringer Woititz in an article from the book *Co-Dependency, An Emerging Issue.* "The distortion is bizarre. I will stay because . . . 'He doesn't beat me.' 'She doesn't run around.' 'He hasn't lost his job.' Imagine getting credit for the behaviors we ordinary mortals do as a matter of course. Even if the worst is true. Even if he does beat you. Even if she does run around. Even if he is no longer working. Even with all this, you will then say, 'But I love him/her!' When I respond, 'Tell me, what is so lovable?' there is no response. The answer doesn't come, but the power of being emotionally stuck is far greater than the power of reason."[2]

I am not suggesting all our intimate relationships are based on insecurities and dependencies. Certainly the power of love overrides common sense, and perhaps that is how it should be at times. By all means, if we love an alcoholic and want to stick with him or her, we should keep loving that person. But the driving force of emotional insecurity can also become far greater than the power of reason or love. Not being centered in ourselves and not feeling emotionally secure with ourselves may trap us.[3] We may become afraid to terminate relationships that are dead and destructive. We may allow people to hurt and abuse us, and that is never in our best interest.

People who feel trapped look for escapes. Codependents who feel stuck in a relationship may begin planning an escape. Sometimes our escape route is a positive, healthy one; we begin taking steps to become undependent, financially and emotionally. "Undependence" is a term Penelope Russianoff uses in her book to describe that desirable balance wherein we acknowledge and meet our healthy, natural needs for people and love, yet we don't become overly or harmfully dependent on them.

We may go back to school, get a job, or set other goals that will bring freedom. And we usually begin setting those goals when we are sick enough of being trapped. Some codependents, however, plan destructive escapes. We may try to escape our prison by using alcohol or drugs. We may become workaholics. We may seek escape by becoming emotionally dependent on another person who is like the person we were attempting to escape—another alcoholic, for example. Many codependents begin to contemplate suicide. For some, ending our lives appears to be the only way out of this terribly painful situation.

Emotional dependency and feeling stuck can also cause problems in salvageable relationships. If we are in a relationship that is still good, we may be too insecure to detach and start taking care of ourselves. We may stifle ourselves and smother or drive away the other person. That much need becomes obvious to other people. It can be sensed, felt.

Ultimately, too much dependency on a person can kill love. Relationships based on emotional insecurity and need, rather than on love, can become self-destructive. They don't work. Too much need drives people away and smothers love. It scares people away. It attracts the wrong kind of people. And our real needs don't get met. Our real needs become greater and so does our despair. We center our lives around this person, trying to protect our source of security and happiness. We forfeit our lives to do this. And we become angry at this person. We are being controlled by him or her. We are dependent on that person. We ultimately become angry and resentful at what we are dependent on and controlled by, because we have given our personal power and rights to that person.[4]

Feeling desperate or dependent can expose us to other risks too. If we let the desperate part of us make our choices, we may unwittingly put ourselves in situations where we expose ourselves to sexually transmitted diseases such as herpes or AIDS (Acquired Immune Deficiency Syndrome). It is not safe to be that needy in intimate relationships.

Sometimes, we may play tricks on ourselves to disguise our dependency. Some of these tricks, according to Colette Dowling, are making someone more than he or she is ("He's such a genius; that's why I stick with him"), making someone less than he or she is ("Men are such babies; they can't take care off themselves"), and—the favorite trick of codependents—caretaking. Dowling demonstrated these characteristics in *The Cinderella Complex*, where she cited the case history of Madeleine, a woman who was extricating herself from a destructive relationship with Manny, her alcoholic husband.

> That is the last trick of the dependent personality—believing that you're responsible for "taking care of" the other one. Madeleine had always felt more responsible for Manny's survival than for her own. As long as she was concentrating on Manny—*his* passivity, *his* indecisiveness, *his* problems with alcohol—she focused all her energy on devising solutions for him, or for "them," and never had to look inside herself. It was why it had taken twenty-two years for Madeleine to catch on to the fact that if things continued as they had always been, she would end up shortchanged. She would end up *never having lived a life.*
>
> . . . From the time she was eighteen until she was forty—years when people are supposed to reap, and grow, and experience the world—Madeleine Boroff had been hanging on, pretending to herself that life was not what it was, that her husband would get his bearings before long, and that she would one day spring free to live her own inner life—peacefully, creatively.
>
> For twenty-two years she had not been able to cope with what it would mean to face down the lie, and so, without intending any harm, but too frightened to live authentically, she turned her back on truth.
>
> It may seem dramatic in its surface details, but in its fundamental dynamic Madeleine's story is not so unusual. The go-along quality she exhibited, the seeming inability to extricate herself, or even *think* of extricating herself, from an utterly draining relationship—these signs of helplessness are characteristic of women who are psychologically dependent.[5]

Why do we do this to ourselves? Why do we feel so uncertain and vulnerable that we can't go about the business of living our lives? Why, when we have proved we are so strong and capable by the sheer fact that many of us have endured and survived what we have, can't we believe in ourselves? Why, when we are experts at taking care of everybody around us, do we doubt our ability to take care of ourselves? What is it about us?

Many of us learned these things because when we were children, someone very important to us was unable to give us the love, approval, and emotional security we needed. So we've gone about our lives the best way we could, still looking vaguely or desperately for something we never got. Some of us are still beating our heads against the cement trying to get this love from people who, like Mother or Father, are unable to give what we need. The cycle repeats itself until it is interrupted and stopped. It's called unfinished business.

Maybe we've been taught to not trust ourselves. This happens when we have a feeling and we're told it's wrong or inappropriate. Or when we confront a lie or an inconsistency and we're told we're crazy. We lose faith in that deep, important part of ourselves that feels appropriate feelings, senses truth, and has confidence in its ability to handle life's situations. Pretty soon, we may believe what we are told about ourselves—that we're off, a tad crazy, not to be trusted. We look at the people around us— sometimes sick, troubled, out-of-control people—and we think, "They're okay. They must be. They told me so. So it must be me. There must be something fundamentally wrong with me." We abandon ourselves and lose faith in our ability to take care of ourselves.

Some women were taught to be dependent. They learned to center their lives around other people and to be taken care of. Even since the women's liberation movement, many women, deep inside, fear being alone.[6] Many people, not just women, fear being alone and taking care of themselves. It is part of being human.

Some of us may have entered an adult relationship with our emotional security intact, only to discover we were in a relationship with an alcoholic. Nothing will destroy emotional security more quickly than loving someone who is alcoholic or has any other compulsive disorder. These diseases demand us to center our lives around them. Confusion, chaos, and despair reign. Even the healthiest of us may begin to doubt ourselves after living with an alcoholic. Needs go unmet. Love disappears. The needs become greater and so does the self-doubt. Alcoholism creates emotionally insecure people. Alcoholism creates victims of us—drinkers and nondrinkers alike—and we doubt our ability to take care of ourselves.

If we have decided, for whatever reason, that we can't take care of ourselves, I have good news. The theme of this book is encouragement to begin taking care of ourselves. The purpose of this chapter is to say we *can* take care of ourselves. We are not helpless. Being ourselves and being responsible for ourselves do not have to be so painful and scare. We can handle things, whatever life brings our way. We don't have to be so dependent on the people around us. Unlike Siamese twins, we can live without any particular human being. As one woman put it: "For years, I kept telling myself I couldn't live without a particular man. I was wrong. I've had four husbands. They're all dead, and I'm still living." Knowing we can live without someone does not mean we *have* to live without that person, but it may free us to love and live in ways that work.

Now, let me give what I shall call the "rest" of the news. There is no magic, easy, overnight way to become undependent.

Emotional security and our present level of insecurity are penetrating issues that we must keep in mind as we make our decisions. Sometimes we become financially as well as emotionally dependent on a person, and we are then faced with two real concerns—two concerns that may or may not be connected.[7] Neither issue is to be taken lightly; each demands consideration. My words or our hopes will not diminish the reality of these facts. If we are financially or emotionally dependent, that is a fact, and facts need to be accepted and taken into account. But I believe we can strive to become less dependent. And I know we can become undependent, if we want to.

Here are some ideas that may help:

1. *Finish business from our childhoods, as best as we can. Grieve. Get some perspective. Figure out how events from our childhoods are affecting what we're doing now.*

A client who has been in committed love relationships with two alcoholics told me the following story. Her father left home when she was five years old. He had been drunk for most of those five years. Although they lived in the same city, she rarely saw her father after he moved out. He visited her a few times after her mother divorced him, but there was no substance to the relationship. As she grew up, she called her father from time to time to tell him about important events in her life: high school graduation, her marriage, the birth of her first child, her divorce, her remarriage, her second pregnancy. Each time she called, her father talked to her for five minutes, mentioned seeing her sometime, then hung up. She said she didn't feel particularly hurt or angry; she expected this from him. He had never been there for her. He never would be there for her. He didn't participate in the relationship. There was nothing, including love, coming back from him. But it was a fact of life, and it did not particularly upset her. She truly thought she had resigned herself to and dealt with her father's alcoholism. This relationship went on this way for years. Her relationships with alcoholics went on for years.

When she was in the midst of her most recent divorce, the phone rang one evening. It was her father. It was the first time he had ever called her. Her heart nearly jumped out of her chest, she reported later. Her father asked how she and her family were—a question he usually avoided. Just as she was wondering if she could tell him about her divorce (something she wanted to do; she had always wanted to cry and be comforted by her father) he began whining about how he had been locked up in a psychiatric ward, he had no rights, it wasn't fair, and couldn't she do something to help him? She quickly wrapped up the conversation, hung up the phone, sat down on the floor, and bawled.

"I remember sitting on the floor screaming: 'You've never been there for me. Never. And now I need you. I let myself need you just once, and you weren't there for me. Instead, you wanted *me* to take care of *you*.'

"When I quit crying, I felt strangely peaceful," she said. "I think it was the first time I ever let myself grieve or get angry at my father. Over the next few weeks, I began to understand—really understand. Of course he had never been there for me. He was an alcoholic. He had never been there for anyone, including himself. I also began to realize that underneath my sophisticated veneer, I felt unlovable. Very unlovable. Somewhere, hidden inside me, I had maintained a fantasy that I had a loving father who was staying away from me—who was rejecting me—because I wasn't good enough. There was something wrong with me. Now I knew the truth. It wasn't me that was unlovable. It wasn't me that was screwed up, although I know I've got problems. It was *he*.

"Something happened to me after that," she said. "I no longer *need* an alcoholic to love me. The truth has indeed set me free."

I am not suggesting that all of this woman's problems were solved when she finished her grieving or by one moment of awareness. She may have more grieving to do; she still needs to deal with her codependent characteristics. But I think what happened helped her.

2. *Nurture and cherish that frightened, vulnerable, needy child inside us. The child may never completely disappear, no matter how self-sufficient we become. Stress may cause the child to cry out. Unprovoked, the child may come out and demand attention when we least expect it.*

I had a dream about this that I think illustrates the point. In my dream, a girl about nine years old had been left alone, abandoned by her mother for several days and nights. Without supervision, the child ran around the neighborhood late at night. She didn't cause any serious problems. She seemed to be looking for something, trying to fill her empty hours. *The child did not want to stay in her house alone when it got dark.* The loneliness was too frightening. When the mother finally returned, the neighbors approached her and complained about this child running all over, unsupervised. The mother became angry, and started yelling at the child for her misbehavior. "I told you to stay in the house while I was gone. I told you to not cause problems, didn't I?" the mother screamed.

The child offered no retort, didn't even cry. She just stood there with downcast eyes and quietly said, "I think I have a stomachache."

Don't pound on that vulnerable child when he or she doesn't want to stay in the dark all alone, when he or she becomes frightened. We don't have to let the child make our choices for us, but don't ignore the child either. Listen to the child. Let the child cry if he or she needs to. Comfort the child. Figure out what he or she needs.

3. *Stop looking for happiness in other people. Our source of happiness and well-being is not inside others; it's inside us. Learn to center ourselves in ourselves.*

Stop centering and focusing on other people. Settle down with and in ourselves. Stop seeking so much approval and validation from others. We don't need the approval of everyone and anyone. We only need *our* approval. We have all the same sources for happiness and making choices inside us that others do. Find and develop our own internal supply of peace, well-being, and self-esteem. Relationships help, but they cannot be our source. Develop personal cores of emotional security with ourselves.

4. *We can learn to depend on ourselves. Maybe other people haven't been there for us, but we can start being there for us.*

Stop abandoning ourselves, our needs, our wants, our feelings, our lives, and everything that comprises us. Make a commitment to always be there for ourselves. We can trust ourselves. We can handle and cope with the events, problems, and feelings life throws our way. We can trust our feelings and our judgments. We can solve our problems. We can learn to live with our unsolved problems, too. We must trust the people we are learning to depend upon—ourselves.

5. *We can depend on God, too. He's there, and He cares. Our spiritual beliefs can provide us with a strong sense of emotional security.*

Let me illustrate this idea. One night, when I lived in a rough neighborhood, I had to walk down the alley behind my house to get to my car. I asked my husband to watch from a window on the second floor to make sure nothing happened to me. He agreed. As I walked across the backyard, away from the security of my home and into the blackness of the night, I began to feel afraid. I turned around and saw my husband in the window. He was watching; he was there. Immediately, the fear left, and I felt comforted and safe. It occurred to me that I believe in God, and I can find the same feelings of comfort and security in knowing that He is always watching over my life. I strive to look to this security.

Some codependents begin to believe God has abandoned us. We have had so much pain. So many needs have gone unmet, sometimes for so long that we may cry out, "Where has God gone? Why has He gone away? Why has He let this happen? Why won't He help? Why has he abandoned me?"

God hasn't abandoned us. We abandoned ourselves. He's there, and He cares. But He expects us to cooperate by caring for ourselves.

6. *Strive for undependence. Begin examining the ways we are dependent, emotionally and financially, on the people around us.*

Start taking care of ourselves whether we are in relationships that we intend to continue, or whether we are in relationships we are trying to get out of. In *The Cinderella Complex,* Colette Dowling suggested doing this with an attitude of "courageous vulnerability."[8] That means: You feel scared, but you do it anyway.

We can feel our feelings, talk about our fears, accept ourselves and our present conditions, and then get started on the journey toward undependence. We *can* do it. We don't have to feel strong all the time to be undependent and taking care of ourselves. We can and probably will have feelings of fear, weakness, and even hopelessness. That is normal and even healthy. Real power comes from feeling our feelings, not from ignoring them. Real strength comes, not from pretending to be strong all the time, but from acknowledging our weaknesses and vulnerabilities when we feel this way.

Many of us have dark nights. Many of us have uncertainty, loneliness, and the pang of needs and wants that beg to be met and yet go seemingly unnoticed. Sometimes the way is foggy and slippery, and we have no hope. All we can feel is fear. All we can see is the dark. I was driving

one night in weather like this. I don't like driving, and I particularly
don't like driving in bad weather. I was stiff and frightened at the wheel.
I could barely see; the headlights were only illuminating a few feet of
the road. I was almost blind. I started to panic. Anything could happen!
Then, a calming thought entered my mind. The path was only lit for a
few feet, but each time I progressed those few feet, a new section was lit.
It didn't matter that I couldn't see far ahead. If I relaxed, I could see as far
as I needed for the moment. The situation wasn't ideal, but I could get
through it if I stayed calm and worked with what was available.

You can get through dark situations, too. You can take care of yourself
and trust yourself. Trust God. Go as far as you can see, and by the time
you get there, you'll be able to see farther.

It's called *One Day at a Time*.

ACTIVITY

1. Examine the characteristics listed on the next two pages, and
decide if you are in a dependent (addicted) or healthy (love)
relationship.

CHARACTERISTICS

Love (Open System)	Addiction (Closed System)
Room to grow, expand—desire for other to grow	Dependent, based on security and comfort—use intensity of need and infatuation as proof of love (may really be fear, insecurity, loneliness)
Separate interests—other friends—maintain other meaningful relationships	Total involvement—limited social life—neglect old friends, interests
Encouragement of each other's expanding—secure in own worth	Preoccupation with other's behavior—dependent on other's approval for own identity and self-worth
Trust—openness	Jealousy, possessiveness, fears competition, "protects supply"
Mutual integrity preserved	One partner's needs suspended for the other's—self-deprivation
Willingness to risk and be real	Search for perfect invulnerability—eliminates possible risks
Room for exploration of feelings in and out of relationship	Reassurance through repeated, ritualized activity
Ability to enjoy being alone	Intolerance—unable to endure separations (even in conflict)—hang on even tighter. Undergo withdrawal—loss of appetite, restless, lethargic, disoriented agony

BREAKUPS

Love *(Open System)*	*Addiction* *(Closed System)*
Accept breakup without feeling a loss of own adequacy and self-worth	Feel inadequate, worthless—often one-sided decision
Wants best for partner, though apart—can become friends	Violent ending—often hate other— try to inflict pain—manipulation to get other back

ONE-SIDED ADDICTION

Denial, fantasy—overestimation of other's commitment

Seeks solutions outside self— drugs, alcohol, new lover, change of situation[9]

10

LIVE YOUR OWN LIFE

Live and let live.

—TWELVE STEP PROGRAM SLOGAN

If I make one point in this book, I hope it is that *the surest way to make ourselves crazy is to get involved in other people's business, and the quickest way to become same and happy is to tend to our own affairs.*

I have discussed concepts and ideas pertaining to that thought. We've examined reactions typical of codependency. We've discussed ways of learning how to react differently using detachment. But, after we've detached and taken our grip off the people around us, what's left? Each of us is left with ourselves.

I remember the day I faced that truth. For a long time I had blamed my unfortunate circumstances on other people. "You are the reason I am the way I am!" I had screeched. "Look what you made me do—with my minutes, my hours, my life." After I detached and took responsibility for myself, I wondered, maybe other people weren't the reason I hadn't been living my own life; maybe they were just the excuse I needed. My destiny—my todays and tomorrows—looked pretty glum.

Living our lives may not be an exciting prospect to some of us either. Maybe we've been so wrapped up in other people that we've forgotten how to live and enjoy our lives.

We may be in so much emotional distress we think we have no life; all we are is our pain. That's not true. We are more than our problems.

We can be more than our problems. We will be more than our problems.[1] Just because life has been this painful so far doesn't mean it has to keep hurting. Life doesn't have to hurt so much, and it won't—if we begin to change. It may not be all roses from here on out, but it doesn't have to be all thorns either. We need to and can develop our own lives. As one friend says, "Get a life."

Some codependents think a life with no future, no purpose, no great shakes, and no great breaks isn't worth living. That's not true, either. I believe God has exciting, interesting things in store for each of us. I believe there is an enjoyable, worthwhile purpose—besides taking care of people and being an appendage to someone—for each of us. I believe we tap into this attitude by taking care of ourselves. We begin to cooperate. We open ourselves up to the goodness and richness available in us and to us.[2]

Throughout this book I have used the phrase *taking care of ourselves*. I have heard that phrase used and abused. I have heard people use it to control, impose upon, or force their wills on people. (I dropped in, uninvited, with my five kids and cat. We're going to spend the week. I'm just taking care of myself!) I have the phrase used manipulatively to justify persecuting and punishing people, instead of dealing appropriately with angry feelings. (I'm going to holler and scream at you all day because you didn't do what I wanted you to do. Don't get mad at me though. I'm just taking care of myself.) I have heard people use these words to avoid responsibility. (I know my son is up in his bedroom shooting heroin, but that's his problem. I'm not going to worry. I'm going to the store and charge $500, and I'm not going to worry about how I'll pay that either. I'm just taking care of myself.)

Those behaviors are not what I mean by taking care of ourselves. Self-care is an attitude toward ourselves and our lives that says, I am responsible for myself. I am responsible for leading or not living my life. I am responsible for tending to my spiritual, emotional, physical, and financial well-being. I am responsible for identifying and meeting my needs. I am responsible for solving my problems or learning to live with those I cannot solve. I am responsible for my choices. I am responsible for what I give and receive. I am also responsible for setting and achieving my goals. I am responsible for how much I enjoy life, for how much pleasure I find in daily activities. I am responsible for whom I love and how I choose to express this love. I am responsible for what I do to others and for what I allow others to do to me. I am responsible for my wants and desires. All of me, every aspect of my being, is important. I count for something. I matter. My feelings can be trusted. My thinking is appropriate. I value my wants and needs. I do not deserve and will not tolerate abuse or constant mistreatment. I have rights, and it is my responsibility to assert these rights. The decisions I make and the way I conduct myself will reflect my high self-esteem. My decisions will take into account my responsibilities to myself.

My decisions will also take into account my responsibilities to other people—my spouse, my children, my relatives, my friends. I will examine and decide exactly what these responsibilities are as I make my decisions. I will also consider the rights of those around me—the right to live their lives as they see fit. I do not have the right to impose on others' rights to take care of themselves, and they have no right to impose on my rights.

Self-care is an attitude of mutual respect. It means learning to live our lives responsibly. It means allowing others to live their lives as they choose, as long as they don't interfere with our decisions to live as we choose. Taking care of ourselves is not as selfish as some people assume it is, but neither is it as selfless as many codependents believe.

In the chapters that follow, we will discuss some specific ways of taking care of ourselves: goal setting, dealing with feelings, working a Twelve Step program, and more. I believe taking care of ourselves is an art, and this art involves one fundamental idea that is foreign to many: giving ourselves what we need.

This may be a shock to us and our family systems at first. Most codependents don't ask for what we need. May codependents don't know or haven't given much thought to what we want and need. (Throughout this book, I have used and will use the terms *needs* and *wants* interchangeably.

I consider wants and needs important, and I will treat these terms with equal respect.)

Many of us have falsely believed our needs aren't important and we shouldn't mention them. Some of us even began to believe our needs are bad or wrong, so we've learned to repress them and push them out of our awareness. We haven't learned to identify what we need, or listen to what we need because it didn't matter anyway—our needs weren't going to get met. Some of us haven't learned how to get our needs met appropriately.

Giving ourselves what we need is not difficult. I believe we can learn quickly. The formula is simple: In any given situation, detach and ask, "What do I need to do to take care of myself?"

Then we need to listen to ourselves and to our Higher Power. Respect what we hear. This insane business of punishing ourselves for what we think, feel, and want—this nonsense of not listening to who we are and what our selves are struggling to tell us—must stop. How do you think God works with us? As I've said before, no wonder we think God has abandoned us; we've abandoned ourselves. We can be gentle with ourselves and accept ourselves. We're not only or merely human, we were created and intended to be human. And we can be compassionate with ourselves. Then, perhaps, we may develop true compassion for others.[3] Listen to what our precious self is telling us about what we need.

Maybe we need to hurry and get to an appointment. Maybe we need to slow down and take the day off work. Maybe we need exercise or a nap. We might need to be alone. We may want to be around people. Maybe we need a job. Maybe we need to work less. Maybe we need a hug, a kiss, or a back rub.

Sometimes giving ourselves what we need means giving ourselves something fun: a treat, a new hairdo, a new dress, a new pair of shoes, a new toy, an evening at the theater, or a trip to the Bahamas. Sometimes, giving ourselves what we need is work. We need to eliminate or develop a certain characteristic; we need to work on a relationship; or we need to tend to our responsibilities to other people or to our responsibilities to ourselves. Giving ourselves what we need does not only mean giving presents to ourselves; it means doing what's necessary to live responsible—not an excessively responsible or an irresponsible existence. Our needs are different and vary from moment to moment and day to day. Are we feeling the crazy anxiety that goes with codependency? Maybe we need to go to an Al-Anon meeting. Are our thoughts negative and despairing? Maybe we need to read a meditation or inspirational book. Are we worried about a physical problem? Maybe we need to go to a doctor. Are the kids going wild? Maybe we need to figure out a family plan for discipline. Are people stomping on our rights? Set some boundaries. Are our stomachs churning with emotions? Deal with our feelings. Maybe we need to detach, slow down, make an amend, do an intervention, initiate a relationship, or file for divorce. It's up to us. What do we think we need to do?

Besides giving ourselves what we need, we begin to ask people for what we need and want from them because this is part of taking care of ourselves and being a responsible human being.

Giving ourselves what we need means we become, as the Reverend Phil L. Hansen suggests, our personal counselor, confidante, spiritual advisor, partner, best friend, and caretaker in this exciting, new venture we have undertaken—living our own lives. The Reverend Hansen is nationally active in the addiction field. We base all our decisions on reality, and we make them in our best interests. We take into account our responsibilities to other people, because that is what responsible people do. But we also know we count. We try to eliminate "shoulds" from our decisions and learn to trust ourselves. If we listen to ourselves and our Higher Power, we will not be misled. Giving ourselves what we need and learning to live self-directed lives requires faith. We need enough faith to get on with our lives, and we need to do at least a little something each day to begin moving forward.

As we learn how to care for and meet our own needs, we forgive ourselves when we make mistakes and we congratulate ourselves when we do well. We also get comfortable doing some things poorly and some

things with mediocrity, for that is part of life, too. We learn to laugh at
ourselves and our humanity, but we don't laugh when we need to cry. We
take ourselves seriously but not too seriously.

Ultimately, we may even discover this astounding truth: Few situations in life are ever improved by not taking care of ourselves and not
giving ourselves what we need. In fact, we may learn most situations are
improved when we take care of ourselves and tend to our needs.

I am learning to identify how to take care of myself. I know many
people who have either learned or are learning to do this too. I believe
all codependents can.

ACTIVITY

1. As you go through the days ahead, stop and ask yourself what
   you need to do to take care of yourself. Do it as often as you
   need to, but do it at least once daily. If you are going through a
   crisis, you may need to do it every hour. Then give yourself what
   you need.

2. What do you need from the people around you? At an appropriate time, sit down with them and discuss what you need from
   them.

11

HAVE A LOVE AFFAIR WITH YOURSELF

This above all:
to thine own self be true,
and it must follow, as the night the day,
thou canst not then be false to any man.

—**WILLIAM SHAKESPEARE**

"Love thy neighbor as thyself." The problem with many codependents is we do just that. What's worse, many of us wouldn't dream of loving or treating other people the way we treat ourselves. We wouldn't dare, and others probably wouldn't let us.

Most codependents suffer from that vague but penetrating affliction, low self-worth. We don't feel good about ourselves, we don't like ourselves, and we wouldn't consider loving ourselves. For some of us, low self-worth is an understatement. We don't merely dislike ourselves, we hate ourselves.[1]

We don't like the way we look. We can't stand our bodies. We think we're stupid, incompetent, untalented, and, in many cases, unlovable.[2] We think our thoughts are wrong and inappropriate. We think our feelings are wrong and inappropriate. We believe we're not important, and even if our feelings aren't wrong, we think they don't *matter.* We're convinced our needs aren't important. And we shame someone else's desires or plans. We think we're inferior to and different from the rest of the world—not unique, but oddly and inappropriately different. We have never come to grips with ourselves, and we look at ourselves not through rose-colored glasses but through a dirty, brownish-gray film.

We may have learned to disguise our true feelings about ourselves by dressing right, fixing our hair right, living in the right home, and working at the right job. We may boast of our accomplishments, but underneath the trappings lies a dungeon where we secretly and incessantly punish and torture ourselves. At times, we may punish ourselves openly before the whole world, by saying demeaning things about ourselves. Sometimes, we even invite others to help us hate ourselves, such as when we allow certain people or religious customs to help us feel guilty, or when we allow people to hurt us. But our worst beatings go on privately, inside our minds.

We pick on ourselves endlessly, heaping piles of shoulds on our conscience and creating mounds of worthless, stinking guilt. Don't confuse this with true, authentic guilt, which motivates change, teaches valuable lessons, and brings us into a close relationship with ourselves, others, and our Higher Power. We constantly put ourselves in impossible situations where we have no choice but to feel badly about ourselves. We think a thought, then tell ourselves we shouldn't think that way. We feel a feeling, then tell ourselves we shouldn't feel that way. We make a decision, act on it, then tell ourselves we shouldn't have acted that way. There is nothing to correct in these situations, no amends to make; we have done nothing wrong. We are engaged in a form of punishment designed to keep us feeling anxious, upset, and stifled. We trap ourselves.

One of my favorite forms of self-torture involves a dilemma between two things to do. I make a decision to do one of them first. The minute I act on this decision, I say: "I should be doing the other thing." So I switch gears, begin doing the other thing, and I start in on myself again: "I really shouldn't be doing this. I should be doing what I was doing before." Another one of my favorites is this: I fix my hair, put on makeup, look in the mirror, and say, "Gee, I look weird. I shouldn't look this way."

Some of us believe we have made such bad mistakes that we can't reasonably expect forgiveness. Some of us believe our lives are a mistake. Many of us believe everything we've done is a mistake. A few of us believe we can't do anything right, but at the same time, we demand perfection of ourselves. We put ourselves in impossible situations, then wonder why we can't get out.

Then we finish the job by shaming ourselves. We don't like what we do, and we don't like who we are. Fundamentally, we are not good enough. For some reason, God created in us a person totally inappropriate for life.

In codependency, as in many other areas of life, everything is connected to everything, and one thing leads to another. In this case, our low self-worth is frequently connected to much of what we do or don't do, and it leads to many of our problems.

As codependents, we frequently dislike ourselves so much that we believe it's wrong to take ourselves into account, in other words, appear selfish. Putting ourselves first is out of the question. Often, we think we're only worth something if we do things for others or caretake, so we never say no. Anyone as insignificant as us must go an extra mile to be liked. No one in their right minds could like and enjoy being with us. We think we have to do something for people to get and keep their friendships. Much of the defensiveness I've seen in codependents comes not because we think we're above criticism, but because we have so little self-worth that any perceived attack threatens to annihilate us. We feel so bad about ourselves and have such a need to be perfect and avoid shame that we cannot allow anyone to tell us about something we've done wrong. One reason some of us nag and criticize other people is because that's what we do to ourselves.

I believe, as Earnie Larsen and other authorities do, that our low self-worth or self-hatred is tied into all aspects of our codependency: martyrdom, refusal to enjoy life; workaholism, staying so busy we can't enjoy life; perfectionism, not allowing ourselves to enjoy or feel good about the things we do; procrastination, heaping piles of guilt and uncertainty on ourselves; and preventing intimacy with people such as running from relationships, avoiding commitment, staying in destructive relationships;

initiating relationships with people who are not good for us, and avoiding people who are good for us.

We can find endless means of torturing ourselves: overeating, neglecting our needs, comparing ourselves to others, competing with people, obsessing, dwelling on painful memories, or imagining future painful scenes. We think, what if she drinks again? What if she has an affair? What if a tornado hits the house? This "what if" attitude is always good for a strong dose of fear. We scare ourselves, then wonder why we feel so frightened.

We don't like ourselves, and we're not going to let ourselves get any of the good stuff because we believe we don't deserve it.

As codependents, we tend to enter into totally antagonistic relationships with ourselves.[3] Some of us learned these self-hating behaviors in our families, possibly with the help of an alcoholic parent. Some of us reinforced our self-disdain by leaving an alcoholic parent and marrying an alcoholic. We may have entered into adult relationships with fragile self-worth, then discovered our remaining self-esteem disintegrated. A few of us may have had our self-worth completely intact until we met him or her or until *that problem* came along; we suddenly or gradually found ourselves hating ourselves. Alcoholism and other compulsive disorders destroy self-worth in alcoholics and codependents. Remember, alcoholism and other compulsive disorders are self-destructive. Some of us may not even be aware of our low self-esteem and self-hatred because we have been comparing ourselves to the alcoholics and other crazy people in our lives; by comparison, we come out on top. Low self-worth can sneak up on us any time we let it.

Actually, it doesn't matter when we began torturing ourselves. We must stop now. Right now, we can give ourselves a big emotional and mental hug. We are okay. It's wonderful to be who we are. Our thoughts are okay. Our feelings are appropriate. We're right where we're supposed to be today, this moment. There is nothing wrong with us. There is nothing fundamentally wrong with us. If we've done wrongs, that's okay; we were doing the best we could.

In all our codependency, with all our controlling, rescuing, and assorted character defects, we are okay. We are exactly as we are meant to be. I've talked a lot about problems, issues, and things to change— these are goals, things we will do to enhance our lives. Who we are right now is okay. In fact, codependents are some of the most loving, generous, good-hearted, and concerned people I know. We've just allowed ourselves to be tricked into doing things that hurt us, and we're going to learn how to stop doing those things. But those tricks are our problems; they are not us. If we have one character defect that is abhorrent, it is the way we hate and pick on ourselves. That is simply not tolerable nor acceptable any longer. We can stop picking on ourselves for picking on ourselves.[4] This habit is not our *fault* either, but it is our *responsibility* to learn to stop doing it.

We can cherish ourselves and our lives. We can nurture ourselves and love ourselves. We can accept our wonderful selves, with all our faults, foibles, strong points, weak points, feelings, thoughts, and everything else. It's the best thing we've got going for us. It's who we are, and who we were meant to be. And it's not a mistake. We are the greatest thing that will ever happen to us. Believe it. It makes life much easier.

The only difference between codependents and the rest of the world is that the other people don't pick on themselves for being who they are. All people think similar thoughts and have a range of feelings. All people make mistakes and do a few things right. So we can leave ourselves alone.

We aren't second-class citizens. We don't deserve to lead second-hand lives. And we don't deserve second-best relationships! We are lovable, and we are worth getting to know. People who love and like us aren't stupid or inferior for doing that. We have a right to be happy.[5] We deserve good things.

The people who look the most beautiful are the same as us. The only difference is they're telling themselves they look good, and they're letting themselves shine through. The people who say the most profound, intelligent, or witty things are the same as us. They're letting go, being who they are. The people who appear the most confident and relaxed are no different from us. They've pushed themselves through fearful situations and told themselves they could make it. The people who are successful are the same as us. They've gone ahead and developed their gifts and talents, and set goals for themselves. We're even the same as the people on television: our heroes, our idols. We're all working with approximately the same material—humanity. It's how we feel about ourselves that makes the difference. It's what we tell ourselves that makes the difference.

We are good. We are good enough. We are appropriate to life. Much of our anxiety and fearfulness stems, I believe, from constantly telling ourselves that we're just not up to facing the world and all its situations. Nathaniel Branden calls this "a nameless sense of being unfit for reality."[6] I'm here to say we are fit for reality. Relax. Wherever we need to go and whatever we need to do, we are appropriate for that situation. We will do fine. Relax. It's okay to be who we are. Who or what else can we be? Just do our best at whatever we are called upon to do. What more can we do? Sometimes, we can't even do our best; that's okay, too. We may have feelings, thoughts, fears, and vulnerabilities as we go through life, but we all do. We need to stop telling ourselves we're different for doing and feeling what everyone else does.

We need to be good to ourselves. We need to be compassionate and kind to ourselves. How can we expect to take care of ourselves appropriately if we hate or dislike ourselves?

We need to refuse to enter into an antagonistic relationship with ourselves. Quit blaming ourselves and being victimized, and take responsible steps to remove the victim. Put the screws to guilt. Shame and guilt serve no long-term purpose. They are only useful to momentarily indicate when we may have violated our own moral codes. Guilt and shame are not useful as a way of life. Stop the "shoulds." Become aware of when we're punishing and torturing ourselves and make a concerted effort to tell ourselves positive messages. If we should be doing something, do it. If we're torturing ourselves, stop it. It gets easier. We can laugh at ourselves, tell ourselves we won't be tricked, give ourselves a hug, then go about the business of living as we choose. If we have real guilt, deal with it. God will forgive us. He knows we did our best, even if it was our worst. We don't have to punish ourselves by feeling guilty to prove to God or anyone else how much we care.[7] We need to forgive ourselves. Take the Fourth and Fifth Steps (see the chapter on working a Twelve Step program); talk to a clergy person; talk to God; make amends; and then be done with it.

We need to stop shaming ourselves. Shame, like guilt, serves absolutely no extended purpose. If people tell us, directly or indirectly, that we ought to be ashamed, we don't have to believe it. Hating or shaming ourselves doesn't help except for a moment. Name one situation that is improved by continuing to feel guilt or shame. Name one time when that has solved a problem. How did it help? Most of the time, guilt and shame keep us so anxious we can't do our best. Guilt makes *everything* harder.

We need to value ourselves and make decisions and choices that enhance our self-esteem.

"Each time you learn to act as if you are valuable, not desperate, you make it easier the next time," advises Toby Rice Drews in *Getting Them Sober.*[8]

We can be gentle, loving, listening, attentive, and kind to ourselves, our feelings, thoughts, needs, wants, desires, and everything we're made of. We can accept ourselves—all of us. Start where we're at, and we will become more. Develop our gifts and talents. Trust ourselves. Assert ourselves. We can be trusted. Respect ourselves. Be true to ourselves. Honor ourselves, for that is where our magic lies. That is our key to the world.

Following is an excerpt from *Honoring the Self,* an excellent book on self-esteem written by Nathaniel Branden. Read closely what he writes.

Of all the judgments that we pass in life, none is as important as the one we pass on ourselves, for that judgment touches the very center of our existence.

. . . No significant aspect of our thinking, motivation, feelings, or behavior is unaffected by our self-evaluation. . . .

The first act of honoring the self is the assertion of consciousness: the choice to think, to be aware, to send the searchlight of consciousness outward toward the world and inward toward our own being. To default on this effort is to default on the self at the most basic level.

To honor the self is to be willing to think independently, to live by our own mind, and to have the courage of our own perceptions and judgments.

To honor the self is to be willing to know not only what we think but also what we feel, what we want, need, desire, suffer over, are frightened or angered by—and to accept our right to experience such feelings. The opposite of this attitude is denial, disowning, repression—self-repudiation.

To honor the self is to preserve an attitude of self-acceptance—which means to accept what we are, without self-oppression or self-castigation, without any pretense about the truth of our own being, pretense aimed at deceiving either ourselves or anyone else.

To honor the self is to live authentically, to speak and act from our innermost convictions and feelings.

To honor the self is to refuse to accept unearned guilt, and to do our best to correct such guilt as we may have earned.

To honor the self is to be committed to our right to exist which proceeds from the knowledge that our life does not belong to others and that we are not here on earth to live up to someone else's expectations. To many people, this is a terrifying responsibility.

To honor the self is to be in love with our own life, in love with our possibilities for growth and for experiencing joy, in love with the process of discovery and exploring our distinctively human potentialities.

Thus we can begin to see that to honor the self is to practice *selfishness* in the highest, noblest, and least understood sense of that word. And this, I shall argue, requires enormous independence, courage, and integrity.[9]

We need to love ourselves and make a commitment to ourselves. We need to give ourselves some of the boundless loyalty that so many codependents are willing to give others. Out of high self-esteem will come true acts of kindness and charity, not selfishness.

The love we give and receive will be enhanced by the love we give ourselves.

ACTIVITY

1. How do you feel about yourself? Write about it. Include the things you like or don't like about yourself. Reread what you have written.

12

LEARN THE ART OF ACCEPTANCE

I'd like to make a motion that we face reality.

—BOB NEWHART, FROM THE *BOB NEWHART SHOW*

Accepting reality is touted and encouraged by most sane people. It is the goal of many therapies, as well it should be. Facing and coming to terms with *what is* is a beneficial act. Acceptance brings peace. It is frequently the turning point for change. It is also much easier said than done.

People, not just codependents, are faced daily with the prospect of either accepting or rejecting the reality of that particular day and present circumstances. We have many things to accept in the course of normal living from the moment we open our eyes in the morning until we close them at night. Our present circumstances include who we are, where we live, who we live with or without, where we work, our method of transportation, how much money we have, what our responsibilities are, what we shall do for fun, and any problems that arise. Some days, accepting these circumstances is a breeze. It comes naturally. Our hair behaves, our kids behave, the boss is reasonable, the money's right, the house is clean, the car works, and we like our spouse or lover. We know what to expect, and what we expect is acceptable. It's okay. Other days might not go so well. The brakes go out on the car, the roof leaks, the kids sass, we break an arm, we lose our job, or our spouse or lover says he or she doesn't love us any more. Something has happened. We have a problem. Things are different. Things are changing. We're *losing* something.

Our present circumstances are no longer as comfortable as they were. Circumstances have been altered, and we have a new situation to accept. We may initially respond by denying or resisting the change, problem, or loss. We want things to be the way they were. We want the problem to be quickly solved. We want to be comfortable again. We want to know what to expect. We are not peaceful with reality. It feels awkward. We have temporarily lost our balance.

Codependents never know what to expect, particularly if we are in a close relationship with an alcoholic, a drug addict, a criminal, a gambler, or any other person with a serious problem or compulsive disorder. We are bombarded by problems, losses, and change. We endure shattered windows, missed appointments, broken promises, and outright lies. We lose financial security, emotional security, faith in the people we love, faith in God, and faith in ourselves. We may lose our physical well-being, our material goods, our ability to enjoy sex, our reputation, our social life, our career, our self-control, our self-esteem, and ourselves.

Some of us lose respect for and trust in the people we love. Sometimes we even lose our love for and our commitment to a person we once loved. This is common. It is a natural, normal consequence of the *disease*. The booklet *A Guide for the Family of the Alcoholic* discusses this:

"Love cannot exist without the dimension of justice. Love must also have compassion which means to bear with or to suffer with a person. Compassion does not mean to suffer because of the injustice of a person. Yet injustice is often suffered repeatedly by families of alcoholics."[1]

Even though this injustice is common, it makes it no less painful. Betrayal can be overwhelming when someone we love does things that deeply hurt us.

Perhaps the most painful loss many codependents face is the loss of our dreams, the hopeful and sometimes idealistic expectations for the future that most people have. This loss can be the most difficult to accept. As we looked at our child in the hospital nursery, we had certain hopes for him or her. Those hopes didn't include our child having a problem with alcohol or other drugs. Our dreams didn't include this. On our wedding day, we had dreams. The future with our beloved was full of wonder and promise. This was the start of something great, something loving, something we had long hoped for. The dreams and promises may have been spoken or unspoken but for most of us, they were there.

"For each couple the beginning is different," wrote Janet Woititz in an article from the book *Co-Dependency, An Emerging Issue.* "Even so, the process that occurs in the chemically dependent marital relationship is essentially the same. For the starting point, let's take a look at the marriage vows. Most wedding services include the following statements—for better or worse—for richer or poorer—in sickness and in health—until death do us part. Maybe that's where all the trouble began. Did you mean what you said when you said it? If you knew at that time that you were going to have not the better but the worse, not the health but the sickness, not the richer but the poorer, would the love that you felt have made it worth it? You may say yes, but I wonder. If you were more realistic than romantic you may have interpreted the vows to mean—through the bad as well as the good, assuming that the bad times would be transitory and the good ones permanent. The contract is entered into in good faith. There is no benefit of hindsight."[2]

The dreams were there. Many of us held on for so long, clutching those dreams through one loss and disappointment after another. We flew in the face of reality, shaking these dreams at the truth, refusing to believe or accept anything less. But one day the truth caught up to us and refused to be put off any longer. This wasn't what we wanted, planned on, asked for, or hoped for. It never would be. The dream was dead, and it would never breathe again.

Some of us may have had our dreams and hopes crushed. Some of us may be facing the failure of something extremely important such as marriage or another important relationship. I know there's a lot of pain at the prospect of losing love or losing the dreams we had. There's nothing we can say to make that less painful or to lessen our grief. It hurts deeply to have our dreams destroyed by alcoholism or any other problem. The disease is deadly. It kills everything in sight, including our noblest dreams. "Chemical dependency destroys slowly, but thoroughly," concluded Janet Woititz.[3] How true. How sadly true. And nothing dies slower or more painfully than a dream.

Even recovery brings losses, more changes we must struggle to accept.[4] When an alcoholic spouse gets sober, things change. Patterns of relating change. Our codependent characteristics, the ways we have been affected, are losses of self-image we must face. Although these are good changes, they are still losses—losses of things that may not have been desirable but may have become oddly comfortable. These patterns became a fact of our present circumstances. At least we knew what to expect, even if that meant not expecting anything.

The losses many codependents must daily face and accept are enormous and ongoing. They are not the usual problems and losses most people encounter as part of normal living. These are losses and problems which are caused by people we care about. Although the problems are a direct result of an illness, condition, or compulsive disorder, they may appear as deliberate and malicious acts. We are suffering at the hands of someone we loved and trusted.

We are continually off balance, struggling to accept changes and problems. We don't know what to expect, nor do we know when to expect it. Our present circumstances are always in a state of flux. We may experience loss or change in all areas. We feel crazy; our kids are upset; our spouse or lover is acting crazy; the car has been repossessed; nobody has worked for weeks; the house is a mess; and the money has dwindled. The losses may come barrelling down all at once, or they may occur gradually. Things then may stabilize briefly, until once more we lose the car, job, home, money, and relationships with the people we care about. We dared to have hope, only to have our dreams smashed again. It doesn't matter that our hopes were falsely based on wishful thinking that the problem would magically go away. Crushed hopes are crushed hopes. Disappointments are disappointments. Lost dreams are dead dreams, and they all bring pain.

Accept reality? Half the time we don't even know what reality is. We're lied to; we lie to ourselves; and our heads are spinning. The other half of the time, facing reality is simply more than we can bear, more than anyone can bear. Why should it be so mysterious that denial is an integral part of alcoholism or any serious problem that causes ongoing losses? We have too much to accept; our present circumstances are overwhelming. Frequently, we are so caught up in crises and chaos trying to solve other people's problems that we're too busy to worry about accepting anything. Yet, we must sometime come to terms with *what is*. If things are ever to be any different, we must accept reality. If we are ever to replace our lost dreams with new dreams and feel sane and peaceful again, we must accept reality.

Please understand acceptance does not mean adaptation. It doesn't mean resignation to the sorry and miserable way things are. *It doesn't mean accepting or tolerating any sort of abuse.* It means, for the present moment, we acknowledge and accept our circumstances, including ourselves and the people in our lives, as we and they are. It is only from that state that we have the peace and the ability to evaluate these circumstances, make appropriate changes, and solve our problems. A person who is being abused will not make the decisions necessary to stop that abuse until he or she acknowledges the abuse. The person must then stop pretending the abuse will somehow magically end, stop pretending it doesn't exist, or stop making excuses for its existence. In a state of acceptance we are able to respond responsibly to our environment. In this state we receive the power to change the things we can. Alcoholics cannot quit drinking until they accept their powerlessness over alcohol and their alcoholism. People with eating disorders cannot solve their food problems until they accept their powerlessness over food. Codependents cannot change until we accept our codependent characteristics—our powerlessness over people, alcoholism, and other circumstances we have so desperately tried to control. Acceptance is the ultimate paradox: we cannot change who we are until we accept ourselves the way we are.

Here is an excerpt from *Honoring the Self* on self-acceptance:

... If I can accept that I am who I am, that I feel what I feel, that I have done what I have done—if I can accept it whether I like all of it or not—then I can accept myself. I can accept my shortcomings, my self-doubts, my poor self-esteem. And when I can accept all that, I have put myself on the side of reality rather than attempting to fight reality. I am no longer twisting my consciousness in knots to maintain delusions about my present condition. And so I clear the road for the first steps of strengthening my self-esteem. ...

So long as we cannot accept the fact of what we are at any given moment of our existence, so long as we cannot permit ourselves fully to be aware of the nature of our choices and actions, cannot admit the truth into our consciousness, we cannot change.[5]

It has also been my experience that my Higher Power seems reluctant to intervene in my circumstances until I accept what He has already given me. Acceptance is not forever. It is for the present moment. But it must be sincere and at gut-level.

How do we achieve this peaceful state? How do we stare at stark reality without blinking or covering our eyes? How do we accept all the losses, changes, and problems that life and people hurl at us?

Not without a little kicking and screaming. We accept things through a five-step process. Elisabeth Kübler-Ross first identified the stages and this process as the way dying people accept their death, the ultimate loss.[6] She called it the grief process. Since then, mental health professionals have observed people go through these stages whenever they face any loss. The loss could be minor—a five-dollar bill, not receiving an expected letter—or it could be significant—the loss of a spouse through divorce or death, the loss of a job. Even positive change brings loss—when we buy a new house and leave the old one—and requires a progression through the following five stages.[7]

1. Denial

The first stage is denial. This is a state of shock, numbness, panic, and general refusal to accept or acknowledge reality. We do everything and anything to put things back in place or pretend the situation isn't happening. There is much anxiety and fear in this stage. Reactions typical of denial include: refusing to believe reality ("No, this can't be!"); denying or minimizing the importance of the loss ("It's no big deal"); denying any feelings about the loss ("I don't care"); or mental avoidance (sleeping, obsessing, compulsive behaviors, and keeping busy).[8] We may feel somewhat detached from ourselves, and our emotional responses may be flat, nonexistent, or inappropriate (laughing when we should be crying; crying when we should be happy).

I am convinced we do most of our codependent behaviors in this stage—obsessing, controlling, repressing feelings. I also believe many of our feelings of "craziness" are connected to this state. We feel crazy because we are lying to ourselves. We feel crazy because we are believing other people's lies. Nothing will help us feel crazy faster than being lied to. Believing lies disrupts the core of our being. The deep, instinctive part of us knows the truth, but we are pushing that part away and telling it, "You're wrong. Shut up." According to counselor Scott Egleston, we then decide there's something fundamentally wrong with us for being suspicious, and we label ourselves and our innermost, intuitive being as untrustworthy.

We are not denying whatever we are denying because we are stupid, stubborn, or deficient. We are not even consciously lying to ourselves. "Denial isn't lying," explained Noel Larsen, a licensed consulting psychologist. "It's not letting yourself know what reality is."

Denial is the bugaboo of life. It's like sleeping. We aren't aware of our actions until we've done them. We, on some level, really believe the lies *we* tell *ourselves*. There is a reason for that, too.

"In times of great stress, we shut down our awareness emotionally, sometimes intellectually, and occasionally physically," explained Claudia L. Jewett in *Helping Children Cope with Separation and Loss*. "A built-in mechanism operates to screen out devastating information and to prevent us from becoming overloaded. Psychologists tell us denial is a conscious or unconscious defense that all of us use to avoid, reduce, or prevent anxiety when we are threatened," Jewett continued. "We use it to shut out our awareness of things that would be too disturbing to know."9

Denial is the shock absorber for the soul. It is an instinctive and natural reaction to pain, loss, and change. It protects us. It wards off the blows of life until we can gather our other coping resources.

2. Anger

When we have quit denying our loss, we move into the next stage: anger. Our anger may be reasonable or unreasonable. We may be justified in venting our wrath, or we may irrationally vent our fury on anything and anyone. We may blame ourselves, God, and everyone around us for what we have lost. Depending on the nature of the loss, we may be a little peeved, somewhat angry, downright furious, or caught in the grips of a soul-shaking rage.

This is why setting someone straight, showing someone the light, or confronting a serious problem often does not turn out the way we expect. If we are denying a situation, we won't move directly into acceptance of reality—we'll move into anger. That is also why we need to be careful about major confrontations.

"The vocation of putting people straight, of tearing off their masks, of forcing them to face the repressed truth, is a highly dangerous and destructive calling," wrote John Powell in Why Am I Afraid To Tell You Who I Am? "He cannot live with some realization. In one way or another, he keeps his psychological pieces intact by some from of self-deception. . . . If the psychological pieces come unglued, who will pick them up and put poor Humpty Dumpty Human Being together again?"10

I have witnessed frightening and violent acts when people finally face a long-denied truth. If we are planning an intervention, we need to seek professional help.

3. Bargaining

After we have calmed down, we attempt to strike a bargain with life, ourselves, another person, or God. If we do such and such or if someone else does this or that, then we won't have to suffer the loss. We are not attempting to postpone the inevitable; we are attempting to prevent it.

Sometimes the deals we negotiate are reasonable and productive: "If my spouse and I get counseling, then we won't have to lose our relationship." Sometimes our bargains are absurd: "I used to think if I just kept the house cleaner or if I cleaned the refrigerator good enough this time, then my husband wouldn't drink any more," recalls the wife of an alcoholic.

4. Depression

When we see our bargain has not worked, when we finally become exhausted from our struggle to ward off reality, and when we decide to acknowledge what life has socked to us we become sad, sometimes terribly depressed. This is the essence of grief: mourning at its fullest. This is what we have been attempting at all costs to avoid. This is the time to cry, and it hurts. This stage of the process begins when we humbly surrender, says Esther Olson, a family counselor who works with the grief or, as she calls it, "forgiveness process." It will disappear, she says, only when the process has been worked out and through.

5. Acceptance

This is it. After we have closed our eyes, kicked, screamed, negotiated, and finally felt the pain, we arrive at a state of acceptance.

"It is not a resigned and hopeless 'giving up,' a sense of 'what's the use?' or 'I just cannot fight it any longer,' though we hear such statements too," wrote Elisabeth Kübler-Ross. "They also indicate the beginning of the end of the struggle, but the latter are not indications of acceptance. Acceptance should not be mistaken for a happy stage. It is almost void of feelings. It is as if the pain had gone, the struggle is over. . . ."[11]

We are at peace with what is. We are free to stay; free to go on; free to make whatever decisions we need to make. We are free! We have accepted our loss, however minor or significant. It has become an acceptable part of our present circumstances. We are comfortable with it and our lives. We have adjusted and reorganized. Once more, we are comfortable with our present circumstances and ourselves.

Not only are we comfortable with our circumstances and the changes we have endured, but we believe we have in some way benefitted from our loss or change even if we cannot fully understand how or why. We have faith that all is well, and we have grown from our experience. We deeply believe our present circumstances—every detail of them—are exactly as they ought to be for the moment. In spite of our fears, feelings, struggles, and confusion, we understand everything is okay even if we lack insight. We accept what is. We settle down. We stop running, ducking, controlling, and hiding. And we know it is only from this point that we can go forward.

This is how people accept things. Besides being called the grief process, counselor Esther Olson calls it the forgiveness process, the healing process, and the "way God works with us." It is not particularly comfortable. In fact, it is awkward and sometimes painful. We may feel like we're falling apart. When the process begins, we usually feel shock and panic. As we go through the stages, we often feel confused, vulnerable, lonely, and isolated. A sense of loss of control is usually present, as is hope, which is sometimes unrealistic.

We will probably go through this process for anything that is a fact in our lives that we have not accepted. A codependent person or a chemically dependent person may be in many stages of the grief process for several losses, all during the same time. Denial, depression, bargaining, and anger may all come rushing in. We may not know what we're trying to accept. We may not even know we're struggling to accept a situation. We may simply feel like we've gone crazy.

We haven't. Become familiar with this process. The entire process may take place in thirty seconds for a minor loss; it may last years or a lifetime when the loss is significant. Because this is a model, we may not go through the stages exactly as I have outlined them. We may travel back and forth: from anger to denial, from denial to bargaining, from bargaining back to denial. Regardless of the speed and route we travel through these stages, we must travel through them. Elisabeth Kübler-Ross says it is not only a normal process, it is a necessary process, and each stage is necessary. We must ward off the blows of life with denial until we are better prepared to deal with them. We must feel anger and blame until we have gotten them out of our system. We must try to negotiate, and we must cry. We don't necessarily have to let the stages dictate our behaviors, but each of us, for our well-being and ultimate acceptance, needs to spend individually appropriate time in each stage. Judi Hollis quoted Fritz Perls, the father of Gestalt therapy, in this manner: "The only way out is through."[12]

We are sturdy beings. But in many ways, we are fragile. We can accept change and loss, but this comes at our own pace and in our own way. And only we and God can determine that timing.

"Healthy are those who mourn," writes Donald L. Anderson, a minister and psychologist, in *Better Than Blessed.* "Only very recently have we begun to realize that to deny grief is to deny a natural human function and that such denial sometimes produces dire consequences," he continues. "Grief, like any genuine emotion, is accompanied by certain physical changes and the release of a form of psychic energy. If that energy is not expended in the normal process of grieving, it becomes destructive within the person. . . . Even physical illness can be a penalty for unresolved grief. . . . Any event, any awareness that contains a sense of loss for you can, and should, be mourned. This doesn't mean a life of incessant sadness. It means being willing to admit to an honest feeling rather than always having to laugh off the pain. It's not only permissible to admit the sadness that accompanies any loss—it's the healthy option."[13]

We can give ourselves permission to go through this process when we face loss and change, even minor losses and changes. Be gentle with ourselves. This is a draining, exhausting process. It can deplete our energy and throw us off balance. Watch how we pass through the stages and feel what we need to feel. Talk to people, people who are safe and will provide the comfort, support, and understanding we need. Talk it out; talk it through. One thing that helps me is thanking God for the loss—for my present circumstances—regardless of how I feel or what I think about them. Another thing that helps many people is the Serenity Prayer. We don't have to act or behave inappropriately, but we need to go through this. Other people do too. Understanding this process helps us be more supportive to other people, and it gives us the power to decide how we will behave and what to do to take care of ourselves when we go through it.

Learn the art of acceptance. It's a lot of grief.

ACTIVITY

1. Are you or is someone in your life going through this grief process for a major loss? Which stage do you think you or that person is in?

2. Review your life and consider the major losses and changes you have gone through. Recall your experiences with the grief process. Write about your feelings as you remember them.

13

FEEL YOUR OWN FEELINGS

When I repress my emotions,
my stomach keeps score . . .[1]

—JOHN POWELL

"I used to facilitate groups to help people deal with their feelings," says the wife of an alcoholic. "I used to openly express my emotions. Now, after eight years in this relationship, I couldn't tell you what I was feeling if my life depended on it."

As codependents, we frequently lose touch with the emotional part of ourselves. Sometimes we withdraw emotionally to avoid being crushed. Being emotionally vulnerable is dangerous. Hurt becomes piled upon hurt, and no one seems to care. It becomes safer to go away. We become overloaded with pain, so we short-circuit to protect ourselves.

We may withdraw emotionally from certain people—people we think may hurt us. We don't trust them, so we hide the emotional part of us when we are around them.

Sometimes we feel forced to withdraw our emotions. Family systems, suffering from the effects of alcoholism and other disorders, reject emotional honesty and at times appear to demand dishonesty. Consider our attempts to tell a drunk how we *felt* about him or her smashing up the car, ruining the birthday party, or throwing up in our bed. Our feelings may provoke unpleasant reactions in others, such as anger. Expressing our feelings may even be dangerous to our physical well-being, because they rock the family boat.

Even families that have no history of alcoholism reject feelings. "Don't feel that way. That feeling is inappropriate. In fact, don't even feel," may be the message we hear. We quickly learn the lie that our feelings don't count, that our feelings are somehow wrong. Our feelings are not listened to, so we quit listening to them, too.

It may appear easier, at times, to not feel. We have so much responsibility because we have taken on so much responsibility for the people around us. We must do what is necessary anyway. Why take the time to feel? What would it change?

Sometimes we try to make our feelings disappear because we are afraid of them. To acknowledge how we really feel would demand a decision—action or change—on our part.[2] It would bring us face to face with reality. We would become aware of what we're thinking, what we want, and what we need to do. And we're not ready to do that yet.

Codependents are oppressed, depressed, and repressed. Many of us can quickly tell what someone else is feeling, why that person is feeling that way, how long they've felt that way, and what that person is probably going to do because of that feeling. Many of us spend our lives fussing about other people's feelings. We try to fix people's feelings. We try to control other people's feelings. We don't want to hurt people, we don't want to upset them, and we don't want to offend them. We feel so responsible for other people's feelings. Yet, we don't know what we are feeling. If we do, we don't know what to do to fix ourselves. Many of us have abandoned or never taken responsibility for our emotional selves.

Just how important are feelings, anyway? Before I answer that question, let me tell you about when I was in treatment for chemical dependency at Willmar State Hospital, Willmar, Minnesota, in 1973. I was faced with kicking a ten-year habit of alcohol, heroin, dilaudid, morphine, methadone, cocaine, barbiturate, amphetamine, marijuana, and any other substance that even remotely promised to change the way I felt.

When I asked my counselor, Ruth Anderson, and other counselors how to do this, they replied: "Deal with your feelings." (They also suggested I attend Alcoholics Anonymous. More on that later.) I did start dealing with my feelings. It felt terrible at first. I had emotional explosions that I thought would rip the top of my head off. But it worked. I experienced my first days and months of sobriety. Then, it came time to leave treatment. I was faced with the unlikely prospect of trying to fit myself into society. I had no resume; it can be difficult for a heroin addict to find and maintain gainful employment. I had to discontinue my relationships with everyone I knew who used chemicals, which was everyone I knew. My family was skeptical about my recovery and still understandably peeved about some of the things I had done. Generally, I had left a trail of destruction and chaos behind me, and I didn't think there was any place in society for me. My life stretched ahead of me, and it held little promise. At the same time, my counselor was telling me to go ahead and start living. Again, I asked her exactly how I should do that. Again, she and others replied: "Keep dealing with your feelings. Go to A.A. And everything will be okay."

It sounded a bit simplistic to me, but I didn't have much choice. Amazingly, and thanks to the help of a Higher Power, it's worked so far. I got into deep water with my codependency when I thought myself too sophisticated to deal with feelings. The moral of this story is that dealing with feelings and going to A.A. can help us recover from chemical dependency. But it goes beyond that, and it answers the question I asked earlier, "How important are feelings?"

Feelings are not the end all and be all to living. Feelings must not dictate or control our behaviors, but we can't ignore our feelings either. They won't be ignored.

Our feelings are very important. They count. They matter. The emotional part of us is special. If we make feelings go away, if we push them away, we lose an important part of us and our lives. Feelings are our source of joy, as well as sadness, fear, and anger. The emotional part of us is the part that laughs as well as cries. The emotional part of us is the center for giving and receiving the warm glow of love. That part of us lets us feel close to people. That part of us lets us enjoy touch and other sensual feelings.

Our feelings are also indicators. When we feel happy, comfortable, warm, and content, we usually know all is well in our world, for the present moment. When we feel uncomfortable with anger, fear, or sadness, our feelings are telling us there's a problem. The problem may be inside us—something we're doing or thinking—or it may be external. But something is going wrong.

Feelings can be positive motivators too. Anger can motivate us to solve a bothersome problem. Fear encourages us to run from danger. Repeated hurt and emotional pain tell us to stay away.

Our feelings can also provide us with clues to ourselves: our desires, wants, and ambitions. They help us discover ourselves, what we are really thinking. Our emotions also tap into that deep part of us that seeks and knows truth, and desires self-preservation, self-enhancement, safety, and goodness. Our emotions are connected to our conscious, cognitive thought process and to that mysterious gift called instinct or intuition.

There is, however, a darker side to emotions. Emotional pain hurts. It can hurt so badly we think all we are or ever will be is our emotional part. Pain and sadness can linger. Fear can be a stopper; it can prevent us from doing the things we want and need to do to live our lives.

Sometimes we can get stuck in emotions—trapped in a well of a certain dark feeling—and think we'll never get out. Anger can fester into resentments and bitterness and threaten to linger indefinitely. Sadness can turn into depression, almost smothering us. Some of us live with fear for long periods of time.

Our feelings can trick us, too. Our emotions can lead us into situations where our heads tell us not to go. Sometimes feelings are like cotton candy; they appear to be more than they actually are.

In spite of the darker side of emotions—the painful ones, the ones that linger, and the tricky ones—there is an even bleaker picture if we choose to become unemotional. Not feeling our feelings, withdrawing emotionally, and pushing that part of us away can be unpleasant, unhealthy, and self-destructive.

Repressing or denying feelings can lead to headaches, stomach disorders, backaches, and generally weakened physical conditions which can open the door to many illnesses. Repressing feelings—particularly if we are doing it during the denial stage of the grief process—can lead us into trouble with overeating, undereating, alcohol and other drug use, compulsive sexual behaviors, compulsive spending, not sleeping enough, sleeping too much, obsessing, controlling gestures, and other compulsive behaviors.[3]

Feelings are energy. Repressed feelings block our energy. We don't do our best when we're blocked.

Another problem with repressed feelings is they don't go away. They linger, sometimes growing stronger and causing us to do many peculiar things. We have to stay one step ahead of the feeling, we have to stay busy, we have to do *something*. We don't dare get quiet and peaceful because we might then feel these emotions. And the feeling might squeak out anyway, causing us to do something we never intended to do: scream at the kids, kick the cat, spill on our favorite dress, or cry at the party. We get stuck in feelings because we're trying to repress them, and like a persistent neighbor, they will not go away until we acknowledge their presence.

The big reason for not repressing feelings is that emotional withdrawal causes us to lose our positive feelings. We lose the ability to feel. Sometimes, this may be a welcome relief if the pain becomes too great or too constant, but this is not a good plan for living. We may shut down our deep needs—our need to love and be loved—when we shut down our emotions. We may lose our ability to enjoy sex, the human touch. We lose the ability to feel close to people, otherwise known as intimacy. We lose our capacity to enjoy the pleasant things in life.

We lose touch with ourselves and our environment. We are no longer in touch with our instincts. We become unaware of what our feelings are telling us and any problems in our environment. We lose the motivating power of feelings. If we aren't feeling, we're probably not examining the thinking that goes with it, and we don't know what our selves are telling us. And if we don't deal with our feelings we don't change and we don't grow. We stay stuck.

Feelings might not always be a barrel of gladness, but repressing them can be downright miserable. So what's the solution? What do we do with these pesky feelings that seem to be both a burden and a delight?

We feel them. We *can* feel. It's okay to feel our feelings. It's okay for us to have feelings—all of them. It's even okay for men to feel. Feelings are not wrong. They're not inappropriate. We don't need to feel guilty about feelings. Feelings are not acts; feeling homicidal rage is entirely different from committing homicide. Feelings shouldn't be judged as either good or bad. Feelings are emotional energy; they are not personality traits.

People say there are hundreds of different feelings, ranging from peeved to miffed to exuberant to delighted and so on. Some therapists have cut the list to four: mad, sad, glad, and scared. These are the four primary feeling groups, and all the rest are shades and variations. For instance, lonely and "down in the dumps" would fall in the sad category; anxiety and nervousness would be variations of the scared theme; tickled pink and happy would qualify as glad. You can call them whatever you want; the important idea is to feel them.

That doesn't mean we have to always be on guard for one feeling or the other. It doesn't mean we have to devote an extraordinary amount of our lives to wallowing in emotional much. In fact, dealing with our feelings means we can move out of the muck. It means if a feeling— emotional energy—comes our way, we feel it. We take a few moments, acknowledge the sensation, and move on to the next step. We don't censor. We don't block. We don't run from. We don't tell ourselves, "Don't feel that. Something must be wrong with me." We don't pass judgment on ourselves for our feelings. We experience them. We allow the energy to pass through our bodies, and we accept it as being our emotional energy, our feeling. We say, "Okay."

Next, we do that mystical thing so many people refer to as "dealing with our feelings." We appropriately respond to our emotion. We examine the thoughts that go with it, and we accept them without repression or censorship.[4]

Then, we decide whether there is a next step. This is where we do our judging. This is where our moral code comes into play. We still don't judge ourselves for having the feeling. We decide what, if anything, we want to do about the feeling and the accompanying thought. We evaluate the situation, then choose a behavior in line with our moral code and our new ideal of self-care. Is there a problem we need to solve? Is our thinking off base? We may need to correct certain disaster-oriented thought patterns, such as: "I feel horribly afraid and sad because the car broke down, and it's the end of the world." It would be more accurate to say: "I feel sad that the car is broken." Is the problem something we can solve? Does it concern another person? Is it necessary or appropriate to discuss the feeling with that person? If so, when? Perhaps it is sufficient to merely feel the emotion and acknowledge the thought. If you are in doubt about what action to take, if the feeling is particularly strong, or if the action you decide to take is radical, I suggest waiting a day or so, until you are peaceful and your mind is consistent. In other words: detach.

Our feelings don't need to control us. Just because we're angry, we don't have to scream and hit. Just because we're sad or depressed, we don't have to lie in bed all day. Just because we're scared, doesn't mean we don't apply for that job. I am not in any way implying or suggesting we allow our emotions to control our behaviors. In fact, what I am saying is the opposite: if we don't feel our feelings and deal with them responsibly, they *will* control us. If we are dealing with our emotions responsibly, we submit them to our intellect, our reason, and our moral and behavioral code of ethics.[5]

Responding appropriately to our feelings also means we are liable for our feelings. Each person's feelings are his or her own. Nobody makes anyone feel; no one is ultimately responsible for our feelings except us, *no matter how much we insist they are.* People might help us feel, but they don't *make* us feel. People also cannot change the way we feel. Only we can do that. Furthermore, we are not responsible for anyone else's feelings, although we are responsible for choosing to be considerate of people's feelings. Responsible people choose to do that, at times. However, most codependents choose to overdo that. We need to be considerate of our feelings, too. Our feelings are reactions to life's circumstances. Thus, etiquette requires that when you discuss a feeling with someone, you say, "I feel such and such when you do such and such because . . ." not "You made me feel . . ."[6]

However, we may want to make another decision about how to deal with our feelings. This is especially true if we are consistently reacting to someone's behavior with a great deal of emotional distress, and even after reporting this distress to the person he or she continues causing us pain. Maybe you don't need that much help to feel. Remember, feelings are indicators and motivators. Watch for patterns in our feelings. They tell us a great deal about ourselves and our relationships.

Sometimes, dealing with feelings means a change of thinking is needed. Many therapies acknowledge a direct correlation between what we think and what we feel.[7] There is a connection. What we think influences how we feel. Sometimes inaccurate, overreactive, or inappropriate thought patterns cause our emotions or cause them to remain longer than necessary. If we think something is awful, will never get better, and just shouldn't be, our feelings will be intense. I call this disaster thinking. That's why it is important, after we feel our emotions, to examine our thinking. Get it out in the light. If it's inappropriate, then we know what we have to do to solve our problem, don't we?

There are times when we may need to discuss our feelings and thoughts with other people. It is not healthy to live our lives in isolation. Sharing the emotional part of us with others creates closeness and intimacy. Also, being accepted by someone else for being who we are helps us accept ourselves. This is always a marvelous experience. Sometimes, we may want to discuss things with a friend who will just listen, while we air things and try to figure out what's going on. Things we lock inside can get too big and too powerful. Letting them out in the air makes them smaller. We gain perspective. It's always fun to share the pleasant feelings too: the joys, the successes, the "tickled-pinks." And if we want an intimate relationship with someone, we need to discuss our persistent feelings with him or her. It's called emotional honesty.

Caution: Intense happy feelings can be as distracting and scary as intense sad feelings, especially to codependents who are not used to happy feelings, according to Scott Egleston. Many codependents believe happy feelings must always be followed by sad feelings, because that is the way it has usually happened in the past. Some codependents believe we can't, shouldn't, and don't deserve to feel happy. Sometimes we do things to create sad feelings after experiencing happy feelings, or whenever the possibility of a happy feeling exists. It's okay to feel happy. It's okay to feel sad. Let the emotional energy pass through, and strive for peace and balance.

There are times when we may need professional help to deal with our emotions. If we are stuck in any particular feeling we should give ourselves what we need. See a counselor, a therapist, a psychoanalyst, or a clergyperson. Take care of ourselves. We deserve it. We may also want to seek professional help if we've been repressing feelings for a long period of time or if we suspect what we've been repressing is intense.

Sometimes, it just takes only a little practice and awareness to awaken the emotional part of us. The following things help me get in touch with my feelings: physical exercise, writing letters I don't intend to send, talking to people I feel safe with, and spending quiet time in meditation. We need to make awareness of ourselves a habit. We need to pay attention to the "shouldn't feel that way" attitudes we tell ourselves; we need to pay attention to our level of comfortableness; we need to listen to what we're thinking and saying and the tone of voice we use; we need to keep an eye on what we're doing. We will find our way to and through our emotions, a way that works for us.

We need to invite emotions into our lives. Then make a commitment to take gentle, loving care of them. Feel our feelings. Trust our feelings and trust ourselves. We are wiser than we think.

ACTIVITY

1. Read through your journal writings. What emotions were squeaking or pouring out as you wrote?

2. Let's play a "what if" game. What if you could be feeling anything you wanted right now, and feeling that way wouldn't make you a bad person. What would you be feeling? Write about it.

3. Find someone who is safe, a good listener, accepting, and non-rescuing, and begin honestly and openly discussing your feelings with that person. Listen to that person's feelings without judgment or caretaking gestures. This is nice, isn't it? If you don't know anybody you feel safe doing that with, join a support group.

14

ANGER

"What is it about me that you hate so much?"
a man asked his wife six months into his sobriety.
"Everything!" she replied with a glare.

—ANONYMOUS QUOTE

For many years I rarely felt anger. I cried. I felt hurt. But anger? No, not me.

After I began my recovery from codependency, I wondered if I would ever *not* be angry.

Janet Woititz described me in this quote from *Marriage on the Rocks:* "You become rigid and mistrustful. Rage consumes you without a satisfying outlet. Anyone who walks into your house can feel the angry vibrations. There is no escape from it. Whoever thought you would turn into such a self-righteous witch?"[1]

Angry feelings are a part of almost everyone's life. Children feel anger; teenagers feel anger; adults feel anger. Sometimes, anger plays a small part in our lives and presents no particular problem. We blow off steam, and we're done with it. We go on with the business of living, and the problem is resolved.

That is usually not the case with codependents, particularly if we are involved with an alcoholic, an addict, or someone with a serious ongoing problem. Anger can become a large part of our lives. It can *become* our lives. The alcoholic is mad, we're mad, the kids are mad, and so is

the dog. Everyone is mad, all the time. Nobody ever seems to blow off
enough steam. Even if we aren't shouting, even if we're trying to pretend
we're not angry, we're mad. We give looks and make little gestures that
give us away. Hostility lurks just below the surface, waiting for a chance
to come out in the open. The anger sometimes explodes like a bomb,
but nobody ever gets done with it. The alcoholic says, "How dare you
become angry with me? I'm the king. I'll get angry with you, but not the
other way around." The codependent says, "After all I've done for you,
I'll get angry any time I please." But silently, the codependent wonders:
Maybe he or she is right. . . . How dare we get angry with the alcoholic?
There must be something wrong with us for feeling this way. We deal
another blow to our self-worth with a little guilt tacked on. Plus, the
anger is still there. The problems don't get resolved; the anger doesn't
blow over. It festers and boils.

Even with the gift of sobriety or recovery from any ongoing problem,
the anger may and usually does linger.[2] Usually, it has reached a peak by
the time the alcoholic gets help. Nobody, including the alcoholic, can
stand the insanity any longer. Sometimes it gets worse. The codependent
may learn for the first time that it *isn't* the codependent's fault. The codependent may even feel new anger for having believed for so long it was!
It may be safe for the first time for the codependent to feel and express
anger. Things may finally have calmed down enough for the codependent
to realize how angry he or she was and is. This can cause more conflicts.
The alcoholic may expect and want to start fresh—minus the dirty laundry from the past—now that he or she has begun a new life.

So the alcoholic says, "How dare you get angry now? We're starting
over."

And the codependent replies, "That's what *you* think. I'm just getting
started."

Then the codependent may add to his or her low self-worth and guilt
another silent, torturing thought: "The alcoholic is right. How dare I be
angry now? I should be ecstatic. I should be grateful. There's something
wrong with *me*."

Then everyone feels guilty, because everyone feels angry. And everyone feels angrier because they feel guilty. The feel cheated and mad because sobriety did not bring the joy it had promised. It was not the turning point for living happily ever after. Don't misunderstand. It's better. It's a lot better when people become sober. But sobriety is not a magical cure for anger and relationship problems. The old anger burns away. New anger fuels the fire. The chemical or problem can no longer be blamed, although it frequently still is. The chemicals can no longer be used to medicate the angry feelings. Often, codependents can no longer even get the sympathy and nurturing we need from friends. We think it's wonderful that the alcoholic has quit drinking or the problem has been solved. What's wrong with us? we ask. Can't we forgive and forget? And once more the codependent wonders, What is wrong with me?

Anger may be a commonplace emotion, but it is tough to deal with. Most of us haven't been taught how to deal with anger, because people show us how they deal with anger; they don't teach us. And most people show us inappropriate ways to deal with anger because they're not sure either.

People may give us good advice. "Be angry, but do not sin; do not let the sun go down on your anger."[3] "Don't seek revenge." Many of us can't adhere to these mandates. Some of us think they mean "Don't be angry." Many of us aren't sure what we believe about anger. Some of us believe lies about anger.

Frequently, codependents and other people believe the following myths about anger:

- It's not okay to feel angry.
- Anger is a waste of time and energy.
- Good, nice people don't feel angry.
- We shouldn't feel angry when we do.
- We'll lose control and go crazy if we get angry.
- People will go away if we get angry with them.
- Other people should never feel anger toward us.
- If others get angry with us, we must have done something wrong.

- If other people are angry with us, we made them feel that way and we're responsible for fixing their feelings.
- If we feel angry, someone else made us feel that way and that person is responsible for fixing our feelings.
- If we feel angry with someone, the relationship is over and that person has to go away.
- If we feel angry with someone, we should punish that person for making us feel angry.
- If we feel angry with someone, that person has to change what he or she is doing so we don't feel angry any more.
- If we feel angry, we have to hit someone or break something.
- If we feel angry, we have to shout and holler.
- If we feel angry with someone, it means we don't love that person any more.
- If someone feels angry with us, it means that person doesn't love us any more.
- Anger is a sinful emotion.
- It's okay to feel angry only when we can *justify* our feelings.[4]

Many people in programs such as Alcoholics Anonymous believe they should never feel angry in their recovery. The idea intended by recovery programs is that people learn to deal appropriately and immediately with anger, before it builds into harmful resentments.

As codependents, we may be frightened of our anger and other people's anger. Maybe we believe one or more of the myths. Or maybe we're frightened of anger for other reasons. Someone may have hit or abused us when he or she was angry. Some of us may have hit or abused someone else when we felt angry. Sometimes just the raw level of energy that accompanies someone's anger can be frightening, particularly if that person is drunk.

We react to anger, both ours and other people's. It is a provocative emotion. It can be contagious. And many of us have so much of it to react to. We have so much of the anger that accompanies grief. We have the anger that comes from the persecution stage of rescuing or caretaking. Many of us are stuck on that corner of the triangle. We have unreasonable anger feelings that may be unjustified and caused by reactive, disastrous thinking: the shoulds, awfuls, nevers, and always. We have justified anger—all the mad feelings anyone would feel if someone did *that* to him or her. We have the anger that covers up hurt and fear. Sad and scared feelings convert into anger, and many of us have so much hurt and fear. We have anger that comes from feeling guilty. Guilt, both earned and unearned, easily converts into anger.[5] Codependents have a lot of that, too. Believe it or not, so do alcoholics. They're just more adept at converting it into anger.

And we have reactive anger. We get angry because the other person feels angry. Then they get angrier, and we get angrier because they got angrier. Soon everybody's angry, and no one is sure why. But we're all mad—and feeling guilty about it.

Sometimes, we prefer to stay angry. It helps us feel less vulnerable and more powerful. It's like a protective shield. If we're angry, we won't feel hurt or scared, at least not noticeably so.

Sadly, many of us have had no place to go with all that anger. We swallow it, bite our tongues, stiffen our shoulders, push it into our stomachs, let it rattle around in our heads, run from it, medicate it, or give it a cookie. We blame ourselves, turn anger into depression, put ourselves to bed, hope to die, and get sick because of it. Finally we ask God to forgive us for being such horrible people for feeling anger in the first place.

Many of us have been in a real dilemma with our anger, especially if we are living in a family system that says, "Don't feel; especially don't feel angry." The alcoholic certainly doesn't want to hear about how mad we feel. He or she probably thinks our anger is unreasonable anyway, and it may bother him or her when we discuss it. Our anger may push the alcoholic's guilt buttons. The alcoholic may even overpower us with his or her anger just to keep us guilty and repressed.

Frequently we can't or don't want to tell our parents how we feel. They may be mad at us for having a friendship with someone who has an alcohol or other drug problem. Or our parents may only see the good side of the alcoholic or addict and think we're unreasonable and unappreciative. Our friends may even become sick of hearing us complain. Some of us may feel so ashamed that we believe we can't tell our pastor or priest how angry we are. The clergy would just call us sinners, and we don't need to hear any more of that. That's all we've been telling ourselves. Many of us wouldn't think of turning to our Higher Power and expressing how angry we are.

So what do we do with all this built-up steam? The same thing we do with almost everything that has to do with us: we repress it and feel guilty about it. Repressed anger, like other repressed emotions, causes problems. Sometimes our anger may leak our inappropriately. We scream at someone we didn't intend to scream at. We wrinkle up our faces, curl our lips, and help people feel like they don't want to be around us. We slam dishes around even though we can't afford to break anything of material value because we've already lost so much.

Other times our anger may show its face in different ways. We may find ourselves not wanting, unable, or refusing to enjoy sex.[6] We may find ourselves unable to enjoy anything. Then we add more self-hatred to our already heaping pile by wondering what is wrong with us and going on our hostile way. When people ask us what's wrong, we tighten our jaw and say, "Nothing. I feel just fine, thank you." We may even start doing little sneaky mean things or big sneaky mean things to get even with those we're angry at.

If anger is repressed long enough, it will ultimately do more than leak out. Unpleasant feelings are like weeds. They don't go away when we ignore them; they grow wild and take over. Our angry feelings may one day come roaring out. We say things we don't mean. Or, as usually happens, we may say what we really mean. We may lose control and unleash ourselves in a fighting, spitting, screeching, hair-pulling, dish-breaking rage. Or we may do something to hurt ourselves. Or the anger may harden into bitterness, hatred, contempt, revulsion, or resentment.

And we still wonder, "What's wrong with me?"

We can repeat it to ourselves as often as necessary: There's nothing wrong with us. Like the book title says, *Of Course You're Angry!*[7] Of course we're *that* angry. We're that steamed because anybody in his or her right mind would be that steamed. An excellent quote from *Marriage on the Rocks* follows:

"You cannot live with active alcoholism without being profoundly affected. Any human being who is bombarded with what you've been bombarded with is to be commended for sheer survival. You deserve a medal for the mere fact that you're around to tell the story."[8]

Anger is one profound effect of alcoholism. It is also an effect of many of the other compulsive disorders or problems codependents find themselves living with.

Even if we're not living with a serious problem or seriously ill person, it is still okay to feel anger when it occurs. Anger is one of the many profound effects life has on us. It's one of our emotions. And we're going to feel it when it comes our way—or else repress it. "I don't trust people who never get mad. People either get mad, or get even," says my friend Sharon George, who is a professional in the mental health field.

We have every right to feel anger. We have every right to feel as angry as we feel. So do other people. But we also have a responsibility—primarily to ourselves—to deal with our anger appropriately.

We're back to our original advice: Deal with our feelings. How do we deal with an emotion as potent as anger? How do we quit feeling that angry? When does it happen? Where does it go? Who can we talk to? Who would want to listen to all that? We probably don't even want to hear it ourselves. After all, the person we're mad at does have a disease. So shouldn't we be feeling compassion and all that good stuff? Is it really all right to be this mad at a sick person?

Yes, we have the right to be mad at a sick person. We didn't ask for the problem. Although the ideal feeling is compassion, we probably won't feel this until we deal with our anger. Somewhere between homicidal rage and biting our tongue because we feel sorry for that sick person is a way to get past our angry feelings—the old ones and the new ones. But I don't believe dealing with repressed emotions will happen overnight.

It may not happen in a month or even a year. How long did it take us to get this angry? Dealing with a significant amount of repressed anger may take time and effort. Dealing with new anger takes practice.

Here are some suggestions for dealing with anger:

- *Address any myths we have subscribe to about anger.* Give ourselves permission to feel angry when we need to. Give other people permission to feel angry, too.
- *Feel the emotion.* Even though it's anger, it's only emotional energy. It is not right or wrong; it calls for no judgment. Anger doesn't have to be justified or rationalized. If the energy is there, feel it. Feel any underlying emotions too, such as hurt or fear.
- *Acknowledge the thoughts that accompany the feeling.* Preferably, say these thoughts aloud.
- *Examine the thinking that goes with the feeling.* Hold it up to the light. See if there are any flaws in it. Watch for patterns and repetitive situations. We'll learn much about ourselves and our environment. Often, recovering alcoholics develop rancid thought patterns, known as stinking thinking, that can indicate the desire to start drinking again.
- *Make a responsible decision about what, if any, action we need to take.* Figure out what our anger is telling us. Is our anger indicating a problem in us or in our environment that needs attention? Sometimes while we're asking God to help us stop feeling angry, He's trying to tell us something. Do we need change? Do we need something from somebody else? Much anger comes from unmet needs. One quick way to resolve anger is to stop screaming at the person we're angry with, figure out what we need from that person, and ask him or her for that. If he or she won't or can't give it to us, figure out what we need to do next to take care of ourselves.
- *Don't let anger control us.* If we find ourselves being controlled by our angry feelings, we can stop ourselves. We don't have to con-

tinue screaming. Don't misinterpret; sometimes screaming helps. Sometimes, however, it doesn't. It's better if we decide, instead of letting our anger decide for us. We don't have to lose control of our actions. It's just energy, not a magical curse over us. Detach. Go to another room. Go to another house. Get peaceful. Then figure out what we need to do. We don't have to let other people's anger control us. I frequently hear codependents say, "I can't do this or that because he (or she) will get angry." Don't jeopardize your safety, but strive to be free from anger's control—your anger or anyone else's. We don't have to react to anger. It's only emotional energy. We don't even have to react by becoming angry, if we don't want to. Try it sometime.

- *Openly and honestly discuss our anger, when it's appropriate.* But don't talk to a drunk when he's drunk. We can make good decisions about expressing our anger openly and appropriately. Beware of how we approach people, though. Anger frequently begets anger. Instead of venting our rage on the person, we can feel our feelings, think our thoughts, figure out what we need from that person, and then go back to him or her and express that need, instead of hollering.

- *Take responsibility for our anger.* We can say: "I feel angry when you do this because . . ." not, "You made me mad." However, I like to give people a little room in communication. We don't always have to say the words exactly right, as if we just walked out of a therapy group. Be ourselves. Just understand we are responsible for our angry feelings—even if they are an appropriate reaction to someone else's inappropriate behavior.

- *Talk to people we trust.* Talking about anger and being listened to and accepted really help clear the air. It helps us accept ourselves. Remember, we can't move forward until we accept where we are. And yes, people care. We may have to leave our house to find them, or go to Al-Anon meetings, but they are out there. If we have angry feelings that have hardened into resentments, we can talk them out with a clergyperson or take a Fourth and Fifth Step. Resentments may be hurting us a lot more than they're helping us.

- *Burn off the anger energy.* Clean the kitchen. Play softball. Exercise. Go dancing. Shovel the snow. Rake the yard. Build a condominium if necessary. Anger is extremely stressful, and it helps to physically discharge that energy.

- *Don't beat ourselves or others for feeling angry.* Don't let other people hit us or abuse us in any way when they feel angry. Don't hurt other people when we're angry. Seek professional help if abuse has occurred.

- *Write letters we don't intend to send.* If we feel guilty about anger, this really helps. Start the letter by asking: "If I could feel angry about anything, nobody would ever know, and it wasn't wrong to feel this way, what I would be angry about is this . . ." Once our anger is out on paper we can get past the guilt and figure out how to deal with it. If we are suffering from depression, this exercise may help too.

- *Deal with guilt.* Get rid of the unearned guilt. Get rid of all of it. Guilt doesn't help. God will forgive us for anything we have done. Besides, I bet He doesn't think we've done as much wrong as we think we have.

Once we begin dealing with anger, we may notice we feel angry much of the time. That's common. We're like kids with a new toy. We'll settle down with it. Be patient. We aren't going to deal with it perfectly. No one does. We'll make mistakes, but we'll also learn from them. The reason we're told to not seek revenge is because getting even is a common response to anger. If we've done or do some inappropriate things, deal with earned guilt and go on from there. Strive for progress.

We need to be gentle with ourselves if we've been repressing loads of angry feelings. Things take time. We may need to be that angry for now. When we don't need to be angry any more, we'll quit feeling angry if we want to. If we think we might be stuck in anger, get professional help.

Some people believe we never have to become angry; if we control our thinking and are appropriately detached, we will never react with or wallow around in anger. That's probably true; however, I prefer to relax and see what happens, rather than guard myself rigidly. And like my friend, I'm leery of people who smile and tell me they never get mad. Don't misunderstand—I'm not advising us to hang onto anger or resentments. I don't believe anger should become our focus in life, nor should we look for reasons to become angry to test ourselves. "It's not good to be angry all the time," says counselor Esther Olson. It's not healthy to act hostile. There is much more to life than anger.

But it's okay to feel anger when we need to.

Activity

1. What do you think would happen if you started feeling your angry feelings?

2. What do you believe deep inside about anger? What myths about anger have you subscribed to? If you need to subscribe to new beliefs about anger, do so. Attack the myths whenever they try to attack you.

3. How do the people in your current family situation deal with anger? How did your mother, father, brothers, and sisters deal with their anger? What's your pattern for dealing with anger?

4. If you have repressed anger, write about it in your notebook. You may need to buy a new notebook and devote it to anger.

5. If anger is a troublesome emotion for you, keep a pencil and paper handy and start writing about your anger as it occurs throughout the day.

15

YES, YOU CAN THINK

For God hath not given us the spirit of fear,
but of power, and of love, and of a sound mind.[1]
—II TIMOTHY 1:7

"What do *you* think I should do?" a client, who was in the throes of her codependency, once asked me. The woman was facing a significant decision regarding her husband and children.

"What do *you* think?" I asked.

"You're asking *me*?" she asked. "It takes me fifteen minutes at the grocery store to decide if I want to buy the 59-cent or the 63-cent bottle of bleach. I can't make the tiniest decisions. How do you expect me to make a big, important one like this?"

As codependents, many of us don't trust our minds. We truly understand the horror of indecision. The smallest choices, such as what to order at the restaurant or which bottle of bleach to purchase, paralyze us. The larger significant decisions we face, such as how to solve our problems, what to do with our lives, and who to live with, can overwhelm us. Many of us simply give up and refuse to think about these things. Some of us allow other people or circumstances to make these choices for us.

This is a short chapter, but it's an important one. Throughout the book, I have been encouraging you to think about things, figure things out, decide what you need, decide what you want, and decide how to solve your problems. Some of you may be wondering if that's possible. The purpose of this chapter is to tell you that you can think, you can figure things out, and you can make decisions—good, healthy decisions. For a variety of reasons, we may have lost faith in our ability to think and reason things out. Believing lies, lying to ourselves (denial), chaos, stress, low self-esteem, and a stomach full of repressed emotions may cloud our ability to think. We become confused. That doesn't mean we *can't* think.

Overreacting may impair our mental functioning. Decisiveness is hindered by worrying about what other people think, telling ourselves we have to be perfect, and telling ourselves to hurry. We falsely believe we can't make the "wrong" choice, we'll never have another chance, and the whole world waits and rises on this particular decision. We don't have to do these things to ourselves.

Hating ourselves, telling ourselves we won't make good decisions, and then throwing in a batch of "shoulds" every time we try to make decisions, doesn't help our thinking process, either.

Not listening to our needs and wants, and telling ourselves that what we desire is wrong, cheats us out of the information we need to make good choices. Second-guessing and "what ifs" don't help either. We're learning to love, trust, and listen to ourselves.

Maybe we've been using our minds inappropriately, to worry and obsess, and our minds are tired, abused, and filled with anxious thoughts. We're learning to stop these patterns also.

Perhaps we lost faith in our ability to think because people have told us we can't think and make good decisions. Our parents may have directly or indirectly done this when we were children. They may have told us we were stupid. Or they may have made all our decisions for us. Maybe they criticized all our choices. Or they could have confused us by denying or by refusing to acknowledge our ability to think when we pointed out problems in the home.

Maybe we had difficulties with subjects in school when we were young; instead of doing what we needed to do to solve the problem, we gave up and told ourselves we couldn't think and figure things out.

People may have put down the intelligence of women, but that's nonsense. We're not stupid. Women can think. Men can think. Children can think. We may be living with people now who are telling us directly or indirectly that we can't think. Some of them may even be telling us we're crazy, but alcoholics do that to people they live with. Maybe we've started wondering if we are crazy! But don't believe any of it for one moment. We can think. Our minds work well. We can figure things out. We can make decisions. We can figure out what we want and need to do and when it is time to do that. And we can make choices that enhance our self-esteem. We're even entitled to opinions! And yes, we do have some of those. We can think appropriately and rationally. We even have the power to evaluate ourselves and our thoughts, so we can correct our thinking when it becomes disastrous or irrational.

We can evaluate our behavior. We can make decisions about what we need and want. We can figure out what our problems are and what we need to do to solve them. We can make little decisions and big decisions. We may feel frustrated when we try to make decisions or solve problems, but that's normal. Sometimes we need to become frustrated to make a breakthrough in our thinking. It's all part of the process.

Remember, decisions don't have to be made perfectly. We don't have to be perfect. We don't even have to be nearly perfect. We can just be who we are. We can make mistakes in our choices. We're not so fragile we can't handle making a mistake. It's no big deal! It's part of living. We can learn from our mistakes, or we can simply make another decision. The following quotation discusses decisiveness in the corporate world, but I believe it applies to other areas of life too.

"If you make a decision, you'll become a hero within the corporate culture. If 30 percent of your decisions are right, you're going to be a big hitter."[2]

We can even change our minds. Then change them again. Then again. Codependents vacillate.[3] As codependents, we are in the midst of upsetting situations. We may go back and forth a lot; we may throw the alcoholic out, then take him or her back. We may leave, then come back, then leave again. This is how we get to where we're going. It's okay. Let's take it one step further—it's normal and often necessary.

"But," a codependent may object, "you don't know my mind. Sometimes I think terrible thoughts. Sometimes I have unspeakable fantasies." We all do, and it's normal, especially if we're living with an alcoholic. We may have attended an alcoholic spouse's funeral 100 times in our minds. Our thoughts are keys to our feelings. Our feelings are keys to our thoughts. We don't have to repress. We need to let the thoughts and feelings pass through, then figure out what we need to do to take care of ourselves.

The following suggestions may help us gain confidence in our mental abilities:

- *Treat our minds to some peace.* Detach. Get calm. If we're facing a decision, big or small, get peaceful first, then decide. Wait until our minds are consistent. If we absolutely can't make a decision on a particular day, then it's obviously not time to make that decision. When it is time, we'll be able to do it. And do it well.
- *Ask God to help us think.* Every morning, I ask Him to give me the right thought, word, or action. I ask Him to send His inspiration and guidance. I ask Him to help me solve my problems.[4] I believe He does help. I know He does. But He expects me to do my part and think. Some days go better than others.
- *Quit abusing our minds.* Worry and obsession constitute mental abuse. Stop doing those things.
- *Feed our minds.* Give our minds information. Get the information we need about problems and decisions, whether that problem is overeating, alcoholism, relationships, or how to buy a computer. Give our minds a reasonable amount of data, then let them sort through things. We will come up with good answers and solutions.

- *Feed our minds healthy thoughts.* Indulge in activities that uplift our thoughts and give us a positive charge. Read a meditation book every morning. Find something that leaves us saying "I can," instead of "I can't."

- *Stretch our minds.* Many of us become so concerned about our problems and other people's problems that we stop reading newspapers, watching documentaries, reading books, and learning new things. Get interested in the world around us. Learn something new. Take a class.

- *Quit saying bad things about our minds.* Stop telling ourselves things like, "I'm stupid," "I can't make good decisions," "I'm really not very smart," "I've never been good at figuring things out," or "I'm not very good at decisions." It's just as easy to say good things about ourselves as it is to say negative things. And, we'll probably start believing the positive things and find out they're true. Isn't that exciting?

- *Use our minds.* Make decisions. Formulate opinions. Express them. Create! Think things through, but don't worry and obsess. We don't have to let anyone make our decisions for us, unless we're wards of the state. And even if we are, we can still think and make some of our choices. Letting people make our decisions for us means we're getting rescued, which means we're feeling like victims. We're not victims. Furthermore, it is not our business to make decisions for other adults. We can take possession of our power to think. And we can let others be responsible for their thinking. We will gain more confidence in ourselves, as we start feeling better and begin to make decisions, small and large. The people around us will grow, as they are allowed to make choices and mistakes.

We can become comfortable with our minds. Become acquainted with them. They're part of us, and they work. Trust them and our ability to think.

ACTIVITY

1. Who makes your decisions for you? How do you feel about that?

2. Did someone important in your life tell you that you couldn't think and make good decisions? Who?

3. Begin doing one thing every day to improve your mind: read an article in the newspaper and formulate an opinion. Later, you might really want to take a risk and tell somebody your opinion on that subject. You may even find yourself in a lively debate.

16

SET YOUR OWN GOALS

Believe that life is worth living and your belief
will create the fact. Be not afraid to live.

—WILLIAM JAMES

The most exciting idea I have discovered in my sobriety and my recovery from codependency is the magic in setting goals. Things happen. Things change. I accomplish important projects. I change. I meet new people. I find myself in interesting places. I make it through difficult times with a minimum of chaos. Problems get solved. My needs and wants get met. Dreams come true.

I am ecstatic about goal setting, and I hope I can transmit my enthusiasm to you. There is nothing in the world like going where we want to go, getting what we want, solving a problem, or doing something we always wanted to do.

Many codependents don't know this joy. It is new to me too. I spent many years of my life not even bothering to think about what I wanted and needed, where I wanted to go, and what I wanted to do. Life was to be endured. I didn't think I deserved good things. I didn't think most good things were within my reach. I wasn't that interested in my life, except as an appendage to other people. I didn't think about living my life; I was too focused on others. I was too busy reacting, rather than acting.

I am not suggesting we can control all the events in our lives. We can't. We don't have final say on much of anything; God does. But I believe we can cooperate with goodness. I believe we can plan, make requests, and start a process in motion.

"Desire, when harnessed, is *power*," writes David Schwartz in his best-seller, *The Magic of Thinking Big*. Failure to follow desire, to do what you want to do most, paves the way to mediocrity. "Success requires heart and soul effort and you can only put your heart and soul into something you really desire."[1]

Goals also give us direction and purpose. I don't get into my car, turn on the ignition, start driving, and hope I get someplace. I decide where I want to go or approximately where I would like to end up, then I steer the car in that general direction. That is how I try to live my life, too. Sometimes things happen, and for a variety of reasons I may not end up where I wanted to go. If I change my mind or problems beyond my control interfere, I find myself doing something other than what I had planned to do. Timing and exact circumstances may vary. That's okay. I usually end up someplace better or someplace that is better for me. That is where acceptance, trust, faith, and letting go come in. But at least I'm not driving aimlessly through life. More of the things I want come to pass. I'm less worried about solving my problems, because I've turned my problems into goals. And I'm starting to think about and consider what *I* want and need.

Goals are fun. They generate interest and enthusiasm in life. They make life interesting and, sometimes, exciting.

". . . Surrender to desire and gain energy, enthusiasm, mental zip, and even better health. . . . energy increases, multiplies, when you set a desired goal and resolve to work toward that goal. Many people, millions of them, can find new energy by selecting a goal and giving all they've got to accomplish that goal. Goals cure boredom. Goals even cure many chronic ailments."[2]

There is magic in setting and writing down goals. It sets into motion a powerful psychological, spiritual, and emotional force. We become aware of and do the things we need to do to achieve and accomplish. Things come to us. Things begin to happen! Following is another excerpt from *The Magic of Thinking Big*.

Let's probe a little deeper into the power of goals. When you surrender yourself to your desires, when you let yourself become obsessed with a goal, you receive the physical power, energy, and enthusiasm needed to accomplish your goal. But you receive something else, something equally valuable. You receive the "automatic instrumentation" needed to keep you going straight to your objective.

The most amazing thing about a deeply entrenched goal is that it keeps you on course to reach your target. This isn't double-talk. What happens is this. When you surrender to your goal, the goal works itself into your subconscious mind. Your subconscious mind is always in balance. Your conscious mind is not, unless it is in tune with what your subconscious mind is thinking. Without full cooperation from the subconscious mind, a person is hesitant, confused, indecisive. Now, with your goal absorbed into your subconscious mind you react the right way automatically. The conscious mind is free for clear, straight thinking.[3]

What are our goals? What do we want to happen in our lives—this week, this month, this year, for the next five years? What problems do we want solved? What material things would we like to possess? What changes do we want to make in ourselves? What would we love to do for a career? What do we want to accomplish?

I'm not going to present a textbook lecture on exactly how you should set goals. Setting goals has been made too boring for too long. Following are some ideas I believe are important. Find a way that works.

- *Turn everything into a goal.* If we have a problem make its solution our goal. We don't have to know the solution. Our goal is solving this problem. Do we want something? A new waterbed, a red sweater, a new car, longer hair, longer nails? Turn it into a goal. Do we want to go someplace—Europe, South America, the circus? Do we want a loving, healthy relationship? Turn that into a goal. Is there something we've always wanted to do—go to school, work for a particular company, make $40,000 a year? Turn it into a goal. Do we need to decide what we want to do for a career? Turn making a decision into a goal. Do we want to grow closer to God, go to church every Sunday, or read the Bible every day? Turn it into a goal. Do we want to change something about ourselves—learn to say no, make a particular decision, resolve some anger? Turn it into a goal. Do we want to improve our relationships with certain people—children, friends, spouse, a relative? Turn it into a goal. Do we want to form new relationships, lose weight, gain weight, quit worrying, stop controlling? Do we want to learn to have fun, learn to enjoy sex, achieve acceptance of some particular person or incident, forgive someone? I believe we can successfully turn every aspect of our lives into a goal. If it bothers us, make it a goal. If we're aware something needs to be changed, make it a goal. If we want it, make it a goal.

- *Omit the shoulds.* We have enough shoulds controlling our lives; we don't need them in our goals. Make it a goal to get rid of 75 percent of our shoulds.

- *Don't limit ourselves.* Go for all of it: everything we want and need, all the problems we want solved, all our desires, and even some of our whims. Don't worry. If we're not supposed to have it, we won't. If we are supposed to have it, I believe we'll stand an improved chance of getting it by turning it into a goal.

- *Write our goals on paper.* There is extraordinary power in jotting down goals, rather than storing them loosely in our minds. We worry less, we have less to think about, and it gives focus and organization to our goals. Recording our goals also helps us direct our energy and be in contact with our Higher Power. We don't have to write our goals neatly or perfectly, or use particular words or systems. Commit them to paper—all of them.

- *Commit our written goals to God.* Tell God these are the things we're interested in, ask for His help, then surrender humbly. It's called, "Thy will be done, not mine."

- *Let go.* Keep our goals close, where we can look at them as we need to but don't worry and obsess about how, when, if, and what if. Some people suggest we monitor our goals daily. I don't, except when I'm setting daily goals. But you can do it any way you choose. Once my goals are on paper, I try to not control or force.

- *Do what we can, one day at a time.* Within the framework of each 24-hour day, do what seems fitting and appropriate. Do God's will for us, that day. Do what we are inspired to do. Do what comes our way that needs to be done. Do it in peace and faith. Marvelous things can and do come to pass this way. Try it. We have to do our part. But I believe we can and will do our part best by doing it *one day at a time.* If it's time to do something, we'll know. If it's time for something to happen, it will. Trust ourselves and God.

- *Set goals regularly and as needed.* I like to do my annual goals at the beginning of each new year. It indicates to me that I am interested in living my life that particular year. I don't believe in New Year's resolutions; I believe in goals. I also write down goals as they occur to me throughout the year. If I am facing a problem, spot a need, feel a new want, I turn it into a goal and add it to my list. I also use goals to get me through crisis times, when I'm feeling shaky. Then, I write down all the things I want and need to accomplish on a daily, weekly, or monthly basis.

- *Check off the goals we reach.* Yes, we will start reaching our goals. Our wants and needs will get met. We will achieve certain things that are important to us. When this happens, cross off that goal, congratulate ourselves, and thank God. We will gain confidence in ourselves, in goal setting, in God, and in the rhythm of life this way. We will see for ourselves that good things do happen to us. Sometimes, we may experience a letdown when we reach a goal, if it's been an important goal that's required much energy or if we've done "magical thinking" about reaching it. (Magical thinking includes thoughts such as, "I will live happily ever after once this problem is solved" or "I will live happily ever after once I get a waterbed.") To avoid a letdown, it's important to have a long list of goals and avoid magical thinking. I've never yet reached a goal or solved a problem that has enabled me to live happily ever after. Life goes on, and I try to live happily and peacefully.

We may never be without a list of problems that we need to turn into goals. We will probably never be without wants and needs. But this process of goal setting, besides making life more enjoyable, helps develop a certain faith in the ebb and flow and general goodness of life. Problems arise. Problems get solved. Wants and needs come into awareness. Wants and needs get met. Dreams are born. Dreams are reached. Things happen. Good things happen. Then, more problems arise. But it's all okay.

- *Be patient.* Trust in God's timing. Don't take an item off the list if it's still important to us just because we didn't achieve or receive something when we thought we should have; the wretched shoulds infiltrate every area of our lives. Sometimes, my goals carry over for years. When I do my annual goal setting, I have looked at my sheet and thought, "Oh, this problem will never get solved. It's been on my list for years." Or, "This dream will never come true. It's the fourth year in a row I've written it down." Or, "I'll never be able to change this character defect of mine." Not true. It just hasn't happened yet. Here is one of the best thoughts I've ever encountered on patience. It is an excerpt from Dennis Wholey's book on alcoholism, *The Courage to Change.*

> I've started to realize that waiting is an art, that waiting achieves things. Waiting can be very, very powerful. Time is a valuable thing. If you can wait two years, you can sometimes achieve something that you could not achieve today, however hard you worked, however much money you threw up in the air, however many times you banged your head against the wall. . . .[4]

Things happen when the time is right—when we're ready, when God is ready, when the world is ready. Give up. Let go. But keep it on our list.

We need to set goals for ourselves. Start today—when you finish this chapter. If you don't have any goals, make your first goal "getting some goals." You probably won't start living happily ever after, but you may start living happily.

ACTIVITY

1. Write your goals on a sheet of paper. Try to think of at least ten items such as wants, problems to be solved, and changes in yourself. Write as many goals as come to mind.

2. Review the checklist of "codependency characteristics" in Chapter Four. Make it a goal to change any of those characteristics that are a problem for you.

17

COMMUNICATION

*When you're doing what's right for you,
it's okay to say it once, simply, and then
refuse to discuss anything further.*[1]

—TOBY RICE DREWS

Read through the following conversations. You may identify with the dialogue, which appears in bold type, and the italicized interpretations, which explain the codependents' intentions and thought patterns.

Danielle is about to call Stacy on the telephone. Danielle wants Stacy to babysit Danielle's three children for the weekend, but she does not intend to ask Stacy to babysit; she intends to manipulate her into doing it. Pay attention to her techniques.

Stacy: **Hello.**

Danielle: **Hi** (mumbled). **Sigh.** *The sigh means, "Poor me. I'm just so helpless. Ask me what's wrong. Rescue me."*

Stacy: (After a long pause.) **Oh, hi, Danielle. Glad you called. How're you doing?** *During the long pause, Stacy thought, "Oh, no. Not her." Sighing and moaning again. "Good heavens, what does she want this time?"*

Danielle: **Sigh. Sigh. I'm doing about the same as always. Problems, you know.** *What Danielle is saying is: "C'mon. Ask me what's wrong."*

Stacy: (Again, after a long pause.) **What's the matter? You sound terrible.** *During the long pause this time, Stacy thought: "I'm not going to ask her what's wrong. I won't get trapped. I refuse to ask her what's wrong." Upon thinking this, Stacy felt angry, then guilty (the rescue feelings), then went on to rescue Danielle by asking her what was wrong.*

Danielle: **Well, my husband just found out he's got to go out of town this weekend on his job, and he's asked me to come with. I would love to go with him. You know I never get to go anywhere. But I don't know who I'd get to watch the kids. I hated to say no, but I had to turn him down. He feels so bad. I hope he doesn't get too mad at me. Oh, well, that's just the way things go, I guess. Sigh. Sigh.** *Danielle is laying it on thick. She wants Stacy to feel sorry for her, guilty, and sorry for her husband. Her words have been carefully chosen. Danielle, of course, told her husband she could go. She told her husband she was going to get Stacy to babysit.*

Stacy: (Long, long pause.) **Well, I suppose I could see if I could maybe help you out.** *During the pause this time, Stacy thought: "Oh, no. No, no, no. I hate watching her kids. She never watches mine. I don't want to. I won't. Darn her for putting me in this spot all the time. Rats. But how could I say no? I should help people. Do unto others. And she needs me so much. God, I don't want her to get angry at me. Besides, if I don't help her out, who will? She leads such a pathetic life. But this is the last time. The last time ever." The feelings were anger, pity, guilt, saintly, and back to anger. Notice how she demeaned Danielle by labeling her helpless; notice her grandiose feelings of responsibility: "I'm the only person in the world who can help her." Also, notice how she worded her response. She was hoping Danielle would notice Stacy's lack of enthusiasm and rescue her by telling her to forget it.*

Danielle: **Would you really babysit? Thanks so much. You're the greatest. I never dreamt you'd actually do this for me.** *"Ah, ha! Got what I wanted."*

Stacy: **No problem. Glad to help.** *"I don't want to do this. Why does this always happen to me?"*

In the next conversation Robert wants his wife, Sally, to call his boss and tell him Robert is sick. Robert was out drinking until 3 A.M. the evening before. His alcoholism is causing increasing problems at home and on the job. During the conversation he feels sick, angry, guilty, and desperate. Sally feels the same way.

Robert: **Good morning, honey. How's my sweetie pie today?** *"Heaven help me, I feel awful. I can't go to work. She's mad. I can't face the boss. Better lather her up, get her to call in for me, and then I'll go back to bed. Better yet, I need another drink. Quick."*

Sally: **I'm fine.** (Said in a clipped, martyred voice after a cold stare, a dirty look, and a long silence.) *What Sally meant was: "I feel hurt. I feel angry. How could you do this to me? You were out again drinking last night. You promised not to do it anymore. Our lives are falling apart, and you don't care. Look at you: You're a mess. I can't stand this!"*

Robert: **Honey, I feel so sick today. I must be getting the flu. I can't even eat breakfast. Call my boss, okay? Tell him I'll be in tomorrow, if I'm better. Could you do that for the old dad? C'mon. Be my little sweetheart. I'm so sick.** *"I'm helpless, and I need you. Take care of me, and do it right now. I know you're angry at me, so I'll try to get you to feel sorry for me."*

Sally: **I really don't think I should call your boss. He likes to talk to you when you're not going to come in. He always has questions about things, and I can't answer them. Don't you think it would be better if you called? After all, you know what you want to say.** *"I hate calling his boss. I hate lying for him. But if I say no, he'll get angry. I'll try to act more helpless than he is."*

Robert: **What's with you, anyway? Can't you do that one little thing for me? Are you that selfish? I know you're mad at me. You're always**

mad at me. It's no wonder I drink, with a wife like you. Go ahead.
Don't call. But if I lose my job, it's your fault. *"How dare she refuse me?"*
he thinks. Then he decides it's time to get tough. He's got to get her to do this.
He decides to throw a big portion of guilt at her, then top it off with a little fear.
He knows she's worried about him losing his job. While he's at it, he lays the
groundwork for today's drinking.

Sally: **Fine. I'll do it. But don't you ever ask me to do it again. And
if you drink one more time, I'm leaving you.** *Feeling trapped, Sally
calls Robert's boss. Robert made his points well. He hit Sally on all her weak
spots. She is afraid of being called selfish because she thinks it would be
terrible if she was selfish; she feels guilty because she knows she is mad all
the time; she feels responsible for Robert's drinking; and she is afraid of him
losing his job. That business about leaving him if he drank again was an
empty threat; she has made no decision to leave Robert. And the next time
Robert asks her, she will call his boss again. After Sally makes the phone
call she flies into a rage at Robert, persecuting him. She then ends up feeling
sorry for herself and victimized. She also continues to feel extremely guilty,
harboring the thought that there is something wrong with her for all her
feelings and reactions, because Robert appears so powerful and she feels so
weak and insecure.*

In this conversation, a counselor is talking to an alcoholic husband and
his wife in a family therapy group. The couple appears to be the perfect
couple. This is not their first time attending this group, but it is the first
time the counselor focuses on them.

Counselor: **Steven and Joanne, I'm glad you're both here tonight.
How are you doing?**

Steven: **We're doing great. Just great. Aren't we, Joanne?**

Joanne: (Smile.) **Yes. Everything's fine.** (Nervous laugh.)

Counselor: **Joanne, you're laughing, but I sense something is wrong.**

It's okay to talk in here. It's okay to talk about your feelings, and it's okay to talk about your problems. This is what this group is for. What's going on underneath your smile?

Joanne: (Her smile crumbles, and she begins crying.) I'm so sick of this. I'm so sick of him hitting me. I'm so sick of being scared of him. I'm sick of the lies. I'm sick of the promises that are never kept. And I'm sick of being slapped around.

Now that we've "listened" to some codependents' talk, let's consider the dialogue we use. Many codependents have poor communication skills. We carefully choose our words to manipulate, people please, control, cover up, and alleviate guilt. Our communication reeks of repressed feeling, repressed thoughts, ulterior motives, low self-worth, and shame. We laugh when we want to cry, we say we're fine when we're not. We allow ourselves to be bullied and buried. We sometimes react inappropriately. We justify, rationalize, compensate, and take others all around the block. We are nonassertive. We badger and threaten, then back down. Sometimes we lie. Frequently, we are hostile. We apologize a lot, and hint at what we want and need.

Codependents are indirect. We don't say what we mean, we don't mean what we say.[2]

We don't do it on purpose. We do it because we've learned to communicate this way. At some point, either in our childhood or adult family, we learned it was wrong to talk about problems, express feelings, and express opinions. We've learned it was wrong to directly state what we want and need. It was certainly wrong to say no, and stand up for ourselves. An alcoholic parent or spouse will be glad to teach these rules; we have been too willing to learn and accept them.

As John Powell asks in the title of his excellent book on communication: *Why Am I Afraid to Tell You Who I Am?* Why are we afraid to tell people who we are? Each of us must answer that question. Powell says it's because who we are is all we've got, and we're afraid of being rejected.[3] Some of us may be afraid because we're not sure who we are and what we want to say. Many of us have been inhibited and controlled by one or more of the family rules I discussed earlier in this chapter. Some of us have had to follow these rules to protect ourselves, to survive. However, I believe most of us are afraid to tell people who we are because we don't believe it is okay to be who we are.

Many of us don't like and don't trust ourselves. We don't trust our thoughts. We don't trust our feelings. We think our opinions stink. We don't think we have the right to say no. We're not sure what we want and need; if we do know, we feel guilty about having wants and needs and we're surely not going to be up front about them. We may feel ashamed for having our problems. Many of us don't even trust our ability to accurately identify problems, and we're more than willing to back down if somebody else insists the problem isn't there.

Communication is not mystical. The words we speak reflect who we are: what we think, judge, feel, value, honor, love, hate, fear, desire, hope for, believe in, and commit to.[4] If we think we're inappropriate to life our communication will reflect this: We will judge others as having all the answers; feel angry, hurt, scared, guilty, needy, and controlled by other people. We will desire to control others, value pleasing others at any cost, and fear disapproval and abandonment. We will hope for everything but believe we deserve and will get nothing unless we force things to happen, and remain committed to being responsible for other people's feelings and behavior. We're congested with negative feelings and thoughts.

No wonder we have communication problems.

Talking clearly and openly is not difficult. In fact, it's easy. And fun. Start by knowing that who we are is okay. Our feelings and thoughts are okay. Our opinions count. It's okay to talk about our problems. And it's okay to say no.

We *can* say no—whenever we want to. It's easy. Say it right now. Ten times. See how easy that was? By the way, other people can say no, too.

It makes it easier if we've got equal rights. Whenever our answer is no, start our response with the word *no,* instead of saying, "I don't think so," or "Maybe," or some other wavering phrase.[5]

Say what we mean, and mean what we say. If we don't know what we mean, be quiet and think about it. If our answer is, "I don't know," say "I don't know." Learn to be concise. Stop taking people all around the block. Get to the point and when we make it, stop.

Talk about our problems. We're not being disloyal to anyone by revealing who we are and what kinds of problems we're working on. All we're doing is pretending by not being who we are. Share secrets with trusted friends who won't use these against us or help us feel ashamed. We can make appropriate decisions about who to talk to, how much to tell them, and when the best time to talk is.

Express our feelings: openly, honestly, appropriately, and responsibly. Let others do the same. Learn the words: I feel. Let others say those words and learn to listen—not fix—when they do.

We can say what we think. Learn to say: "This is what I think." Our opinions can be different from other people's opinions. That doesn't mean we're wrong. We don't have to change our opinions, and neither does the other person, unless either of us wants to.

We can even be wrong.

We can say what we expect, without demanding that other people change to suit our needs. Other people can say what they expect, and we don't have to change to suit them, either—if we don't want to.

We can express our wants and needs. Learn the words: "This is what I need from you. This is what I want from you."

We can tell the truth. Lying about what we think, how we feel, and what we want isn't being polite—it's lying.

We don't have to be controlled by what other people say; we don't have to try to control them with our words and special effects. We don't have to be manipulated, guilted, coerced, or forced into anything. We can open our mouths and take care of ourselves! Learn to say: "I love you, but I love me, too. This is what I need to do to take care of *me.*"

We can, as Earnie Larsen says, learn to ignore nonsense. We can refuse to talk to someone's illness, whether it is alcoholism or another compulsive disorder. If it doesn't make sense, it doesn't make sense. We don't have to waste our time trying to make sense out of it or trying to convince the other person that what he or she said didn't make sense. Learn to say, "I don't want to discuss this."

We can be assertive and stand up for ourselves without being abrasive or aggressive. Learn to say: "This is as far as I go. This is my limit. I will not tolerate this." And mean those words.

We can show compassion and concern without rescuing. Learn to say, "Sounds like you're having a problem. What do you need from me?" Learn to say, "I'm sorry you're having that problem." Then, let it go. We don't have to fix it.

We can discuss our feelings and problems without expecting people to rescue us too. We can settle for being listened to. That's probably all we ever wanted anyway.

One common complaint I hear from codependents is, "Nobody takes me seriously!" Take ourselves seriously. Balance that with an appropriate sense of humor and we won't have to worry about what anyone else is or isn't doing.

Learn to listen to what people are saying and not saying. Learn to listen to ourselves, the tone of voice we use, the words we choose, the way we express ourselves, and the thoughts going through our minds.

Talking is a tool and a delight. We talk to express ourselves. We talk to be listened to. Talking enables us to understand ourselves and helps us understand other people. Talking helps us get messages to people. Sometimes we talk to achieve closeness and intimacy. Maybe we don't always have something earth-shattering to say, but we want contact with people. We want to bridge the gap. We want to share and be close. Sometimes we talk to have fun—to play, enjoy, banter, and entertain. There are times when we talk to take care of ourselves—to make it clear that we will not be bullied or abused, that we love ourselves, and that we have made decisions in our best interests. And sometimes we just talk.

We need to take responsibility for communication. Let our words reflect high self-esteem and esteem for others. Be honest. Be direct. Be open. Be gentle and loving when that's appropriate. Be firm when the situation calls for firmness. Above all else, be who we are and say what we need to say.

In love and dignity, speak the truth—as we think, feel, and know it—and it shall set us free.

ACTIVITY

1. Read these books: *Why Am I Afraid to Tell You Who I Am?* by John Powell, and *How to Be an Assertive (Not Aggressive) Woman in Life, in Love, and on the Job,* by Jean Baer. *How to Be an Assertive Woman* is an excellent book for men, too.

18

WORK A TWELVE STEP PROGRAM

"How do the Twelve Steps work?"
"They work just fine, thank you."

—ANONYMOUS A.A./AL-ANON QUOTE

I detest the disease of alcoholism. Chemical dependency and other compulsive disorders destroy people—beautiful, intelligent, sensitive, creative, loving, caring people who do not deserve to be destroyed. The illnesses kill love and dreams, hurt children, and tear apart families. Alcoholism leaves in its wake sheared, fragmented, bewildered victims. Sometimes the early death it brings to the drinker causes far less pain than the wretched illness caused during his or her lifetime. It is a horrid, cunning, baffling, powerful, and deadly disease.

I unabashedly love Twelve Step programs. I have great respect for all of them: Alcoholics Anonymous, for people with a desire to stop drinking; Al-Anon, for people affected by someone else's drinking; Alateen, for teenagers affected by someone's drinking; Al-Atots, for children affected by someone's drinking; and Narcotics Anonymous, for people addicted to drugs.

Other Twelve Step programs that I respect include Nar-Anon, for people affected by another's chemical addiction; Overeaters Anonymous, for people with eating disorders; O-Anon, for people affected by others' eating disorders; Families Anonymous, for people concerned about the use of chemicals and/or related behavioral problems in a relative or friend;

Adult Children of Alcoholics, for adult children of alcoholics; Emotions Anonymous, for people with a desire to become well emotionally.

Other good Twelve Step programs include Sex Addicts Anonymous, for people with compulsive sexual behavior; Co-SA, for people affected by another person's sexual addiction; Gamblers Anonymous, for people with a desire to stop gambling; Gam-Anon, for people affected by another person's gambling; Parents Anonymous, for parents who are abusive, neglectful, or afraid of becoming so, or for adolescents who are encountering problems due to past or current abuse; and Sex Abusers Anonymous. There may also be other programs which I have either over-looked or which have sprung into origin since the writing of this book.

Twelve Step programs are not merely self-help groups that help people with compulsive disorders stop doing whatever it is they feel compelled to do (drinking, helping the drinker, etc.). The programs teach people how to live—peacefully, happily, successfully. They bring peace. They promote healing. They give life to their members—frequently a richer, healthier life than those people knew before they developed whatever problem they developed. The Twelve Steps are a way of life.

In this chapter I am going to focus on the programs for people who have been affected by another person's compulsive disorder, because this is a book on codependency and that's what codependency is about. I am going to refer specifically to the Al-Anon program, because that is one program I "work." (I will discuss that little piece of jargon, "working a program," later.) However, with a bit of creativity on your part, the information I present can be applied to any of the Twelve Step programs.

THE TWELVE STEPS

The Twelve Steps are at the heart of the Twelve Step programs. The Steps, in their basic forms (following in italics), belong to various programs. But all of the programs adapted their Steps from those of Alcoholics Anonymous.

The interpretations following the Steps are my personal opinions and are not related to, endorsed by, or affiliated with any Twelve Step program. The programs also have Traditions, which guard the purity of the programs to ensure that they continue to operate effectively. The Eleventh Tradition in the Al-Anon program says, "Our public relations policy is based on attraction rather than promotion. . . ."[1] Please understand I am not promoting this program or any program. I am just saying what I think, and I happen to think highly of the Twelve Steps.

1. *We admitted we were powerless over alcohol—that our lives had become unmanageable.* This is an important Step. It must be taken first. That is why it is the First Step. Much of our struggle to accept whatever it is we must accept—a loved one's alcoholism or eating problem, for example, brings us to this door. My denial, my bargains, my efforts to control, my rescuing, my anger, my hurt, my grief propelled me to this place. Not once, but twice in my lifetime, I had tried to do the impossible. I tried to control alcohol. I had battled with alcohol in my own drinking and using days; I went to war again with alcohol when people I loved were using and abusing it. Both times, I lost. When will I learn to quit fighting lions? Both times, alcohol gained control of me—once directly, through my own imbibing; the second time, indirectly, through another person's use of the substance. It didn't matter, though, how it had gained control. It had. My thoughts, emotions, behaviors—my life—were regulated and directed by alcohol and its effects on another person's life. People were controlling me, but those people were being controlled by alcohol. Once the light was turned on, it wasn't difficult to see who was boss. The bottle was. Once I saw that, I could easily see my life had become unmanageable. Indeed, it had. Spiritually, emotionally, mentally, behaviorally, I was out of control. My relationships with people were unmanageable. My career was unmanageable. I couldn't even keep my house clean.

If this Step sounds like giving up, that's because it is. It is where we surrender to the truth. We are powerless over alcohol. We are powerless over the disease of alcoholism. We are powerless over another person's drinking and the effects of alcoholism in his or her life. We are powerless over people—what they do, say, think, feel, or don't do, say, think, or feel. We have been trying to do the impossible. At this point we understand this and make a rational decision to quit trying to do what we cannot ever do, no matter how hard we try. At this point we turn our eyes to ourselves—to the ways we have been affected, to our characteristics, to our pain. It sounds hopeless and defeatist, but it isn't. It is acceptance of what is. We can't change things we can't control, and trying to do that will make us crazy. This Step is appropriately humbling. It is also the bridge to the Second Step. For with our admission of powerlessness over that which we are truly powerless over, we receive the power which is appropriately ours—our own power to change ourselves and live our lives. When we quit trying to do the impossible, we are allowed to do the possible.

2. *Came to believe that a Power greater than ourselves could restore us to sanity.* If the First Step left us despairing, this Step will bring hope. I did not doubt for a minute that I was crazy, once I stopped comparing myself to the crazy people around me. The way I had been living was insane; the way I had not been living my life was insane. I needed to believe I could become sane. I needed to believe the pain I felt could somehow be lessened. Listening to, talking with, and actually seeing people who had been as upset as I was, and seeing they had found peace in circumstances sometimes worse than mine, helped me come to believe. There is no substitute for visualization. As someone once said, seeing is believing.

And, yes, this is a spiritual program. Thank God we aren't left to our own devices any longer. This is not a do-it-yourself program. This is not a do-it-yourself book. Do it yourself at your own risk. We are spiritual beings. We need a spiritual program. This program meets our spiritual needs. We are not talking about religion here; the word I used was *spiritual.* We select and come to terms with a Power greater than ourselves.

3. *Made a decision to turn our will and our lives over to the care of God as we understood Him.* I had turned my will and my life over to the care of alcohol and other drugs; I had turned my will and life over to the care of other human beings (usually alcoholics); I had spent many years trying to impose my own plan onto the scheme of things. It was

time to remove myself from anyone or anything's control (including my own) and place myself in the hands of an extraordinarily loving God. "Take it," I said, "All of it—who I am, what's happened to me, where I shall go, and how I'll get there." I said it once. I say it every day. Sometimes, I say it every half hour. This Step does not mean we resign ourselves to a bunch of shoulds and ought tos, and don our sackcloth. It in no way implies a continuation of martyrdom. The exciting thing about this Step is it means there is a purpose and a plan—a great, perfectly wonderful, usually enjoyable, and worthwhile plan that takes into account our needs, wants, desires, abilities, talents, and feelings—for each of our lives. This was good news to me. I thought I was a mistake. I didn't think there was anything of significance planned for my life. I was just stumbling around, trying to make the best out of being here when I learned this: We are here to live as long as we are alive, and there is a life for each of us to live.

4. *Made a searching and fearless moral inventory of ourselves.* We take our eyes off the other person and look at ourselves. We see just what we're working with, how we have been affected, what we are doing, what *our* characteristics are, and we write on a piece of paper what we see. We look fearlessly, not in self-hate and self-castigation, but in an attitude of love, honesty, and self-care. We may even discover that hating ourselves, not loving ourselves enough, has been a real moral problem. We root out any other problems, including earned guilt. We also look at our good qualities. We examine our hurts and angers. We examine ourselves and the part we have played in our lives. This Step also gives us an opportunity to examine the standards we judge ourselves by, choose those we believe to be appropriate, and disregard the rest. We are now on our way to dumping our earned guilt, getting rid of our unearned guilt, accepting the package we call ourselves, and starting on the path to growth and change.

5. *Admitted to God, to ourselves, and to another human being the exact nature of our wrongs.* Confession is good for the soul. There is nothing like it. We don't have to hide any longer. We tell our worst, most shameful

secrets to a trusted person skilled in listening to the Fifth Step. We tell someone how hurt and angry we are. Someone listens. Someone cares. We are forgiven. Wounds begin to heal. We forgive. This Step is liberating.

6. *Were entirely ready to have God remove all these defects of character.* We realize some of the things we've been doing to protect ourselves have been hurting us and possibly others. We decide we're ready to take a risk, and let go of these outdated behaviors and attitudes. We become willing to be changed and to cooperate in the process of change. I use this and the next Step as daily tools to rid myself of any defects that come to my attention. I consider my low self-worth a defect, and I use this Step on it too.

7. *Humbly asked Him to remove our shortcomings.* From my experience, *humbly* seems to be the key here.

8. *Made a list of all persons we had harmed and became willing to make amends to them all. Willingness* is the important word here, although I suspect it's directly connected to humility. Don't forget to put ourselves on the list. Note that, as Jael Greenleaf writes: "The Eighth Step does not read 'Made a list of all persons we had harmed and became willing to feel guilty about it.'"² This is our chance to take care of our earned guilt. This is an important Step in a tool that will be available to us all our lives so we no longer have to feel guilty.

9. *Made direct amends to such people wherever possible except when to do so would injure them or others.* This is a simple Step in a simple program. Sometimes the simplest things help us feel happy.

10. *Continued to take personal inventory and when we were wrong promptly admitted it.* We keep our eyes on ourselves. We continually and regularly evaluate our behavior. We figure out what we like about ourselves, what we've done right and good. Then we either congratulate ourselves, feel good about it, thank God, or do all three. We figure out what we don't like that we've been doing, then we figure out how to accept and take care of that without hating ourselves for it. Here's the difficult part: if *we're* wrong, we say so. If we have worked Steps Eight and Nine and dumped all our guilty feelings, we will know when we need to say "I'm wrong" and "I'm sorry." We will feel earned guilt, and we will be able to

notice it. If, however, we are still feeling guilty all the time, it may be difficult to distinguish when we do something wrong because we're feeling guilty all the time and we don't feel any different. It's just one more shovel of guilt thrown onto an already heaping pile. The moral of that story is: Dump guilt. If we get some, take care of it immediately.

11. *Sought through prayer and meditation to improve our conscious contact with God* **as we understood Him,** *praying only for knowledge of His will for us and the power to carry that out.* This Step, used daily and as needed, will successfully take us through our entire lives. This Step requires we learn the difference between *rumination* and *meditation.* It also requires us to decide whether we believe God is benevolent. We need to decide if we believe God "knows where we live," as another friend says. Get quiet. Detach. Pray. Meditate. Ask Him what He wants us to do. Ask to be given the power to do that. Then let go and watch what happens. Usually, His will is an appropriate, common-sense approach to life. Sometimes, we get surprises. Learn to trust this Higher Power to whom we have given the guardianship of our lives. Become sensitive to how He works with us. Learn to trust ourselves. He works through us too.

12. *Having had a spiritual awakening as the result of these steps, we tried to carry this message to others, and to practice these principles in all our affairs.* * We will awaken spiritually. We will learn to spiritually take care of ourselves—not religiously, although that certainly is part of life. This program will enable us to love ourselves and other people, instead of rescuing and being rescued. Carrying the message does not mean we become evangelists; it means our lives become a light. We will learn how to shine. If we apply this program to all areas of our lives, it will work in all areas of our lives.

---

* The Twelve Steps printed here are those of Al-Anon, adapted from the Twelve Steps of Alcoholics Anonymous, found in *Alcoholics Anonymous,* A.A. World Services, New York, NY, pp. 59–60. Reprinted with permission.

WORKING THE PROGRAM

Now that we are familiar with the Steps, let's discuss what "working the program" and "working the Steps" mean. All over the world, "anonymous" people meet at a variety of locations—churches, homes, and barber shops. They might meet once a day, twice a week, or seven nights a week. They don't preregister or register. They simply find out where a particular group meets that focuses on the problem these people are having troubles with. At the meeting, they don't have to identify their last names or where they or their spouse work; they don't have to say anything if they don't want to. They don't have to pay money, although they can make a donation of any amount to help pay for coffee and meeting room rent expenses—*if they want to*. They don't have to sign up. They don't have to fill out a card. They don't have to answer any questions. They just walk in and sit down. This is called going to a meeting. It is an essential part of working the program.

One nice thing about meetings is that people can be who they are. They don't have to pretend they don't have a particular problem, because everybody there has the same problem. If they didn't have that problem, they wouldn't be there.

Meeting formats vary with each particular group. Some groups sit around a table and the people who want to talk, discuss feelings or problems. Some meetings are speaker meetings, where one person gets up in front of everyone and talks about a Step or an experience. At some groups, the Steps are the theme and the people just put their chairs in a circle and each person gets a chance to say something about whatever Step is the theme that day. There are many meeting variations, but usually the meetings have something to do with the Steps, the Traditions, or topics related to the problem. People learn about the Steps at the meetings, and they learn what the Steps mean to other people. They also hear slogans. Al-Anon and A.A. slogans include such catchy little sayings as *Let Go and Let God, Easy Does It,* and *One Day at a Time.* The reason these sayings have become slogans is because they are true. And even if people get sick of saying and hearing these slogans, they keep repeating and listening to them because they are so true. And the slogans help people feel better. After the meeting is over, people usually stay and chat or go out to a restaurant and have a soda or coffee. Learning the Steps and slogans, listening to other people's experiences, sharing personal experiences, and fellowship, are parts of working the program.

At the meetings, books, pamphlets, and literature are sold at cost. These books contain information on the problems common to that group. Some groups sell meditation books which contain suggestions for approaching each day. Reading the literature and reading the daily meditation books are parts of working the program. People have something to take home and do through the literature. They are reminded of what they learned at the meeting, and sometimes they learn new things.

During their daily routines, the people who go to these meetings think about the Steps and slogans. They try to figure out how the Steps and slogans apply to them, what they're feeling, what they're doing, and what's going on in their lives at that particular time. They do this regularly and when a problem arises. Sometimes, they call someone they met at the meeting and discuss a problem with that person or tell that person how they're doing that day. Sometimes, these people do the things a Step suggests they do, such as write out an inventory, make a list of people they have harmed, or make appropriate amends. If these people think about and work these Steps enough, eventually the Twelve Steps may become habits—habitual ways of thinking, behaving, and handling situations—much the same as codependent characteristics become habits. When they become habits, the program becomes a way of life. This is called working the Steps and working the program.

That's all there is to working a program. Twelve Step programs are simple and basic. People don't graduate and go on to more complicated things—they stick with the basics. Twelve Step programs work because they are simple and basic.

I get excited about such simple things as going to meetings and working the Steps. I can try to explain, but words only convey a little bit of the important idea here. Something happens if we go to these meetings and work a program. A peace and a healing sets in. We start to change and feel better. The Steps are something we work on, but they also work on us. There is magic at these meetings.

We never have to do anything we are unable to do, truly find offensive, or don't want to do. When it is time to do or change a certain thing, we will know it is time and we will want to do it. There will be a rightness and an appropriateness to it. Our lives begin to work this way, too. Healing—growth—becomes a natural process. The Twelve Steps capture and are a formula for man's natural healing process.[3] Upon reading them, we may not think the Steps look like much and certainly not like enough to get as excited as I am about them, but when we work them something happens. They appear. Their power appears. We may not understand until it happens to us.

The best description of the Twelve Steps I have heard was the "invisible boat" story, told by a man at a meeting I attended recently. He was talking about A.A., but his story applies to Al-Anon and other groups. I have changed some of his words so his idea fits Al-Anon, but here is the essence of his analogy:

> Picture ourselves standing on the shore. Way across the water is an island called serenity, where peace, happiness, and freedom exist from the despair of alcoholism and other problems. We really want to get to that island, but we've got to find a way to get across the water—that huge void that stands between us and where we want to be.
>
> We have two choices. In the water is an ocean liner, a cruise ship that looks real posh and cozy. It's called treatment, therapy. Next to it, on the beach, sits a group of odd-looking people. They appear to be rowing a boat, but we can't see a boat, and we can't see the oars. We only see these happy people sitting on the beach, rowing an invisible boat with invisible oars. The invisible boat is called Al-Anon (or A.A. or any other Twelve Step program). The ocean liner honks, summoning us aboard the treatment and therapy cruise.

We can see the people on board: they're happy and waving to us. Then there's these goofy people hollering at us to join them in their invisible boat. Would we choose the liner or the invisible boat? Of course, we'll get on the ocean liner, the luxury cruise. The next thing we know, we're heading toward that island of happiness.

The problem is about mid-way across the water, the ocean liner stops, turns around, and heads back to the shore where we started from. Then the captain orders everyone off the ship. When we ask, "Why?" he says, "Our cruise only goes so far. The only way you can ever get to that island is by getting in the invisible boat (called Al-Anon)."

So we shrug our shoulders and walk over to the people in the boat. "Get in!" they holler. "We can't see any boat to get into!" we holler back. "Get in anyway," they say. So we get in, and pretty soon they say, "Pick up an oar and start rowing (working the Steps)." "Can't see any oars," we holler back. "Pick 'em up and start rowing, anyway!" they say. So we pick up invisible oars and start rowing, and pretty soon we see the boat. Before we know it, we see the oars too. Next thing we know, we're so happy rowing the boat with the goofy people we don't care if we ever get to the other side.[4]

That is the magic of the Twelve Step programs—they work. I am not saying, implying, or suggesting treatment and therapy are not helpful. They are. For many of us, treatment or a little therapy is just what we need to get *started* on our journey. But that ride ends and if we have a compulsive disorder or love someone with a compulsive disorder, we may discover we need to get on the invisible boat with those happy people.

At the end of this chapter, I have included tests we can take to help determine if we are candidates for Al-Anon, Alateen, or O-Anon. I have also included further questions from Adult Children of Alcoholics (ACOA). Please understand that the "anon" and ACOA groups are not for people with the drinking problem; they are for people who have been affected by someone else's problem. People frequently misunderstand this. Also, many chemically dependent people who attend A.A. find they also need to go to Al-Anon or ACOA to deal with their codependent characteristics. If you believe you might be a candidate for any of the Twelve Step programs—if you even suspect you have a problem common to one of the groups discussed at the beginning of this chapter—find a group and start going to meetings. It will help you feel better.

I know it's difficult to go to meetings. I know it's difficult to present ourselves to a group of strangers and hold up our problem for the world to see. I know many of us probably don't understand how going to meetings could help anything—especially if the *other person* has the problem. But it will help. I was so angry when I started attending Al-Anon meetings. I was already working a program for my alcoholism. I didn't want or need another program or another problem in my life to work on. Besides, I felt I had already done enough to help the alcoholics in my life. Why should *I* have to go to meetings? The alcoholics were the ones who needed help. At my first meeting, some cheery little woman walked up to me, talked to me for a few minutes, smiled, and said, "Aren't you lucky? You're a double winner. You get to work both programs!" I wanted to choke her. Now, I agree. I am lucky. I am a double winner.

Some of us may be reluctant to go to meetings because we feel we've already done enough for the *other people* in our lives. Well, we're right. We probably have. That's why it's important to go to our meetings. We're going for ourselves.

Others of us may want to go only to help the *other people,* and may feel disappointed that the meetings expect us to work on ourselves. That's okay, too. Health begets health. If we start working on ourselves, our good health may rub off on the other people, in the same fashion that their illness rubbed off on us.

Some of us may be embarrassed to go. All I could do at the first meetings I attended was sit and cry, and I felt terribly awkward. But for once, it was a good cry. My tears were tears of healing. I needed to sit and cry. When I stopped crying and looked around, I saw other people crying too. Al-Anon is a safe place to go and be who we are. The people there understand. So will you.

I've addressed most of the common objections I've heard to attending meetings. There may be other objections, but if we qualify for membership in a program, go anyway. I won't be talked down. The Twelve Steps are God's gift to people with compulsive disorders and to people who love people with compulsive disorders. If you're feeling crazy and reacting to people and things, go. If you don't like the first group you attend, find another meeting and go there. Each group has its own personality. Continue going to different groups until you find one that feels comfortable. If you used to go to meetings but stopped going, go back. If you start going, go for the rest of your life. Alcoholism is a lifetime illness that requires a lifetime of treatment. Our codependent characteristics become habits and may be tendencies we lean toward for the rest of our lives. Go whether the other people in your life get better or sicker.

Go until you feel grateful that you can go. In the words of one man, "Isn't it nice they have these meetings and they *let* me come to them? Nobody else wants me around when I get this crazy. The people here just smile, shake my hand, and say: 'We're glad you're here. Please come again.'"

Go until you see the boat and the oars and you get happy. Go until the magic works on you. And don't worry—if you go long enough, the magic will work.

ACTIVITY

1. Complete the tests or read over the list of characteristics on the following pages.

2. If you are a candidate for any of the programs discussed in this chapter, look in the phone book or call an appropriate human services organization in your community. Find out where and when meetings are being held, then go.

AL-ANON: IS IT FOR YOU?

Millions of people are affected by the excessive drinking of someone close. The following twenty questions are designed to help you decide whether or not you need Al-Anon.

1. Do you worry about how much someone else drinks?   Yes   No

2. Do you have money problems because of someone else's drinking?   Yes   No

3. Do you tell lies to cover up for someone else's drinking?   Yes   No

4. Do you feel that drinking is more important to your loved one than you are?   Yes   No

5. Do you think that the drinker's behavior is caused by his or her companions?   Yes   No

6. Are mealtimes frequently delayed because of the drinker?   Yes   No

7. Do you make threats, such as, "If you don't stop drinking, I'll leave you"?   Yes   No

8. When you kiss the drinker hello, do you secretly try to smell his or her breath?   Yes   No

9. Are you afraid to upset someone for fear it will set off a drinking bout?   Yes   No

10. Have you been hurt or embarrassed by a drinker's behavior?   Yes   No

11. Does it seem as if every holiday is spoiled because of drinking?   Yes   No

12. Have you considered calling the police because of drinking behavior?   Yes   No

13. Do you find yourself searching for hidden liquor?   Yes   No

14. Do you feel that if the drinker loved you, he or she
    would stop drinking to please you?   Yes   No

15. Have you refused social invitations out of fear or
    anxiety?   Yes   No

16. Do you sometimes feel guilty when you think
    of the lengths you have gone to to control the
    drinker?   Yes   No

17. Do you think that if the drinker stopped drinking,
    your other problems would be solved?   Yes   No

18. Do you ever threaten to hurt yourself to scare the
    drinker into saying, "I'm sorry" or "I love you"?   Yes   No

19. Do you ever treat people (children, employees,
    parents, co-workers, etc.) unjustly because you are
    angry at someone else for drinking too much?   Yes   No

20. Do you feel there is no one who understands your
    problems?   Yes   No

If you answered yes to three or more of these questions, Al-Anon or Alateen may help. You can contact Al-Anon or Alateen by looking in your local telephone directory.[5]

ARE YOU AN EATING DISORDER CODEPENDENT?
Use this questionnaire from *Fat Is a Family Affair* to evaluate the extent of
your involvement with an under- or overeater.

Do you force diets?

Do you threaten to leave due to weight?

Do you check on the diet?

Do you make promises based on pounds lost or gained?

Do you hide food from an overeater?

Do you worry incessantly about an undereater?

Have you "walked on eggshells" so as not to upset the over/undereater?

Do you throw food away so the overeater won't find it?

Have you excused the erratic, sometimes violent, mood swings resulting
from sugar binges?

Do you change social activities so the overeater won't be tempted?

Do you manipulate budgets to control spending on food and clothing?

Do you purchase and promote eating the "right" foods?

Do you promote gyms, health spas, and miracle cures?

Do you break into emotional tirades when you catch the overeater
bingeing?

Are you constantly disappointed when you see relapse?

Are you embarrassed by the over/undereater's appearance?

Do you falsely console the over/undereater when he or she is embarrassed?

Do you set up tests of willpower to test the over/undereater?

Have you lowered your expectations of what you might like?

Does your weight fluctuate with your loved one's (you up, he or she
down)?

Have you stopped attending to your own grooming?

Do you have many aches and pains, and preoccupation with health?

Are you drinking heavily or using sleeping pills or tranquilizers?

Do you bribe with food?

Do you talk about the eater's body to him or her or to others?

Do you feel life will be perfect if the over/undereater shapes up?

Are you grateful you aren't "that bad"?

Does his or her eating disorder give you license to run away?

Does his or her eating disorder give you an excuse to stay?

Do you "subtly" leave "helpful" literature around the house?

Do you read diet books though you have no weight problem?

Do you think you have the perfect home, except for the over/under-eater?

Do you use pills to get to sleep and escape worry?

Have you spent much time in your own therapy talking about the over/undereater?

PROGRESSION OF A CODEPENDENT PERSONALITY

This is also from *Fat Is a Family Affair.* It is meant to be used as a checklist to monitor your own progression.

Early Stages

___ Often born of dysfunctional family and learned to "care" for others as measure of self-worth.

___ Failed to cure parents so will "cure" the over/undereater.

___ Finds over/undereater who is "needy" so controls.

___ Begins doubting own perceptions and wants to control eating to show decisiveness.

___ Social life affected. Isolated self from community to "help" over/undereater.

Obsession

___ Makes pleas and threats related to the eating behavior.

___ Judges self and feels the cause of eating/starving.

___ Hides food.

___ Attempts controlling eating, hiding food, idle threats, nagging, scolding.

___ Shows anger and disappointment regarding the over/undereater's promises.

Secret Life

___ Becomes obsessed with watching and covering up.

___ Takes over responsibilities of the over/undereater.

___ Takes pivotal role in communications, excluding contact between the over/undereater and others.

___ Expresses anger inappropriately.

Out of Control

___ Makes violent attempts to control eating. Fights with the over/undereater.

___ Lets self go physically and mentally.

___ Has extramarital affairs such as infidelity, workaholism, obsession with outside interests.

___ Becomes rigid, possessive. Appears angry most of the time and careful and secretive about home life.

___ Has related illness and drug abuse: ulcers, rashes, migraines, depression, obesity, tranquilizer use.

___ Constantly loses temper.

___ Becomes sick and tired of being sick and tired.[6]

ADULT CHILDREN OF ALCOHOLICS

Are you an adult child of an alcoholic? Following are fourteen questions you may find relevant to your life and personality.

1. Do I often feel isolated and afraid of people, especially authority figures?

2. Have I observed myself to be an approval seeker, losing my own identity in the process?

3. Do I feel overly frightened of angry people and personal criticism?

4. Do I often feel I'm a victim in personal and career relationships?

5. Do I sometimes feel I have an overdeveloped sense of responsibility, which makes it easier to be concerned with others rather than myself?

6. Do I find it hard to look at my own faults and my own responsibility to myself?

7. Do I get guilt feelings when I stand up for myself instead of giving in to others?

8. Do I feel addicted to excitement?

9. Do I confuse love with pity and tend to love people I can pity and rescue?

10. Do I find it hard to feel or express feelings, including feelings such as joy or happiness?

11. Do I find I judge myself harshly?

12. Do I have a low sense of self-esteem?

13. Do I often feel abandoned in the course of my relationships?

14. Do I tend to be a reactor, instead of an actor?

THE TWELVE STEPS OF A.A.*

1. We admitted we were powerless over alcohol—that our lives had become unmanageable.

2. Came to believe that a Power greater than ourselves could restore us to sanity.

3. Made a decision to turn our will and our lives over to the care of God *as we understood Him.*

4. Made a searching and fearless moral inventory of ourselves.

5. Admitted to God, to ourselves, and to another human being the exact nature of our wrongs.

6. Were entirely ready to have God remove all these defects of character.

7. Humbly asked Him to remove our shortcomings.

8. Made a list of all persons we had harmed, and became willing to make amends to them all.

9. Made direct amends to such people wherever possible, except when to do so would injure them or others.

10. Continued to take personal inventory and when we were wrong promptly admitted it.

11. Sought through prayer and meditation to improve our conscious contact with God *as we understood Him,* praying only for knowledge of His will for us and the power to carry that out.

12. Having had a spiritual awakening as the result of these Steps, we tried to carry this message to alcoholics, and to practice these principles in all our affairs.

---

* The Twelve Steps are taken from *Alcoholics Anonymous*, 3rd ed., published by A.A. World Services, New York, NY, pp. 59–60. Reprinted with permission.

19

PIECES AND BITS

*When Prince Charming does come along, I'll
probably be down at the pond kissing frogs.*[1]

This chapter contains miscellaneous tidbits about codependency and
self-care.

DRAMA ADDICTS

Many codependents become what some people call drama or crises
addicts. Strangely enough, problems can become addicting. If we live
with enough misery, crises, and turmoil long enough, the fear and
stimulation caused by problems can become a comfortable emotional
experience. In her excellent book *Getting Them Sober, Volume II,* Toby
Rice Drews refers to this feeling as "excited misery."[2] After a while, we
can become so used to involving our emotions with problems and crises
that we may get and stay involved with problems that aren't our concern.
We may even start making troubles or making troubles greater than they
are to create stimulation for ourselves. This is especially true if we have
greatly neglected our own lives and feelings. When we're involved with
a problem, we know we're alive. When the problem is solved, we may
feel empty and void of feeling. Nothing to do. Being in crisis becomes a
comfortable place, and it saves us from our humdrum existence. It's like
getting addicted to soap operas, except the daily crises occur in our lives
and the lives of our friends and family. "Will Ginny leave John?" "Can we
save Herman's job?" "How will Henrietta survive this dilemma?"

After we have detached and begun minding our own business and our lives finally become serene, some codependents still occasionally crave a little of the old excitement. We may at times find our new way of life boring. We are just used to so much turmoil and excitement that peace seems bland at first. We'll get used to it. As we develop our lives, set our goals, and find things to do that interest us, peace will become comfortable—more comfortable than chaos. We will no longer need nor desire excited misery.

We need to learn to recognize when we are seeking out "excited misery." Understand that we don't have to make problems or get involved with others' problems. Find creative ways to fill our need for drama. Get enjoyable jobs. But keep the excited misery out of our lives.

EXPECTATIONS

Expectations can be a confusing topic. Most of us have expectations. We entertain certain notions, on some level of consciousness, about how we hope things will turn out or how we want people to behave. But it is better to relinquish expectations, so we can detach. It is better to refrain from forcing our expectations on others or refrain from trying to control the outcome of events, since doing so causes problems and is usually impossible anyway. So where do we go with our expectations?

Some people strive to relinquish all expectations and live moment to moment. That is admirable. But I think the important idea here is to take responsibility for our expectations. Get them out into the light. Examine them. Talk about them. If they involve other people, talk to the people involved. Find out if they have similar expectations. See if they're realistic. For example, expecting healthy behavior from unhealthy people is futile; expecting different results from the same behaviors, according to Earnie Larsen, is insane. Then, let go. See how things turn out. Let things happen—without forcing. If we are constantly disappointed, we may have a problem to solve—either with ourselves, another person, or a situation.

It's okay to have expectations. At times, they are real clues to what we want, need, hope for, and fear. We have a right to expect good things and appropriate behavior. We will probably get more of these things (the good stuff and the appropriate behavior) if we consistently expect these things. If we have expectations, we will also realize when they are *not* being met. But we need to realize these are only expectations; they belong to us, and we're not always boss. We can make sure our expectations are realistic and appropriate and not let them interfere with reality or let them spoil the good things that are happening.

FEAR OF INTIMACY

Most people want and need love. Most people want and need to be close to people. But fear is an equally strong force, and it competes with our need for love. More specifically, this force is fear of intimacy.

For many of us, it feels safer to be alone or in relationships where we are "unemotionally involved" than it does to be emotionally vulnerable, close, and loving. I understand that. In spite of the range of needs and wants that go unmet when we don't love, it may feel safer to not love. We don't risk the uncertainty and vulnerability of closeness. We don't risk the pain of loving, and for many of us love has caused a great deal of pain. We don't risk being trapped by ourselves in relationships that don't work. We don't risk having to be who we are, which includes being emotionally honest and the possible rejections of that. We don't risk people abandoning us; we don't risk. And we don't have to go through the awkwardness of initiating relationships. When we don't get close to people, at least we know what to expect: nothing. Denial of love feelings protects us from the anxiety caused by loving. Love and closeness often bring a sense of loss of control. Love and closeness challenge our deepest fears about who we are and whether it is okay to be ourselves, and about who others are and whether that is okay. Love and closeness—involvement with people—are the greatest risks a man or woman can take. They require honesty, spontaneity, vulnerability, trust, responsibility, self-acceptance, and acceptance of others. Love brings joy and warmth, but it also requires us to be willing to occasionally feel hurt and rejection.

Many of us have learned to run from closeness, rather than take the risks involved. We run from love or prevent closeness in many ways. We push people away or do hurtful things to them so they won't want to be close to us. We do ridiculous things in our minds to talk ourselves out of wanting to be close. We find fault with everyone we meet; we reject people before they have a chance to reject us. We wear masks and pretend to be something other than who we are. We scatter our energies and emotions among so many relationships that we don't get too close or vulnerable to anyone—a technique called "watering down the milk" by one person. We settle for artificial relationships, where we will not be expected nor asked to be close. We play roles instead of being a real person. We withdraw emotionally in our existing relationships. Sometimes, we prevent closeness by simply refusing to be honest and open. Some of us sit, paralyzed by fear, unable to initiate relationships or enjoy closeness in existing relationships. Some of us run; we physically remove ourselves from any situation where love, emotional vulnerability, and risk are or might be present. As a friend says, "We all have a pair of track shoes in our closet."

We run from intimacy for many reasons. Some of us, particularly those of us who grew up in alcoholic family situations, may never have learned how to initiate relationships and how to be close once a relationship begins. Closeness was not safe, taught, or allowed in our families. For many people, caretaking and chemical use became substitutes for intimacy.

Some of us allowed ourselves to get close once or twice, then got hurt. We may have decided (on some level) that it was better and safer not to get close, not to risk being hurt again.

Some of us learned to run from relationships that aren't good for us. But for some of us, running from or avoiding closeness and intimacy may have become a habit, a destructive habit that prevents us from getting the love and closeness we really want and need. Some of us may be tricking ourselves, so we're not even aware we're running or what we're running from. We may be running when it isn't necessary.

Closeness to people may look like scary, mind-boggling business, but it doesn't have to be that scary. And it's not that difficult. It even feels good, when we relax and let it happen.

It's okay to feel afraid of closeness and love, but it's also okay to allow ourselves to love and feel close to people. It's okay to give and receive love. We can make good decisions about who to love and when to do that. It's okay for us to be who we are around people. Take the risk of doing that. We can trust ourselves. We can go through the awkwardness and friction of initiating relationships. We can find people who are safe to trust. We can open up, become honest, and be who we are. We can even handle feeling hurt or rejected from time to time. We can love without losing ourselves or giving up our boundaries. We can love and think at the same time. We can take off our track shoes.

We can ask ourselves, are we preventing closeness in our existing relationship? How are we doing that? Is it necessary? Why? Do we know someone we want to be close to—someone who would be safe to be close to? Why don't we take steps to get close to that person? Would we like to initiate some new relationships? How could we do that? Are we needing and wanting more intimacy in our relationships but settling for less? Why?

FINANCIAL RESPONSIBILITY

Some codependents become financially dependent on other people. Sometimes this is by agreement; for example, a wife stays home and raises the children while the husband works and provides the money. Sometimes this is not by agreement. Some codependents become so victimized that we believe we cannot take care of ourselves financially. Many codependents were, at one time, financially responsible, but as alcoholism or another problem progressed in a loved one we simply became too upset to work. Some of us just gave up: "If you don't care about the money, then neither do I."

Sometimes, codependents become financially responsible for other adults. I have frequently seen a codependent wife work two or even three jobs, while her husband brings home not one penny—yet he continues to eat, watch television, and live rent free.

Neither way is preferable. Each person is financially responsible for him- or herself as well as in all other ways. That does not mean housewives have to work at paying jobs to be financially responsible.

Homemaking is a job, a heroic and admirable one. If that is what a man or woman chooses to do, then I believe that person is earning his or her share. Being financially responsible also does not mean all things have to be equal. Assuming financial responsibility for oneself is an attitude. It means figuring out exactly what our responsibilities are, then setting out to take care of those responsibilities. It also means we allow—even insist—other people be financially responsible for themselves. That includes becoming familiar with all areas of one's finances and deciding which task belongs to which person. Which bills need to be paid? When? When are taxes due? How much money has to last for how long? What's our part in all this? Are we doing less or more than our appropriate share? If it is not our responsibility to hold a salaried job, do we at least understand we may someday need to work? Do we feel financially responsible for ourselves? Or does this frighten us? Are the people around us assuming appropriate financial responsibility for themselves, or are we doing it for them?

Taking care of money is part of life. Earning money, paying bills, and feeling financially responsible is part of taking care of ourselves. Many codependents who have quit a job to control a spouse or who have otherwise centered their lives around a person and neglected their own careers, have discovered even a low-paying, part-time job does wonders for their self-esteem. We forgot we are worth money and someone will actually pay for our abilities. Many of us codependents, who have been financially dependent on a spouse, also like the freedom of having our own money. It's called a good feeling. It's something to think about as we begin living our own lives.

Being financially dependent on a person can trigger emotional dependency. Emotional dependency on a person can trigger financial dependency.[3] Becoming financially responsible for ourselves—however we accomplish that—can help trigger undependence.

FORGIVENESS

Compulsive disorders such as alcoholism twist and distort many good things, including the great principle of forgiveness. We repeatedly forgive the same people. We hear promises, we believe lies, and we try to forgive some more. Some of us may have reached a point where we cannot forgive. Some of us may not want to, because to forgive would leave us vulnerable to further hurt and we believe we cannot endure more pain. Forgiveness turns on us and becomes a painful experience.

Some of us may be truly trying to forgive; some of us may think we have forgiven, but the hurt and anger just won't disappear.

Some of us can't keep up with the things we need to forgive; the problems are happening so fast we barely know what's going on. Before we can register the hurt and say, "I forgive," another nasty thing has been dumped on us.

Then we feel guilty because someone asks, "Why can't you just forgive and forget?" People uninformed about the disease of alcoholism and other compulsive disorders frequently ask that. For many of us, the problem is not forgetting. Forgiving and forgetting feed our denial system. We need to think about, remember, understand, and make good decisions about what we are forgiving, what can be forgotten, and what is still a problem. And forgiving someone does not mean we have to let that person keep hurting us. An alcoholic doesn't need forgiveness; he or she needs treatment. We don't need to forgive the alcoholic, at least not initially. We need to step back so he or she can't keep stomping on our toes.

I am not suggesting we adopt an unforgiving attitude. We all need forgiveness. Grudges and anger hurt us; they don't help the other person much either. Forgiveness is wonderful. It wipes the slate clean. It clears up guilt. It brings peace and harmony. It acknowledges and accepts the humanness we all share, and it says, "That's okay. I love you anyway." But I believe we codependents need to be gentle, loving, and forgiving with ourselves before we can expect to forgive others. But I believe codependents need to think about how, why, and when we dole out forgiveness.

Also, forgiveness is closely tied into the acceptance or grief process. We cannot forgive someone for doing something if we have not fully accepted what this person has done. It does little good to forgive an alcoholic for going on a binge, if we have not yet accepted his or her disease of alcoholism. Ironically, the kind of forgiveness we often give to soothe an alcoholic's "morning after" remorse may help him or her continue drinking.

Forgiveness comes in time—in its own time—if we are striving to take care of ourselves. Don't let other people use this principle against us. Don't let other people help us feel guilty because they think we should forgive someone, and we are either not ready or believe forgiveness is not the appropriate solution. Take responsibility for forgiveness. We can dole out forgiveness appropriately based on good decisions, high self-esteem, and knowledge of the problem we are working on. Don't misuse forgiveness to justify hurting ourselves; don't misuse it to help other people continue hurting themselves. We can work our program, live our own lives, and take the Fourth and Fifth Steps. If we are taking care of us, we will understand what to forgive and when it's time to do that.

While we're at it, don't forget to forgive ourselves.

The Frog Syndrome

There is an anecdote circulating through codependency groups. It goes like this: "Did you hear about the woman who kissed a frog? She was hoping it would turn into a prince. It didn't. She turned into a frog, too."

Many codependents like to kiss frogs. We see so much good in them. Some of us even become chronically attracted to frogs after kissing enough of them. Alcoholics and people with other compulsive disorders are attractive people. They radiate power, energy, and charm. They promise the world. Never mind that they deliver pain, suffering, and anguish. The words they say sound so good.

If we don't deal with our codependent characteristics, probabilities dictate we will continue to be attracted to and kiss frogs. Even if we deal with our characteristics, we may still lean toward frogs, but we can learn not to jump into the pond with them.

FUN

Fun does not go hand in hand with codependency. It is difficult to have fun when we hate ourselves. It is difficult to enjoy life when there is no money for groceries because the alcoholic has drunk it all up. It is almost impossible to have fun when we are bottled up with repressed emotions, worried sick about someone, saturated with guilt and despair, rigidly controlling ourselves or someone else, or worried about what other people are thinking about us. However, most people aren't thinking about us; they're worried about themselves and what we think of them.

As codependents, we need to learn to play and enjoy ourselves. Arranging for and allowing ourselves to have fun is an important part of taking care of ourselves. It helps us stay healthy. It helps us work better. It balances life. We deserve to have fun. Fun is a normal part of being alive. Fun is taking time to celebrate being alive.

We can schedule fun into our routine. We can learn to recognize when we need to play and what kinds of things we enjoy doing. If we don't do this, we can make "learning to have fun" an immediate goal. Start doing things just for ourselves, just because we want to. It might feel uncomfortable at first, but after a while it'll feel better. It'll become fun.

We can let ourselves enjoy life. If we want something and can afford it, buy it. If we want to do something that is legal and harmless, do it. When we're actually involved with doing something that is recreational, don't find ways to feel bad. Let go and enjoy life. We can find things we enjoy doing, then let ourselves enjoy doing them. We can learn to relax and enjoy the things we do daily, not just the recreational activities. Martyrdom can interfere with our ability to feel good long after the alcoholic has stopped helping us feel miserable. Suffering can become habitual, but so can enjoying life and being good to ourselves. Try it.

LIMITS/BOUNDARIES

Codependents, it has been said, have boundary problems. I agree. Most of us don't have boundaries.

Boundaries are limits that say: "This is how far I shall go. This is what I will or won't do for you. This is what I won't tolerate from you."

Most of us began relationships with boundaries. We had certain expectations, and we entertained certain ideas about what we would or wouldn't tolerate from those people. Alcoholism and other compulsive disorders laugh in the face of limits. The diseases not only push on our boundaries, they step boldly across them. Each time the disease pushes or steps across our limits we give in. We move our boundaries back, giving the disease more room to work. As the disease pushes more, we give in more until we are tolerating things we said we would never tolerate and doing things we said we would never do.[4] Later, this process of "increased tolerance" of inappropriate behaviors may reverse. We may become totally intolerant of even the most human behaviors. In the beginning, we make excuses for a person's inappropriate behavior; toward the end, there is no excuse.

Not only do many of us begin tolerating abnormal, unhealthy, and inappropriate behaviors, we take it one step further: we convince ourselves these behaviors are normal and what we deserve. We may become so familiar with verbal abuse and disrespectful treatment that we don't even recognize when these things are happening. But deep inside, an important part of us knows. Our *selves* know and will tell us if we will listen. Sometimes living with subtle problems, such as a nondrinking alcoholic who is not in any recovery program, can be harder on our *selves* than the more blatant problems. We sense something is wrong. We start feeling crazy, but we can't understand why because we can't identify the problem.

Codependents need boundaries. We need to set limits on what we shall do to and for people. We need to set limits on what we will allow people to do to and for us. The people we relate to need to know we have boundaries. It will help them and us. I am not suggesting we become tyrants. I also advise against absolute inflexibility, but we can understand our limits. As we grow and change, we may want to change our boundaries too. Here are some examples of boundaries common to codependents who are recovering:

- I will not allow anyone to physically or verbally abuse me.
- I will not knowingly believe or support lies.
- I will not allow chemical abuse in my home.
- I will not allow criminal behavior in my home.
- I will not rescue people from the consequences of their alcohol abuse or other irresponsible behavior.
- I will not finance a person's alcoholism or other irresponsible behavior.
- I will not lie to protect you or me from your alcoholism.
- I will not use my home as a detoxification center for recovering alcoholics.
- If you want to act crazy that's your business, but you can't do it in front of me. Either you leave or I'll walk away.
- You can spoil your fun, your day, your life—that's your business—but I won't let you spoil my fun, my day, or my life.

Sometimes it is necessary to set a certain boundary that applies to a particular relationship, such as, "I won't babysit Mary Lou's children anymore, because I don't want to and she takes advantage of me in that area."

Set boundaries, but make sure they're our boundaries. The things we're sick of, can't stand, and make threats about, may be clues to some boundaries we need to set. They may also be clues to changes we need to make within ourselves. Mean what we say, and say what we mean. People may get angry at us for setting boundaries; they can't use us anymore. They may try to help us feel guilty so we will remove our boundary and return to the old system of letting them use or abuse us. Don't feel guilty and don't back down. We can stick to our boundaries and enforce them. Be consistent. We will probably be tested more than once on every boundary we set. People do that to see if we're serious, especially if we haven't meant what we said in the past. As codependents, we have made many empty threats. We lose our credibility, then wonder why people don't take us seriously. Tell people what our boundaries are—once, quietly, in peace. Watch our level of tolerance, so the pendulum doesn't swing too far to either extreme.

Some codependents, particularly those of us in the latter stages of a relationship with an alcoholic, may find we have a difficult time setting and enforcing limits with children, as well as with the trouble adults in our lives. Setting limits takes time and thought; enforcing limits takes energy and consistency.

But boundaries are worth every bit of time, energy, and thought required to set and enforce them. Ultimately, they will provide us with more time and energy.

What are our limits? What boundaries do we need to establish?

PHYSICAL CARE

Sometimes in the latter stages of codependency, we codependents neglect our health and grooming. It's okay to look the best we possibly can! We can get our hair styled or cut, for example. That's a normal part of living. We can dress in a manner that helps us feel good about ourselves. Look in the mirror; if we don't like what we see, fix it. If we can't fix it, we can stop hating ourselves and accept it.

Don't abandon the importance of exercise. If we're sick, go to a doctor. If we're overweight, figure out what we need to do to take care of ourselves. The less we care for our bodies, the worse we will feel about ourselves. Sometimes, doing little things can help us feel a lot better. Get in touch with the physical parts of us. Listen to them. Give them what they need. Taking care of ourselves means taking care of our bodies and grooming. Make both a daily practice.

Taking care of our emotional selves is also connected to our bodies. The more we take care of our emotional selves—the more we get our needs met—the less we find ourselves sick. If we refuse long enough to take care of ourselves, our bodies will rebel and become sick, forcing us and the people around us to give us the caretaking we need. It's easier to take care of ourselves before we get sick.

PROFESSIONAL HELP

We need to seek professional help if:

- We are depressed and thinking about suicide.
- We want to do an intervention and confront an alcoholic or other troubled person.
- We have been the victim of physical or sexual abuse.
- We have been physically or sexually abusing somebody else.
- We are experiencing problems with alcohol or other drugs.
- We can't seem to solve our problems or get "unstuck" by ourselves.
- For any other reason, we believe we might benefit from professional help.

We can remember to trust ourselves when we go to professionals and pay attention to our feelings. If we are not comfortable with the agency or person we're working with, if we don't agree with the direction the counseling is taking, or if we in any way don't trust the help we are receiving or not receiving, find another professional. We may be experiencing a normal resistance to change, but it could be the person we're working with is not right for us. Not all professionals are able to work well with codependency, compulsive disorders, or chemical dependency.

One woman sought help from a private therapist because her daughter's chemical dependency and behavioral problems were disrupting the family. The therapist pulled the whole family into counseling, then began devoting most of the session time to trying to convince the parents that the reason the daughter was misbehaving was because the parents smoked cigarettes. The therapist had a prejudice against smoking. The goal of therapy switched from "daughter behaving" to "Mom and Dad stopping smoking." The parents were a little baffled and not entirely comfortable with the setup, but they were desperate for help. And they assumed the therapist knew more than they did. After spending three months and $50 a week on this nonsense, the parents finally realized they were going nowhere and the trip was costing them a lot of money. I'm not saying it's not good to stop smoking—but it was not the problem this family sought help for.

If we seek help and it doesn't seem right for us, seek different help. If we honestly make an effort to try something and it doesn't work, try something else. We don't have to give up our power to think, feel, and make good decisions to anyone—including someone with a Ph.D. after his or her name.

We can get ourselves the best care possible.

STROKES

I'm not talking about heart problems; *strokes* is a Transactional Analysis term that caught on in therapy circles years ago. Most of us need people. Most of us have at least a few relationships. When we are with these people, we can either generate warm, loving feelings; no feeling; or cold, hostile feelings. We can say honest, tender, appreciative things, and they can say those things back to us. We can lie, and people can lie back to us. We can talk about unimportant, superficial stuff, and others can do the same. Or we can say nasty things, and they can respond in the same way. Most of us do a little of all those things from time to time.

The idea is to strive for good relationships. If we don't have people to be honest, tender, loving, and appreciative with, find some. If people say mean things to us, causing us to retaliate, stop retaliating and try to get the person to quit talking that way. If we can't get this person to change, find someone else to talk to. We need to be treated nicely. It helps us grow, and it feels good.

Strive for good physical treatment too. We don't ever have to let people hit us. And we don't have to hit people. Hug them instead. Or, if a hug isn't appropriate, touch them in gentle, loving ways that communicate positive energy. For those who think hugging is a waste of time or an unnecessary activity indulged in by overly-sentimental people, read the following excerpt from *Fat Is a Family Affair* and think again:

. . . In the early 1970s, doctors began studying a mechanism within the nervous system which produces a morphine-like effect helping to alleviate pain and subduing trauma and shock. These morphine-like substances are called endorphins and they are secreted to soothe pain, take the edge off, and promote general well-being. Some research indicates that overeaters and alcoholics produce fewer of these endorphins than normal people. . . . Since you produce fewer endorphins, you often feel on a raw edge. Eating sugar increases endorphin production, so when you eat, the rawness vanishes. . . .

If anorexic, you get the same kind of soothing from the "high" of not eating. That exuberant feeling comes from the endurance high of pushing yourself beyond your limits, much like the "runner's high" . . . there is an alternative method to increased endorphin production. . . . It involves hugging. That's right, hugging. When you turn to a fellow human being and you put your arms around one another, this starts the endorphins flowing and the raw edges are removed by the warmth of a loving friend. Your dog is no dummy when he jumps up for a rub on the chest or a pat on the head. He's getting his endorphins up and keeping himself mellow.[5]

Codependents also frequently have difficulties accepting compliments—positive strokes. We can stop fighting the fact that we are good people with good qualities. If someone tells us something good about ourselves, we can accept it unless instinct tells us the person has ulterior motives. Even if he or she is trying to manipulate us, take the compliment and refuse to be manipulated. Let it go all the way down to the heart and let the warm glow come. We deserve compliments. We need them. We all need them. They help us believe what we are working so hard to believe: we are good people. The beauty of compliments is, the more good things we believe about ourselves, the better we get.

We can also pass out compliments and spread around some positive energy. We can share what we like about people and say what we appreciate in them. Make it honest, but make it good.

We can learn to recognize when we need to give a stroke. Learn to recognize when we need to be around people and get some strokes. Choose friends that can give us the good stuff. Sometimes codependents get involved with friends who see them as victims, helpless people who can't take care of themselves. These friends give sympathy, which is probably better than nothing, but it's not the same as strokes. Real love says, "You're having problems. I care, and I'll listen, but I won't and can't do it for you." Real friendship says, "I think so highly of you that I'll let you figure out how to do it for yourself. I know you can."

TRUST

Codependents frequently aren't certain whom or when to trust. "Harvey's been in treatment for alcoholism two weeks. He's lied to me 129 times. Now he's mad at me because I say I don't trust him. What should I do?"

I've repeatedly heard variations of this from codependents. My answer is usually the same: There's a difference between trust and stupidity. Of course you don't trust Harvey. Quit trying to make yourself trust someone you don't trust.

Throughout the book I have repeated this phrase, and I will say it again: we can trust ourselves. We can trust ourselves to make good decisions about whom to trust. Many of us have been making inappropriate decisions about trust. It is not wise to trust an alcoholic to never drink again if that alcoholic has not received treatment for the disease of alcoholism. It is not even wise to trust an alcoholic never to drink again if he or she has received treatment—there are no guarantees on human behavior. But we can trust people to be who they are. We can learn to see people clearly.

Figure out if people's words match their behaviors. Is what they *say* the same as what they *do*? As one woman puts it, "He's looking real good, but he's not acting any better."

If we pay attention to ourselves and the messages we receive from the world, we will know whom to trust, when to trust, and why to trust a particular person. We may discover we've always known whom to trust—we just weren't listening to ourselves.

SEX

In one breath, a codependent will tell me her marriage is falling apart. In the next breath, she will ask if it's normal to have sexual problems when things get that bad.

Yes, it's normal to have sexual problems. Many people have problems with sex. Many codependents experience sexual problems. Alcoholism and the whole range of compulsive disorders attack all areas of intimacy.[6] Sometimes, the physical expression of love is the last and final loss we suffer—the blow that tells us the problem won't go away, no matter how long we close our eyes.

Sometimes the alcoholic has the problem. He becomes impotent, or she loses her sexual desire. This can happen both before and after recovery. Frequently, it is the codependent who has problems with sex. There is a range of difficulties that can be encountered in the bedroom. We may be unable to achieve orgasm, fear loss of control, or lack trust in our partner. We may withdraw emotionally from our partner, be unwilling to be vulnerable with our partner, or lack desire for our partner. We may feel revulsion toward our partner, or we don't get needs met because we're not asking to get these needs met. The relationship probably isn't going to be much better in bed than it is outside the bedroom. If we're caretaking in the kitchen, we'll probably be caretaking in the bedroom. If we're angry and hurt before we make love, we'll probably feel angry and hurt after we make love. If we don't want to be in the relationship, we won't want to have sex with that person. The sexual relationship will echo and reflect the overall tone of the relationship.

Sexual problems can sneak up on people. For a while, sex can be the salvation of a troubled relationship. Sex can be a way of making up after an argument. Talking seems to clear the air, and sex makes it all better.

After a certain point, though, talking may no longer clear the air. Talking just fogs it up more, and sex stops making it better. Instead, sex can make things worse. For some, sex may become a purely clinical act that provides approximately the same emotional satisfaction as brushing one's teeth. For others, it can become a time of humiliation and degradation: another chore, another duty, something else we should do but don't want to. It becomes one more area that isn't working, that we feel guilty and ashamed about, that we try to lie to ourselves about. We have one more area in our lives that causes us to wonder, "What's wrong with me?"

I am not a sex therapist. I have no cures or technical advice—just some common sense. I believe taking care of ourselves means we apply the same principles in the bedroom as we do in any other area of our lives. First, we stop blaming and hating ourselves.

Once we understand that, we get honest with ourselves. We stop running, hiding, and denying. We gently ask ourselves what we are feeling and thinking, then we trust our answers. We respectfully listen to ourselves. We don't abuse and punish ourselves. We understand the problem we are experiencing is a normal response to the system we have been living in. Of course we're having that problem—it's a normal part of the process. It would be abnormal to not feel revulsion, withdrawal, lack of trust, or other negative feelings. There's nothing wrong with us.

After we have sorted things out, we get honest with our partner. We tell him or her what we are thinking and feeling, and what we need from him or her. We explore possibilities, negotiating and compromising when appropriate. If we cannot solve our problems by ourselves, we seek professional help.

Some of us may have sought comfort in extramarital affairs. We need to forgive ourselves and figure out what we need to do to take care of ourselves. Take the Fourth and Fifth Steps; talk to a clergyperson. We can try to understand our actions were common reactions to the problems we have been living with.

Some of us may be trying to run from our problems by having a series of unsatisfactory sexual relationships. That frequently occurs during the denial stage, when compulsive behaviors tend to set in. We don't have to continue doing that. We can face and solve our problems in other ways. We can forgive ourselves and quit hurting ourselves. Some of us may be looking for love and coming up with sex instead. Understand what we need and figure out how to best meet our needs. Some of us may need to start asking for what we need. Others may need to learn to say no. Some of us may be trying to force love back into a dead relationship by trying to force sexual enjoyment. That technique may not work. Sex isn't love; it is sex. It doesn't make love exist if the love wasn't there to start with. Sex can only express the love that already exists.

Some of us may have given up and decided sex isn't that important. I happen to believe sex is important. It's not the most important thing in life, but it's an important part of my life.

Sex is a powerful force, a great source for intimacy and for pleasure. We can take care of ourselves if our sex life isn't working the way we would like it to. We are responsible for our sexual behavior—for our enjoyment or lack of pleasure in bed. We can ask ourselves, what are our sex lives telling us about our relationships?

20

LEARNING TO LIVE AND LOVE AGAIN

At least I don't run around actively
seeking my own demise any more.

—AL-ANON MEMBER

Originally I planned to separate the material in this chapter into two chapters: Learning to Live Again and Learning to Love Again. However, I decided separately addressing living and loving was not the issue. The problem many codependents encounter is learning to do both at the same time.

According to Earnie Larsen and others, the two deepest desires most people have are: to love and be loved, and to believe they are worthwhile and know someone else believes that also.[1] I have also heard this phrased more simply, with one item added: To be happy we need someone to love, something to do, and something to look forward to.

I am not going to split hairs over whether those desires are needs or wants. I think they're important. Whether we have been aware of these desires or not, they probably have been driving forces in our lives. Most of us have been trying, on some level of consciousness, to meet these needs. To protect ourselves, some of us may have blocked or shut off these needs. They are still there, whether we acknowledge or repress them. Understanding ourselves and our desires is powerful information. What we, as codependents, need to learn to do is fulfill these desires, needs, and wants in ways that don't hurt ourselves or other people, in ways that allow maximum enjoyment of life.

For many of us, that means we need to do things differently, because the ways we have gone about getting our needs met haven't worked. We've talked about some concepts that will help us do that: detachment, a non-rescuing approach to people, not controlling the object of our attention, directness, paying attention to ourselves, working a Twelve Step program, and becoming undependent. I believe as we get healthier, love will be different. I believe love will be better, perhaps better than ever before, if we let it and if we insist on it.

I don't think love has to hurt as much as it did in the past. I don't think we have to allow love to hurt us as much as it has. We certainly don't have to let it destroy us. As one woman so aptly phrases it, "I'm sick of being addicted to pain. I'm sick of being addicted to suffering. And I'm sick of letting men work out their unfinished business in my life!" It's not God's will that we stay miserable and stay in miserable relationships. That's something we've been doing to ourselves. We don't have to stay in relationships that cause us pain and misery. We are free to take care of ourselves.

We can learn to recognize the difference between relationships that do and don't work. We can learn to leave destructive relationships and enjoy the good ones. We can learn new behaviors that will help our good relationships work better.

I believe God allows certain people to come into our lives. But I also believe we are responsible for our choices and behaviors in initiating, maintaining, and discontinuing these relationships when appropriate. We may want and need love, but we don't need destructive love. And when we believe that, our message will come across clearly.

I believe our professional lives can be different and better. We can learn to take care of ourselves and our needs on the job. And if we are not so absorbed in other people and their business, if we believe we are important, we are free to set our own goals and reach our dreams. We are able to capture a vision for our own lives. That's exciting because good things can, do, and will happen to us if we allow those things to happen and if we are open to and believe we deserve those things. The good things probably won't happen without some struggle and pain, but at least we will be struggling and stretching for something worthwhile, instead of simply suffering.

It's okay to succeed, to have good things, and to have loving relationships that work. These things may not come easily or naturally. We may struggle and kick and want to hide our heads in the sand along the way. That's okay. That's how growth feels. If it feels too comfortable, too natural, or too easy, we're not growing and we're not doing anything different. We're doing the same things we always have, and that's why it feels so comfortable.

Learning to live and love again means finding a balance: learning to love and, at the same time, living our own lives; learning to love without getting so emotionally entangled with the object of our affection; and learning to love others without forfeiting love for ourselves. We need to learn to live, love, and have fun so each activity does not unreasonably interfere with any of the others.

Much of recovery is finding and maintaining balance in all areas of our lives. We need to watch the scales so they do not tip too far to either side as we measure our responsibilities to ourselves and to others. We need to balance our emotional needs with our physical, mental, and spiritual needs. We need to balance giving and receiving; we need to find the dividing line between letting go and doing our part. We need to find a balance between solving problems and learning to live with unsolved problems. Much of our anguish comes from having to live with the grief of unsolved problems, and having things not go the way we hoped and expected. We need to find a balance between letting go of our expectations and remembering we are important, valuable people who deserve to lead decent lives.

GETTING STARTED

Frequently I am asked, where do I start? How do I get started? How do I even get my balance?

I've discussed many suggestions and ideas in this book, and some of us may feel overwhelmed.

For some of us, getting our balance may seem impossible. We may feel like we are lying flat on the floor of a dark cellar, and we cannot possibly crawl out. We can. Alcoholics Anonymous and Al-Anon offer a simple three-part formula for doing this. It's called "HOW": Honesty, Openness, and Willingness to try. Earlier, I wrote change begins with awareness and acceptance. The third step in changing human behavior is assertive action.[2] For us that means doing things differently. Get honest, keep an open mind, and become willing to try to do things differently, and we will change.

Choose one behavior to work on and when that becomes comfortable go on to another item. I have heard we need to repeat an action 21 times to make it a habit. That's a rule of thumb to keep in mind. The checklist in Chapter Four may provide some clues about where to start. The activities at the end of the chapters may give us some ideas. Figure out where we want to start and begin there. Start where we're at. If we can't figure out where to start, start by going to Al-Anon meetings, or another appropriate group. If we're in the basement, start crawling out. We'll learn to walk; we'll get our balance.

Getting started is both difficult and fun. When I began my recovery from codependency, I felt hopelessly trapped in myself and my relationships. Gloom surrounded me, and depression seemed to have permanently confined me to my bed. One morning, unhappy about being alive and awake, I dragged myself into the bathroom to get dressed and comb my hair, when my son insisted I follow him to another part of the house. I discovered a raging fire was consuming my bedroom. It had spread to the curtains, the ceiling, and the carpet. As in the past, I thought I could handle things myself; I thought the fire was not the disaster it appeared to be, so I grabbed a fire extinguisher and emptied it on the flames. Too little, too late. The fire raged on as we left the house.

My house was gutted by the time the fire department arrived. It was two weeks before Christmas, and my family and I had to move into a small apartment minus most of our clothing and the most basic of comforts. I hit my peak of despondency and anxiety. I had already lost so much, including myself. My home had been my nest, my remaining source of emotional security, and now I had lost that too. I had lost everything.

As the weeks passed, life began to require a little activity from me. Insurance inventories, negotiations, cleanup, and rebuilding plans demanded my attention. I felt anxious and insecure, but I had no choice. I had to think. I had to get busy. I had to do certain things. Once the actual reconstruction began, I had to do even more. I made choices about how to spend thousands of dollars. I worked hand in hand with the crews, doing everything I was able to do to help cut costs and expedite the project. That included physical activity, a part of my life that had become nonexistent. The busier I got, the better I felt. I began to trust my decisions. I worked off lots of anger and fear. By the time my family and I moved back into our home, my balance had been restored. I had begun living my own life, and I wasn't going to stop. It felt good!

The important concept here is, get started. Light a fire under yourself.

Growing Forward

Once we have gotten started, moving forward will become a natural process, if we continue to move. Sometimes, we will take a few steps backward. That's okay too. Sometimes it's necessary. Sometimes it's part of going forward.

Some of us may be facing tough decisions, decisions about ending relationships that are miserable and destructive. According to Earnie Larsen, if the relationship is dead, bury it. We can take our time, work on ourselves, and we will be able to make the right decision when the time is right.

Some of us may be trying to repair damaged but still alive relationships. Be patient. Love and trust are fragile, living entities. They do not automatically regenerate upon command if they have been bruised. Love and trust do not automatically reappear if the other person gets sober or solves whatever problem he or she had.[3] Love and trust must be allowed to heal in their own time. Sometimes they heal; sometimes they don't.

Some of us may be without a special person to love. That can be difficult, but it is not an impossible situation. We may want and need someone to love, but I think it helps if we love ourselves enough. It's okay to be in a relationship, but it's also okay to not be in a relationship. Find friends to love, be loved by, and who think we are worthwhile. Love ourselves and know we are worthwhile. Use our time alone as a breather. Let go. Learn the lessons we are to be learning. Grow. Develop. Work on ourselves, so when love comes along, it enhances a full and interesting life. Love shouldn't be the concern of our whole life or an escape from an unpleasant life. Strive toward goals. Have fun. Trust God and His timing. He cares and knows all about our needs and wants.

Whatever our situation, we can go slowly. Our hearts may lead us where our heads say we shouldn't go. Our heads may insist we go where our hearts don't want to follow. Sometimes our attraction to frogs may take us where neither our hearts nor heads choose to be. That's okay. There are no rules about whom we should or shouldn't love and relate to. We can love whomever we love, however we want to. But slow down and take the time to do it in a way that doesn't hurt us. Pay attention to what's happening. Love from our strengths, not from our weaknesses, and ask others to do the same. Make good decisions each day about what we need to do to take care of ourselves. Between our Higher Power and ourselves, we will be able to figure out what to do. I hope we will find people we enjoy loving—people who enjoy loving us and challenge us to grow. I hope we find enjoyable work that challenges us to grow.

A word of caution. From time to time, we may lose our balance. We may start running, skipping, and jumping, then suddenly find ourselves with our noses on the cement. All the old crazy feelings come rushing in. Don't be frightened. This is normal. Codependent characteristics, ways of thinking, and feelings become habits. Those habitual feelings and thoughts may surface on occasion. Change (even good change), certain circumstances reminiscent of alcoholic insanity, and stress, may provoke codependency. Sometimes the craziness returns unprovoked. See it through. Don't be ashamed and don't hide. We can pick ourselves up again. We will get through it. Talk to trusted friends; be patient and gentle with ourselves. Just keep doing the things we know we need to do. It will get better. Don't stop taking care of *us* no matter what happens.

Getting our balance and keeping it once we have found it is what recovery is all about. If that sounds like a big order, don't worry. We can do it. We can learn to live again. We can learn to love again. We can even learn to have fun at the same time.

EPILOGUE

I am not a teacher, but an awakener.

—ROBERT FROST

I wanted to write this book many years before I began it.

Originally, I wanted to write a book about codependency because when I was in so much pain with my codependency, I couldn't find a book that explained what had happened. I wanted to write a book for other hurting people that would explain codependency, help them understand, and ease their pain.

That motive got squelched when I was "beaten to the punch." Other people began writing about codependency. Also, some literature had been available; I just hadn't found it.

Later, my motive for writing this book changed. I not only wanted to ease other people's pain; I wanted to redeem my suffering. It was a bargain I was trying to strike on my somewhat extended path to acceptance: If I write a book about this, then that part of my life won't be such a loss.

That motive was squelched too. Before I wrote the book, I accepted what had happened to me. It was okay, whether I did or didn't write about it. I also realized I had gained more than I had lost. Through my experience with codependency, I found my *self.* Everything from our pasts has prepared and propelled us to this moment; today prepares us for tomorrow. And it all works out for the good. Nothing's wasted.

By the time I actually sat down to write this book, my motive was about the same as it had been originally. I wanted to write something that would help codependent people, and I thought I had a few worthwhile ideas to pass along. However, this book is just an opinion, and my thoughts and ideas are just that—thoughts and ideas. To illustrate this point, let me quote Garrison Keillor. He was discussing fiction, but his statement applies to nonfiction, self-help books, as well:

"It's tough to tell the truth especially when . . . we're not absolutely sure of the truth. You're looking for the truth, and you are just putting out some markers."[1]

I hope this book has marked some truth for you. I hope I have helped awaken you to your *self*.

NOTES

Introduction

1. Janet Geringer Woititz, "Co-Dependency: The Insidious Invader of Intimacy," in *Co-Dependency, An Emerging Issue* (Hollywood, FL: Health Communications, 1984), 59.
2. Toby Rice Drews, *Getting Them Sober* (South Plainfield, NJ: Bridge Publishing, 1980), vol.1, xv.

Chapter 3

1. Paraphrase based on a quote by Joan Wexler and John Steidll (teachers of psychiatric social work at Yale University), quoted by Colette Dowling, *The Cinderella Complex: Women's Hidden Fear of Independence* (New York: Pocket Books, 1981), 145.
2. Robert Subby, "Inside the Chemically Dependent Marriage: Denial and Manipulation," in *Co-Dependency, An Emerging Issue* (Hollywood, FL: Health Communications, 1984), 26.
3. Robert Subby and John Friel, "Co-Dependency: A Paradoxical Dependency," in *Co-Dependency, An Emerging Issue,* 31.
4. Al-Anon Family Groups, *Al-Anon Faces Alcoholism* (New York: Al-Anon Family Group Headquarters, 1977).
5. Al-Anon protects the anonymity of its members and keeps no official record of membership data. However, the Minneapolis Intergroup office agreed this figure was probably accurate.
6. Terence T. Gorski and Merlene Miller, "Co-Alcoholic Relapse:

Family Factors and Warning Signs," in *Co-Dependency, An Emerging Issue*, 78.
7. Earnie Larsen; Subby, "Inside the Chemically Dependent Marriage."
8. Subby and Friel, "Co-Dependency."
9. Charles L. Whitfield, "Co-Dependency: An Emerging Problem Among Professionals," in *Co-Dependency, An Emerging Issue*, 53; Joseph L. Kellerman, *The Family and Alcoholism: A Move from Pathology to Process* (Center City, MN: Hazelden, 1984).
10. Wayne W. Dyer, *Your Erroneous Zones* (New York: Funk and Wagnalls, 1976); Theodore I. Rubin with Eleanor Rubin, *Compassion and Self-Hate: An Alternative to Despair* (New York: David McKay Company, 1975).

Chapter 4
1. Nathaniel Branden, *Honoring the Self: Personal Integrity and the Heroic Potentials of Human Nature* (Boston: Houghton Mifflin Company, 1983), 162.
2. Dennis Wholey, *The Courage to Change* (Boston: Houghton Mifflin Company, 1984), 207.
3. Judi Hollis, *Fat Is a Family Affair* (San Francisco: Harper/Hazelden, 1986), 55.
4. Ibid., 53.
5. Robert Subby and John Friel, "Co-Dependency: A Paradoxical Dependency," in *Co-Dependency, An Emerging Issue* (Hollywood, FL: Health Communications, 1984), 32.

Chapter 5
1. This quote is excerpted from a handout entitled "Detachment," which contains a collection of writings by anonymous Al-Anon members.
2. Wayne W. Dyer, *Your Erroneous Zones* (New York: Funk and Wagnalls, 1976), 89.

3. Al-Anon Family Groups, *One Day at a Time in Al-Anon* (New York: Al-Anon Family Group Headquarters, Inc., 1976).
4. Judi Hollis, *Fat Is a Family Affair* (San Francisco: Harper/Hazelden, 1986), 47.
5. Terence Williams, *Free to Care: Therapy for the Whole Family* (Center City, MN: Hazelden, 1975).
6. Hollis, *Fat Is a Family Affair.*
7. Carolyn W., *Detaching with Love* (Center City, MN: Hazelden, 1984), 5.
8. Lois Walfrid Johnson, *Either Way, I Win: A Guide to Growth in the Power of Prayer* (Minneapolis: Augsburg, 1979).
9. Earnie Larsen does a similar meditation exercise at the end of his seminars.

Chapter 6
1. William Backus and Marie Chapian, *Telling Yourself the Truth* (Minneapolis: Bethany Fellowship, 1980).

Chapter 7
1. Eda LeShan, "Beware the Helpless," *Woman's Day,* 26 April 1983.

Chapter 8
1. Claude M. Steiner, *Scripts People Live* (New York: Grove Press, 1974).
2. *Ibid.*; Claude M. Steiner, *Games Alcoholics Play* (New York: Grove Press, 1971); and Claude M. Steiner, *What Do You Say After You Say Hello?* (New York: Grove Press, 1972).

Chapter 9
1. Penelope Russianoff, *Why Do I Think I'm Nothing Without a Man?* (New York: Bantam Books, 1982); Theodore I. Rubin with Eleanor Rubin, *Compassion and Self-Hate; An Alternative to Despair* (New York: David McKay Company, 1975), 278.

2. Janet Geringer Woititz, "Co-Dependency: The Insidious Invader of Intimacy," in Co-Dependency, An Emerging Issue (Hollywood, FL: Health Communications, 1984), 56.
3. Rubin, Compassion, 196.
4. Colette Dowling, The Cinderella Complex: Women's Hidden Fear of Independence (New York: Pocket Books, 1981).
5. Ibid., 152–53.
6. Ibid.
7. Russianoff, Why Do I Think I'm Nothing.
8. Dowling, The Cinderella Complex, 22.
9. Kathy Capell-Sowder, "On Being Addicted to the Addict: Co-Dependent Relationships," in Co-Dependency, 23. See also Stanton Peele and Archie Brodsky, Love and Addiction (New York: New American Library, 1975).

Chapter 10

1. Nathaniel Branden, Honoring the Self: Personal Integrity and the Heroic Potentials of Human Nature (Boston: Houghton Mifflin Company, 1983), 53.
2. Theodore I. Rubin with Eleanor Rubin, Compassion and Self-Hate: An Alternative to Despair (New York: David McKay Company, 1975), 65.
3. Ibid.

Chapter 11

1. Theodore I. Rubin with Eleanor Rubin, Compassion and Self-Hate: An Alternative to Despair (New York: David McKay Company, 1975); Nathaniel Branden, Honoring the Self: Personal Integrity and the Heroic Potentials of Human Nature (Boston: Houghton Mifflin Company, 1983).
2. Robert Subby and John Friel, "Co-Dependency: A Paradoxical Dependency," in Co-Dependency, An Emerging Issue (Hollywood, FL: Health Communications, 1984), 40.
3. Rubin, Compassion.

4. *Ibid.*
5. Branden, *Honoring the Self.*
6. *Ibid.*, 76.
7. Wayne W. Dyer, *Your Erroneous Zones* (New York: Funk and Wagnalls, 1976).
8. Toby Rice Drews, *Getting Them Sober* (South Plainfield, NJ: Bridge Publishing, 1980), vol.1, xxi.
9. Branden, *Honoring the Self,* 1–4.

Chapter 12

1. Joseph L. Kellerman, *A Guide for the Family of the Alcoholic* (New York: Al-Anon Family Group Headquarters, 1984), 8–9.
2. Janet Geringer Woititz, "Co-Dependency: The Insidious Invader of Intimacy," in *Co-Dependency, An Emerging Issue* (Hollywood, FL: Health Communications, 1984), 55.
3. *Ibid.*, 59.
4. Harold A. Swift and Terence Williams, *Recovery for the Whole Family* (Center City, MN: Hazelden, 1975).
5. Nathaniel Branden, *Honoring the Self: Personal Integrity and the Heroic Potentials of Human Nature* (Boston: Houghton Mifflin Company, 1983), 62–65.
6. Elisabeth Kübler-Ross, *On Death and Dying* (New York: MacMillan Publishing, 1969).
7. Melody Beattie, *Denial* (Center City, MN: Hazelden, 1986).
8. Claudia L. Jewett, *Helping Children Cope with Separation and Loss* (Harvard, MA: The Harvard Common Press, 1982), 29.
9. *Ibid.*, 23, 29.
10. John Powell, *Why Am I Afraid to Tell You Who I Am?* (Allen, TX: Argus Communications, 1969), 116–17.
11. Kübler-Ross, *On Death and Dying,* 99–100.
12. Judi Hollis, *Fat Is a Family Affair* (San Francisco: Harper/Hazelden, 1986), 80.

13. Donald L. Anderson, *Better Than Blessed* (Wheaton, IL: Tyndale House Publishers, 1981), 11.

Chapter 13
1. John Powell, *Why Am I Afraid to Tell You Who I Am?* (Allen, TX: Argus Communications, 1969), 155.
2. Jael Greenleaf, "Co-Alcoholic/Para-Alcoholic: Who's Who and What's the Difference?" in *Co-Dependency, An Emerging Issue* (Hollywood, FL: Health Communications, 1984), 9.
3. Scott Egleston; Powell, *Why Am I Afraid*; Toby Rice Drews, *Getting Them Sober* (South Plainfield, NJ: Bridge Publishing, 1980), vol. 1.
4. Nathaniel Branden, *Honoring the Self: Personal Integrity and the Heroic Potentials of Human Nature* (Boston: Houghton Mifflin Company, 1983).
5. Powell, *Why Am I Afraid*.
6. *Ibid.*
7. Albert Ellis and Robert A. Harper, *A New Guide to Rational Living* (Hollywood, CA: Wilshire Book, 1975); William Backus and Marie Chapian, *Telling Yourself the Truth* (Minneapolis: Bethany Fellowship, 1980).

Chapter 14
1. Janet Geringer Woititz, "The Co-Dependent Spouse: What Happens to You When Your Husband Is an Alcoholic," in *Co-Dependency, An Emerging Issue* (Hollywood, FL: Health Communications, 1984), 90.
2. Gayle Rosellini and Mark Worden, *Of Course You're Angry* (San Francisco: Harper/Hazelden, 1986).
3. Ephesians 4:26 RSV.
4. Toby Rice Drews, *Getting Them Sober* (South Plainfield, NJ: Bridge Publishing, 1980), vol.1; Rosellini and Worden, *Of Course You're Angry*; and Scott Egleston.

5. Frederick S. Perls, *Gestalt Therapy Verbatim* (New York: Bantam Books, 1969).

6. Claude M. Steiner, *Scripts People Live* (New York: Grove Press, 1979).

7. Rosellini and Worden, *Of Course You're Angry.*

8. Woititz, "The Co-Dependent Spouse," 83.

Chapter 15

1. 2 Timothy 1:7 New Scofield Reference Bible.

2. Aron Kahn, "Indecision Decidedly in Vogue," *St. Paul Pioneer Press and Dispatch* (1 April 1986, sec. C).

3. Toby Rice Drews, *Getting Them Sober* (South Plainfield, NJ: Bridge Publishing, 1980), vol. 1.

4. Paraphrase of material in *Alcoholics Anonymous,* 3d ed. *"The Big Book"* (New York: Alcoholics Anonymous World Services, 1976)

Chapter 16

1. David J. Schwartz, *The Magic of Thinking Big* (New York: Cornerstone Library, 1959), 162–63.

2. *Ibid.*, 163–64.

3. *Ibid.*, 164.

4. Dennis Wholey, *The Courage to Change* (Boston: Houghton Mifflin Company, 1984), 39.

Chapter 17

1. Toby Rice Drews, *Getting Them Sober* (South Plainfield, NJ: Bridge Publishing, 1980), vol. 1, 77–78.

2. *Ibid.*, 76.

3. John Powell, *Why Am I Afraid to Tell You Who I Am?* (Allen, TX: Argus Communications, 1969), 12.

4. *Ibid.*, 8.

5. Jean Baer, *How to Be an Assertive (Not Aggressive) Woman in Life, in Love, and on the Job* (New York: New American Library, 1976).

Chapter 18

1. Al-Anon Family Groups, *Al-Anon's Twelve Steps and Twelve Traditions* (New York: Al-Anon Family Group Headquarters, 1981), 131.
2. Jael Greenleaf, "Co-Alcoholic/Para-Alcoholic: Who's Who and What's the Difference?" in *Co-Dependency, An Emerging Issue* (Hollywood, FL: Health Communications, 1984), 15.
3. George E. Vaillant, *The Natural History of Alcoholism* (Cambridge, MA: Harvard University Press, 1983).
4. Warren W. told this story in Minneapolis 23 August 1985, borrowing it from circuit speaker Clancy Imislund who operates the Midnight Mission and lives in Venice, California.
5. Al-Anon Family Groups, *Al-Anon: Is It for You?* (New York: Al-Anon Family Group Headquarters, 1983). Reprinted by permission of Al-Anon Family Group Headquarters, Inc.
6. Judi Hollis, *Fat Is a Family Affair* (San Francisco: Harper/Hazelden, 1986), 49–52.

Chapter 19

1. Paraphrased quote based on a greeting card and poster sold years ago; author is unknown.
2. Toby Rice Drews, *Getting Them Sober* (South Plainfield, NJ: Bridge Publishing, 1980), vol. 2, 52.
3. Penelope Russianoff, *Why Do I Think I'm Nothing Without a Man?* (New York: Bantam Books, 1982).
4. Kathy Capell-Sowder, "On Being Addicted to the Addict: Co-Dependent Relationships," in *Co-Dependency, An Emerging Issue* (Hollywood, FL: Health Communications, 1984), 20–21.
5. Judi Hollis, *Fat Is a Family Affair* (San Francisco: Harper/Hazelden, 1986), 30–31.
6. Ideas discussed in this section are drawn from several articles in *Co-Dependency, An Emerging Issue* (Hollywood, FL: Health Communications, 1984); Janet Geringer Woititz, "The Co-Dependent Spouse: What Happens to You When Your Husband

Is an Alcoholic"; Gerald Shulman, "Sexuality and Recovery: Impact on the Recovering Couple"; Marilyn Mason, "Bodies and Beings: Sexuality Issues During Recovery for the Dependent and Co-Dependent"; and Janet Geringer Woititz, "Co-Dependency: The Insidious Invader of Intimacy."

Chapter 20

1. Abraham H. Maslow, ed., *Motivation and Personality,* 2d ed. (New York: Harper & Row, 1970); Benjamin Wolman, ed., *International Encyclopedia of Psychiatry, Psychology, Psychoanalysis, & Neurology* (New York: Aesculapius Publishers, 1977), vol. 7, 32–33.

2. Nathaniel Branden, *Honoring the Self: Personal Integrity and the Heroic Potentials of Human Nature* (Boston: Houghton Mifflin Company, 1983), 162.

3. Janet Geringer Woititz, "Co-Dependency: The Insidious Invader of Intimacy," in *Co-Dependency, An Emerging Issue* (Hollywood, FL: Health Communications, 1984), 59.

Epilogue

1. Michael Schumacher, "Sharing the Laughter with Garrison Keillor," *Writer's Digest* (January 1986), 33.

BIBLIOGRAPHY

Books

Alcoholics Anonymous World Services. *Alcoholics Anonymous* ("The Big Book"), 3d ed. New York: Alcoholics Anonymous World Services, 1976.

Al-Anon Family Groups. *Al-Anon: Is It for You?* New York: Al-Anon Family Group Headquarters, 1983.

————. *Al-Anon's Twelve Steps and Twelve Traditions.* New York: Al-Anon Family Group Headquarters, 1981.

————. *Al-Anon Faces Alcoholism.* New York: Al-Anon Family Group Headquarters, 1977.

————. *One Day at a Time in Al-Anon.* New York: Al-Anon Family Group Headquarters, 1974.

————. *The Dilemma of the Alcoholic Marriage.* New York: Al-Anon Family Group Headquarters, 1971.

Anderson, Donald L. *Better Than Blessed.* Wheaton, IL: Tyndale House Publishers, 1981.

Backus, William, and Marie Chapian. *Telling Yourself the Truth.* Minneapolis: Bethany Fellowship, 1980.

Baer, Jean. *How to Be an Assertive (Not Aggressive) Woman in Life, in Love and on the Job.* New York: New American Library, 1976.

Branden, Nathaniel. *Honoring the Self: Personal Integrity and the Heroic Potentials of Human Nature.* Boston: Houghton Mifflin Company, 1983.

DeRosis, Helen A., and Victoria Y. Pellegrino. *The Book of Hope: How Women Can Overcome Depression.* New York: MacMillan Publishing, 1976.

Dowling, Colette. *The Cinderella Complex: Women's Hidden Fear of Independence.* New York: Pocket Books, 1981.

Drews, Toby Rice. *Getting Them Sober, Volume 1.* South Plainfield, NJ: Bridge Publishing, 1980.

———. *Getting Them Sober, Volume 2.* South Plainfield, NJ: Bridge Publishing, 1983.

Dyer, Wayne W. *Your Erroneous Zones.* New York: Funk and Wagnalls, 1976.

Ellis, Albert, and Robert A. Harper. *A New Guide to Rational Living.* Hollywood, CA: Wilshire Books, 1975.

Fort, Joel. *The Addicted Society: Pleasure-Seeking and Punishment Revisited.* New York: Grove Press, 1981.

Hafen, Brent Q., with Kathryn J. Frandsen. *The Crisis Intervention Handbook.* Englewood Cliffs, NJ: Prentice-Hall, 1982.

Hazelden. *Day by Day.* San Francisco: Harper/Hazelden, 1986.

———. *Twenty-Four Hours a Day.* San Francisco: Harper/Hazelden, 1985.

Health Communications. *Co-Dependency, An Emerging Issue.* Hollywood, FL: Health Communications, 1984.

Hollis, Judi. *Fat Is a Family Affair.* San Francisco: Harper/Hazelden, 1986.

Hornik-Beer, Edith Lynn. *A Teenager's Guide to Living with an Alcoholic Parent.* Center City, MN: Hazelden, 1984.

Jewett, Claudia L. *Helping Children Cope with Separation and Loss.* Harvard, MA: The Harvard Common Press, 1982.

Johnson, Lois Walfrid. *Either Way, I Win: A Guide to Growth in the Power of Prayer.* Minneapolis: Augsburg Publishing House, 1979.

Kimball, Bonnie-Jean. *The Alcoholic Woman's Mad, Mad World of Denial and Mind Games.* Center City, MN: Hazelden, 1978.

Kübler-Ross, Elisabeth. *On Death and Dying.* New York: MacMillan Publishing, 1969.

Landorf, Joyce. *Irregular People.* Waco, TX: Word, 1982.

Lee, Wayne. *Formulating and Reaching Goals.* Champaign, IL: Research Press Company, 1978.

Maslow, Abraham H., ed. *Motivation and Personality,* 2d ed. New York: Harper & Row, 1970.

Maxwell, Ruth. *The Booze Battle.* New York: Ballantine Books, 1976.

McCabe, Thomas R. *Victims No More.* Center City, MN: Hazelden, 1978.

Perls, Frederick S. *Gestalt Therapy Verbatim.* New York: Bantam Books, 1969.

Pickens, Roy W., and Dace S. Svikis. *Alcoholic Family Disorders: More Than Statistics.* Center City, MN: Hazelden, 1985.

Powell, John S. *Why Am I Afraid to Tell You Who I Am?* Allen, TX: Argus Communications, 1969.

Restak, Richard M. *The Self Seekers.* Garden City, NY: Doubleday and Company, 1982.

Rosellini, Gayle, and Mark Worden. *Of Course You're Angry.* San Francisco: Harper/Hazelden, 1986.

Rubin, Theodore I. *Reconciliations: Inner Peace in an Age of Anxiety.* New York: The Viking Press, 1980.

Rubin, Theodore I., with Eleanor Rubin. *Compassion and Self-Hate: An Alternative to Despair.* New York: David McKay Company, 1975.

Russianoff, Penelope. *Why Do I Think I Am Nothing Without a Man?* New York: Bantam Books, 1982.

Schwartz, David J. *The Magic of Thinking Big.* New York: Cornerstone Library, 1959.

Steiner, Claude M. *Games Alcoholics Play: The Analysis of Life Scripts.* New York: Grove Press, 1971.

———. *Healing Alcoholism.* New York: Grove Press, 1979.

———. *Scripts People Live.* New York: Grove Press, 1974.

———. *What Do You Say After You Say Hello?* New York: Grove Press, 1972.

Valliant, George E. *The Natural History of Alcoholism: Causes, Patterns and Paths to Recovery.* Cambridge, MA: Harvard University Press, 1982.

Vine, Phyllis. *Families in Pain: Children, Siblings, Spouses and Parents of the Mentally Ill Speak Out.* New York: Pantheon Books, 1982.

Wallis, Charles L., ed. *The Treasure Chest.* New York: Harper & Row, 1965.

Wholey, Dennis. *The Courage to Change.* Boston: Houghton Mifflin Company, 1984.

Woititz, Janet Geringer. *Adult Children of Alcoholics.* Hollywood, FL: Health Communications, 1983.

Wolman, Benjamin B., ed. *International Encyclopedia of Psychiatry, Psychology, Psychoanalysis & Neurology,* vol. 7. New York: Aesculapius Publishers, 1977.

York, Phyllis and David, and Ted Wachtel. *Toughlove.* Garden City, NY: Doubleday and Company, 1982.

Pamphlets

Beattie, Melody. *Denial* Center City, MN: Hazelden, 1986.

Burgin, James E. *Help for the Marriage Partner of an Alcoholic.* Center City, MN: Hazelden, 1976.

Emotions Anonymous International Services. *The Enormity of Emotional Illness: The Hope Emotions Anonymous Has to Offer.* St. Paul, MN: Emotions Anonymous International Services, 1973.

H., Barbara. *Untying the Knots: One Parent's View.* Center City, MN: Hazelden, 1984.

Harrison, Earl. *Boozlebane on Alcoholism and the Family.* Center City, MN: Hazelden, 1984.

Hazelden Educational Materials. *Teen Drug Use: What Can Parents Do?* Center City, MN: Hazelden. (Reprinted with permission of Department of Public Instruction, Bismarck, ND, Drug Abuse Education Act of 1970.)

————. *No Substitute for Love: Ideas for Family Living.* Center City, MN: Hazelden. (Reprinted with permission of Special Action Office for Drug Abuse Prevention, Executive Office of the President, Washington, DC, in conjunction with the Drug Abuse Prevention Week in 1973.)

———. *Step Four: Guide to Fourth Step Inventory for the Spouse.* Center City, MN: Hazelden, 1976.

———. *Learn about Families and Chemical Dependency.* Center City, MN: Hazelden, 1985.

Kellerman, Joseph L. *The Family and Alcoholism: A Move from Pathology to Process.* Center City, MN: Hazelden, 1984.

———. *A Guide for the Family of the Alcoholic.* New York: Al-Anon Family Group Headquarters, 1984.

Nakken, Jane. *Enabling Change: When Your Child Returns Home from Treatment.* Center City, MN: Hazelden, 1985.

Schroeder, Melvin. *Hope for Relationships.* Center City, MN: Hazelden, 1980.

Scientific Affairs Committee of the Bay Area Physicians for Human Rights. *Guidelines for AIDS Risk Reduction.* San Francisco: The San Francisco AIDS Foundation, 1984.

Swift, Harold A., and Terence Williams. *Recovery for the Whole Family.* Center City, MN: Hazelden, 1975.

Timmerman, Nancy G. *Step One for Family and Friends.* Center City, MN: Hazelden, 1985.

———. *Step Two for Family and Friends* Center City, MN: Hazelden, 1985.

W., Carolyn. *Detaching with Love.* Center City, MN: Hazelden, 1984.

Williams, Terence. *Free to Care: Therapy for the Whole Family of Concerned Persons.* Center City, MN: Hazelden, 1975.

Articles

Anderson, Eileen. "When Therapists Are Hooked on Power." *The Phoenix,* vol. 5, no. 7, July 1985.

"Author's Study Says CoAs Can't Identify Their Needs." *The Phoenix* (from Family Focus, published by the U.S. Journal of Drug and

Alcohol Dependence), vol. 4, no. 11, November 1984.

Bartell, Jim. "Family Illness Needs Family Treatment, Experts Say." *The Phoenix,* vol. 4, no. 11, November 1984.

Black, Claudia. "Parental Alcoholism Leaves Most Kids Without Information, Feelings, Hope." *The Phoenix,* vol. 4, no. 11, November 1984.

Hamburg, Jay. "Student of Depression Sights a Silver Lining." *St. Paul Pioneer Press and Dispatch (Orlando Sentinel),* 23 September 1985.

Jeffris, Maxine. "About the Word Co-Dependency." *The Phoenix,* vol. 5, no. 7, July 1985.

Kahn, Aron. "Indecision Decidedly in Vogue." *St. Paul Pioneer Press and Dispatch,* 1 April 1986.

Kalbrener, John. "We Better Believe That Our Children Are People, Says Children Are People." *The Phoenix,* vol. 4, no. 11, November 1984.

LeShan, Eda. "Beware the Helpless." *Woman's Day,* 26 April 1983.

Ross, Walter S. "Stress: It's Not Worth Dying For." *Reader's Digest,* January 1985, 76.

Schumacher, Michael. "Sharing the Laughter with Garrison Keillor." *Writer's Digest,* January 1986, 33.

Strick, Lisa Wilson. "What's So Bad About Being So-So?" *Reader's Digest,* August 1984, 78 (reprinted from *Woman's Day,* 3 April 1984).

Miscellaneous

"Adult Children of Alcoholics," handout, author unknown.

"Detachment," handout written by anonymous Al-Anon members.

Jourard, Sidney, with Ardis Whitman. "The Fear That Cheats Us of Love," handout.

Larsen, Earnie. "Co-Dependency Seminar," Stillwater, MN, 1985.

Wright, Thomas. "Profile of a Professional Caretaker," handout.

About the Author

Melody Beattie is one of America's most beloved self-help authors and a household name in addiction and recovery circles. Her international best-selling book, *Codependent No More,* introduced the world to the term codependency in 1986. Millions of readers have trusted Melody's words of wisdom and guidance because she knows firsthand what they're going through. In her lifetime, she has survived abandonment, kidnapping, sexual abuse, drug and alcohol addiction, divorce, and the death of a child. "Beattie understands being overboard, which helps her throw bestselling lifelines to those still adrift," said *Time* magazine.

Melody was born in St. Paul, Minnesota, in 1948. Her father left home when she was a toddler, and she was raised by her mother. "My mother was a classic codependent," Melody recalls. Spanning more than twenty years, her writing career has produced fifteen books published in twenty languages and hundreds of newspaper and magazine articles. She has been a frequent guest on many national television shows, including *Oprah.* She and her books continue to be featured regularly in national publications including *Time, People,* and other major periodicals around the world.

Although it almost destroyed her when her twelve-year-old son Shane died in a ski accident in 1991, eventually Melody picked up the pieces of her life again. "I wanted to die, but I kept waking up alive," she says. She began skydiving, mountain climbing, and teaching others what she'd learned about grief.

Hazelden, a national nonprofit organization founded in 1949, helps people reclaim their lives from the disease of addiction. Built on decades of knowledge and experience, Hazelden offers a comprehensive approach to addiction that addresses the full range of patient, family, and professional needs, including treatment and continuing care for youth and adults, research, higher learning, public education and advocacy, and publishing.

A life of recovery is lived "one day at a time." Hazelden publications, both educational and inspirational, support and strengthen lifelong recovery. In 1954, Hazelden published *Twenty-Four Hours a Day*, the first daily meditation book for recovering alcoholics, and Hazelden continues to publish works to inspire and guide individuals in treatment and recovery, and their loved ones. Professionals who work to prevent and treat addiction also turn to Hazelden for evidence-based curricula, informational materials, and videos for use in schools, treatment programs, and correctional programs.

Through published works, Hazelden extends the reach of hope, encouragement, help, and support to individuals, families, and communities affected by addiction and related issues.

For questions about Hazelden publications,
please call **800-328-9000**
or visit us online at **hazelden.org/bookstore.**